JAMESTOWN, THE BURIED TRUTH

# JAMES

# TOWN

## THE BURIED TRUTH

William M. Kelso

UNIVERSITY OF VIRGINIA PRESS
Charlottesville and London

Publication of this volume was made possible with the generous support of the Office of the President of the University of Virginia and the Association for the Preservation of Virginia Antiquities.

All illustrations unless otherwise noted appear courtesy of the Association for the Preservation of Virginia Antiquities.

University of Virginia Press
Printed in the United States of America on acid-free paper

First published 2006

9 8 7 6 5 4 3 2 1

LIBRARY OF CONGRESS CATALOGING-IN-PUBLICATION DATA
Kelso, William M.
  Jamestown, the buried truth / William M. Kelso.
    p.   cm.
  Includes bibliographical references and index.
  ISBN-13: 978-0-8139-2563-9 (cloth : alk. paper)
    1. Jamestown (Va.)—History. 2. Jamestown (Va.)—Antiquities. 3. Excavations (Archaeology)—Virginia—Jamestown.   4. Colonial National Historical Park (Va.)—Antiquities. I. Title.
F234.J3K46 2006
973.2′1—dc22                                                  2006004093

*For Ellen*

# CONTENTS

Acknowledgments   *ix*

Introduction   *1*

1  Reimagining Jamestown   *9*

2  Rediscovering Jamestown   *44*

3  Recovering Jamestownians   *125*

4  Reanimating Jamestown   *169*

5  Royal Jamestown   *191*

Notes   *215*

Index   *231*

# Acknowledgments

The achievements of the Jamestown Rediscovery® project at Historic James-towne®, Virginia, are due in large measure to the many individuals and organizations who have provided leadership, generous financial support, scholarly advice, and expertise.

Among the hundreds who could be acknowledged, I highlight a few here for special recognition: The Jamestown Rediscovery National Advisory Board, especially chairman Dr. Warren M. Billings, Dennis B. Blanton, Dr. Edward Bond, Frederick Faust, Dr. Jeffrey P. Brain, Dr. Cary Carson, Dr. Kathleen Deagan, Dr. Rex M. Ellis, Dr. Alaric Faulkner, Dr. William W. Fitz-hugh, Ms. Camille Hedrick, Dr. James Horn, Dr. Jon Kukla, Dr. Douglas Owsley, Dr. David Orr, Mr. Oliver Perry, Dr. Carmel Schrire, Dr. George Stuart, Dr. Sandra Treadway, Dr. Edwin Randolph Turner, Mr. Robert Wharton, Ms. Roxane Gilmore; APVA Preservation Virginia's Trustees, es-pecially Presidents Peter I. C. Knowles II, Ivor Massey Jr., and William B. Kerkam III; Executive Director Elizabeth S. Kostelny, the staff and mem-bership for their constant interest and support; and our special partner, the National Park Service. Generous benefactors to recognize include: the U.S. Congress, the Commonwealth of Virginia, National Geographic Soci-ety, National Endowment for the Humanities, Virginia Foundation for the Humanities, James City County, City of Williamsburg, the Mellon Founda-tion, the Mary Morton Parsons Foundation, Jessie Ball duPont Fund, 1772 Foundation, the Morgan Foundation, an anonymous Richmond founda-tion, the Garden Club of Virginia, the William Byrd and Colonial Capital Branches of the APVA, the Beirne Carter Foundation, Anheuser-Busch,

Dominion Resources, Universal Leaf Corporation, Wachovia, Verizon, the William M. Grover Jr. family, Mr. Ivor Massey Jr., Mr. and Mrs. Peter I. C. Knowles II, Mr. and Mrs. John H. Guy IV, Mr. and Mrs. D. Anderson Williams, Mr. and Mrs. John A. Prince, the Alan M. Voorhees Family, Mrs. T. Eugene Worrell, the Edward Maria Wingfield Family Society, the Fontaine C. Stanton Estate, William G. Beville, Mr. and Mrs. John H. Van Landingham III, Mr. and Mrs. Martin Kirwan King, Mr. and Mrs. William Garber, especially Patricia Cornwell for her generosity, and many other generous individuals.

The project has been very much a staff team effort from the start and now very much an experienced team effort. With an open mind to ways of improving the process, over the initial ten years of the project the staff has had the opportunity to fine-tune the way things have been done. I am especially grateful for their ability to decipher together the ever-widening archaeological story at Historic Jamestowne. I am indebted to senior curator Bly Straube for her unequaled and ever-expanding understanding of postmedieval material culture and for her disciplined and insightful reading of seventeenth-century Jamestown documents; former senior staff archaeologist Eric Deetz for his growing mastery of fieldwork, insight into postmedieval vernacular architecture, and education of students and visitors; senior staff archaeologist and graphic artist Jamie May for her skillful direction of fieldwork, her exceptional artistic eye on the computer, for organizing and creating the insightful images for this publication, and for her skillful reading of the archaeological signs in the soil of Jamestowne; staff archaeologist and information technologist David Givens for his vast field experience, for his insight into Virginia Indian archaeology, for creating our GIS archives, and for his many and varied mechanical skills; staff archaeologists Danny Schmidt and Carter Hudgins for their increasing field skills, interpretive insight, and commitment to the archives and historical research; Douglas W. Owsley for teaching me what careful forensic science is and for his steadfast honesty; Ashley McKeown for her dedication, insight, and ability to unravel the art and mystery of Historic Jamestowne's skeletal biology; conservator/photographer Michael Lavin for his uniquely experienced conservation touches and photographic eye; Dan Gamble for his ever-diligent and talented conservation work; Caroline Taylor for her careful artifact processing; Catherine Correll-Walls for accumulating the insightful Early Jamestown Biographies database; and to the many, many skilled archaeologists along the way, for their diligent and talented fieldwork, especially Nick Luccketti, Luke Peccarero, Seth Mallios, Sarah Stroud, Heather Lapham, and conservator and information technologist Elliott Jordan. The efforts of eleven seasons of University of Virginia annual field schools are especially recognized and appreciated as are the public relations work of Paula Neely and the managerial talent of program co-coordinator Ann Berry. I also want to acknowledge the talented and instructive editing of this volume by Kenny Marotta and my 2004 Virginia Foundation for the Humanities fellowship, which gave me some much-needed writing time in residence at Charlottesville. I am especially grateful for the stalwart and always encouraging corps of Historic Jamestowne interpreters and the field and lab volunteers. Andrew Scott, James Halsall, and Edward and Joanna Martin made the Gosnold DNA study in England possible.

And I am forever indebted to Ivor Noël Hume for first revealing to me the rigorous process of historical archaeology, the thrill of archaeological discovery, and the archaeological possibilities at Jamestown. Without the original support of past APVA presidents Mary Douthat Higgins and Shirley Van Landingham, Jamestown Rediscovery archaeology at APVA Jamestown would never have happened.

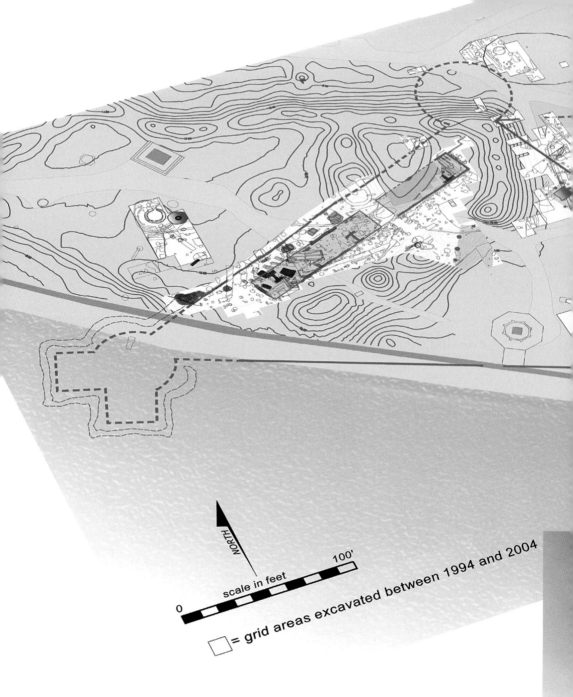

NORTH

scale in feet

0          100'

□ = grid areas excavated between 1994 and 2004

Artist's reconstruction of James Fort as
it may have looked ca. 1611, based on
1994–2005 archaeological excavations
and documentary history.

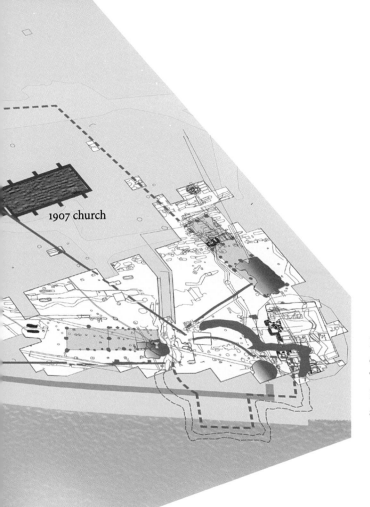

1907 church

Plan of archaeological
excavations, 1994–2005.
Those dating to the James
Fort period (1607–1624)
are in red.

# INTRODUCTION

The American dream was born on the banks of the James River. Lured by the promise of a better life, in 1607 a band of adventurers established the first enduring English settlement in the New World: Jamestown. By 1620—the year the Pilgrims reached Plymouth—much of the James River basin, from the mouth of the Chesapeake Bay to within twenty miles of the site of modern Richmond, had been settled by the English under the sponsorship of the Virginia Company. The year before, a governmental body composed of men elected from the scattered settlements of Virginia had met for the first time on Jamestown Island. This assembly was the first expression of English representative government in North America.

Important as these accomplishments were, the written records pertaining to them are scarce, ambiguous, and sometimes conflicting: maps of questionable accuracy; a few letters and official reports; published accounts written by interested parties (most famous among them John Smith, his account including the dubious tale of his own dramatic rescue by the Indian maiden Pocahontas). Still, certain facts can be gleaned from these records. The colony's early history was evidently a troubled one, beginning with an alleged mutiny during the crossing from England (blamed on John Smith) and continuing through many struggles for power and incidents of civil unrest. The colony faced other trials and hardships as well, including a major battle with the local Indians within weeks of arrival, an unfamiliar semitropical climate, lack of fresh water, meager and spoiled food, drought, and accidents. The Virginia Company's goals—to find a route to the Orient, convert the New World natives to Christianity, find gold, and export raw and manufactured goods—were at best only slightly fulfilled. The hoped-for precious minerals and short, all-water route to the riches of the Orient were never found; the native population was far from willing to embrace the Church of England; and initial manufacturing projects did not prove lucrative.

These early years also witnessed periods of renovation, repopulation, and restructuring of the colony. The introduction of Caribbean tobacco by John Rolfe in 1613 did at last establish a cash crop that helped insure the survival of the Virginia colony, although the success of hinterland plantations depleted the Jamestown population. A 1622 Indian revolt and the resulting death of nearly 350 colonists led to the end of the Virginia Company's rule, as Jamestown itself became a Royal Colony.

The documentary evidence of the precariousness of life in early Jamestown and of the gap between the founders' intentions and the colony's achievements led to a story of Jamestown that emphasized its shortcomings: "The adventurers who ventured capital lost it. Most of the settlers who ventured their lives lost them. And so did most of the Indians who came near them. Measured by any of the objectives announced for it, the colony failed."[1] In this interpretation, the colony's failure was ascribed to poor planning by the sponsoring Virginia Company, the incompetence or laziness of the colonists (qualities supposedly explained by the upper-class origin of half of the original settlers), and mistaken cultural assumptions about the Indians. This story, which continues to be told, has been held responsible for the diminished importance of Jamestown itself in American popular consciousness.[2] A comprehensive textbook survey concluded that "textbooks downplay Jamestown because it was a disaster."[3]

To call Jamestown a failure, let alone a disaster, is to oversimplify. Even the scanty documents, with their record of the colony's important firsts, its periods of thriving, and the energy and intelligence unceasingly invested in it, hint at a more complex story. The assertion of the textbook survey is correct to this extent, however: as the complex actuality of the early Jamestown experience faded with time, the importance of Jamestown to American history faded, too. Significant memories, significant truths were lost—seemingly forever.

My own engagement with Jamestown began over four decades ago, far from Virginia. An undergraduate at Ohio's Baldwin-Wallace College, I decided

In 1611 Ralph Hamor reports that "most" of the citizens of Jamestown were found at their usual pursuits of "bowling in the streets," much like the skittle players in this seventeenth-century Jan Steen painting. Such references led many historians to conclude that it was the "lazy" lifestyle of the gentlemen that turned the Jamestown settlement effort into a "fiasco." (National Gallery, London)

to cheer myself up one gray March day by reading about Virginia, where I had heard that the sun usually shone and that American colonial history, second only to football as a passion in my life, was considered a serious subject. On a well-worn magazine cover, an aerial photo of Jamestown Island spread out before me. I was mesmerized. The color image showed a network of open archaeological trenches laying bare the foundations of the buried town. This gridwork was part of an effort in 1955 by the National Park Service to uncover remains of Jamestown for a 1957 exhibition celebrating the 350th anniversary of Jamestown's founding. Inspecting the strict order of archaeological trenches crisscrossing the park-like expanse of hallowed ground between unspoiled woodland and the spacious James River, I was amazed that archaeology could happen so close to my own time and place in history. At that time, all my knowledge of archaeology had come from *National Geographic* photo essays on the pyramids.

Never much of a spectator, I could not help imagining digging with my own hands in that Jamestown soil. When I arrived at the College of William and Mary in Williamsburg, Virginia, as a graduate student interested in early American history, I naturally sought out the ruins at nearby Jamestown Island. I was especially curious about the 1607 fort that must surely have been uncovered in the 1955 excavations, the fort that first defined the limits of colonial Jamestown. At the excavation site, owned by the Association for the Preservation of Virginia Antiquities (APVA), I saw the moss-covered church reconstructed by the APVA, statues of Pocahontas and Captain John Smith, and, in the side of the nearby earthen Civil War fort, a curious windowed exhibit. The glass protected some exposed layers of dirt in the fort bank, showing the actual soil surfaces that made up the

An aerial view of excavations at Jamestown conducted by the National Park Service in the mid-1950s. This grid of search trenches located a number of seventeenth-century brick building sites, ditches, trash pits, and wells in preparation for the 350th anniversary of the founding of Jamestown in 1957. (National Park Service, Colonial National Historical Park)

bank: the Civil War zone, complete with lead bullets; beneath it the dark band of colonial trash; and the deepest deposit, a lighter soil containing arrow points and prehistoric Indian pottery. I was clearly seeing a layer cake of time, pre-Jamestown at the bottom, the colonial period in the middle, and the Civil War era on top. I took in the simple lessons. What is older is deeper; artifacts tell time; the earth can be an index of American history.

I asked a park ranger where the old fort site was. He pointed to a lone cypress tree growing way off shore and said, "Unfortunately, you're too late. It's out there—and lost for good."

I was disappointed to hear that this historic site had been swallowed by the waters that eroded the riverbank. I was confused, too. Looking back at the dirt under glass that said "colonial," I asked again, "But what about here?"

He thought for a moment and replied with a shrug of his shoulders that I took as a "could be."

I did not forget James Fort in the ensuing years when I became an archaeologist specializing in the British Colonial America period, learning with my colleagues about that often-forgotten American century, the 1600s. Most of our work focused on rescuing farm sites along the James River, which were being rediscovered by real estate developers and resettled by retirees. The more we learned from the earth about the seventeenth century, the more we thought that the "colonial level" under the glass exhibit at the Civil War fort might be a sign that the 1607 James Fort was there. The likelihood seemed greater when Nicholas Luccketti, Bly Straube, and I restudied the field notes from the 1955 National Park Service excavations, the artifacts those excavations had uncovered, and some disturbances in the soil nearby.[4] Might those disturbances be vestiges of narrow slot trenches that had held seventeenth-century wooden palisade fort walls of the sort we had found elsewhere on the James? The bits of iron and pottery found with such trenches were old and military enough to have been part of James Fort.

When the APVA decided to investigate its property on Jamestown Island archaeologically—this time in preparation for the 400th anniversary of

A cross-sectional trench dug into the dirt bank of Jamestown's Civil War earthwork fort showing (A) Civil War period, (B) Colonial period, (C) pre-1607 Virginia Indian period (*background*) and an L-shaped excavated ditch of unknown origin (*foreground right*). This excavated cross-section was left visible to Jamestown visitors as an archaeological exhibit for some years after the 1955 digging. (National Park Service, Colonial National Historical Park)

The first Jamestown Rediscovery excavation season, in which visiting professional historical archaeologists and University of Virginia field school students aided, uncovered the first sign of James Fort, the dark soil trace of a wall line.

Jamestown in 2007—I enthusiastically volunteered for the job. There was not much of a line ahead of me. Most archaeologists discounted any chance of finding traces of the early James Fort. At best there would only be signs that it had long since dissolved as the shoreline retreated before nearly four centuries of waves. So it happened that, thirty years to the day after I had first set foot on Jamestown Island, I found myself putting shovel to ground one hundred feet from the glassed-in cross-section that had originally inspired my curiosity. I did not have to miss out on digging at Jamestown after all.

An archaeologist must often practice more than one kind of patience. One September day in 1994, my digging was interrupted by a pair of tourists.

"What are you doing?"

I had been lost in the act of scraping loose dirt from a dark streak in the yellow clay. The accent of the speaker left no doubt that he was British.

"Archaeology," I answered, hoping to end the conversation so that I could get on with my digging. No luck.

"Have you found anything?"

He spoke so earnestly that I felt compelled to give a serious answer.

"Absolutely. See this black stain in the clay? Well, that's what's left of a 1607 fort wall . . . maybe from James Fort."

"Really?"

Silence for a moment. Then the man's companion said, "You mean that's it? That's all there is? America, the last of the world's superpowers, began as . . . just dirt?"

"I never thought about it quite like that," I said, "but yes, I guess it was just dirt."

"But," she continued, "shouldn't there have been a ruined castle or some marble columns or . . . something real?"

"No, there was just dirt," I answered. "But you know what else? I guess plenty of, well, just hope."

"Oh, brilliant!" they said in unison. "Brilliant indeed!"

The British visitors moved on, having grasped the concept that national stature was not necessarily synonymous with highly visible architectural ruins. The archaeologist exploring the beginnings of the United States discovers no medieval castles, classical temples, or Egyptian pyramids. "Just dirt" held out hope for the landless English immigrant, offering a way to break into an otherwise closed society based on the inheritance of family estates. "Just dirt" holds out hope to the archaeologist as well. Marks in the soil of Jamestown Island are the traces of a native people and English immigrants, evidence that has survived the ground-disturbing activities of succeeding generations and the eroding effects of the adjacent river. So we dig, in the faith that these traces bear America's richest heritage.

This hope and faith have now been justified. The excavations at Jamestown have turned up more evidence than anyone had expected—most important, the site of James Fort, so long thought unrecoverable. Nor are these physical remains the only treasure to be discovered.

Discovery of aligned pockets of dark soil formed by rotting upright logs in narrow trenches revealed the architectural footprint of James Fort.

The soil has yielded a new understanding of the early years of Jamestown; a new picture of its settlers, of their abilities, their lives, and their accomplishments; and a new story of the interdependence between the English settlers and the Virginia Indians.

This volume chronicles my effort to unearth this once-lost treasure by the methods of historical archaeology. In chapter 1 I review what can be learned about the nature and extent of the first Jamestown settlement and its settlers from documentary evidence alone. Chapter 2 recounts the exciting and painstaking discovery of James Fort and rereads the documents in the light of this archaeological discovery. In chapter 3 the recovery of early Jamestown burials becomes a means to understand more about the people of James Fort, the Jamestownians. Through an examination of the James Fort artifacts, chapter 4 corrects earlier and simpler notions of the nature and causes of what has been called Jamestown's failure, showing how the people of James Fort both acted out their preconceptions of Virginia and adapted to the realities of the New World. These uncovered artifacts illustrate the process by which Englishmen and -women began to be transformed into Americans. Moving beyond the confines of earliest Jamestown, chapter 5 documents the recovery of the fragmentary remains of the places where representative government was born and developed in the seventeenth century, continuing the process whereby Americans invented themselves.

Throughout these chapters, readers will become acquainted with the tools of the archaeologist: the arts of computer manipulation, dendrochronology, forensic sculpting, and x-ray, chemical, and DNA analysis; a knowledge of soil and water ecology and of the history of technology, architecture, and fashion; and, above all, the tireless practice of deductive reasoning. Put simply, my hope is that this book will give readers an opportunity to glimpse, from an archaeological perspective, the genesis of the American dream.

Admittedly the dream will, at times, be a nightmare even more vivid than the one earlier historians have portrayed. On the whole, however, the new archaeology offers a more balanced account of Jamestown's beginning. Jamestown's precarious attempt to plant English roots in the New World was a tale of trial and error. It was a story, too, of individual success and endurance by our nation's founding grandfathers. Modern America took root for good at Jamestown. The pages that follow trace the story of the search and recovery of those telltale roots.

The buried truth lies ahead. Like any search for something buried, this search requires a map. So the quest begins not in the earth but in the library.

# REIMAGINING JAMESTOWN

*T* *he soil was good and fruitful, with excellent good timber. There are*
   *also great store of vines in bigness of a man's thigh, running up to the*
*tops of the trees, in great abundance . . . many squirrels, conies, blackbirds*
*with crimson wings and divers other fowls and birds of divers and sundry*
*colors of crimson, watchet, yellow, green, murrey and of divers other hues*
*naturally without any art using.*[1]

The exuberant eyewitness description given above of the Virginia wonder-
land came from the pen of George Percy, one of the first Jamestown settlers, who was to become governor of the colony almost by default when
the dreamland turned into a nightmare two and one-half years later. Percy's account of the voyage to the New World is the most complete of the
firsthand descriptions of the founding of Jamestown and the fate of the
colonists during the first spring and summer in Virginia.

Eyewitness testimonies carry great weight in any search for the truth. A
reading of the documents pertaining to early Jamestown is essential if we
are to discover its buried secrets. But documents must be read carefully:
the testimony even of eyewitnesses must be scrutinized, keeping in mind
that the authors were not immune to dreams of gold and glory that might
distort their accounts. It is important to ask, for instance, how much of the
fruitful abundance Percy describes in his first sighting might have been
merely an expression of the hopes of a new settler rather than reality.

An examination of the documents contemporary with Jamestown's
founding offers hints of the precise location, configuration, and artifacts

*Top:* George Percy, highest-ranking original settler and lieutenant governor during the "starving time" winter of 1609. By Herbert Luther Smith. (Virginia Historical Society, Richmond) *Bottom:* Captain John Smith, by Simon de Passe. (The Library of Virginia)

of James Fort. In all, only a half dozen first-hand descriptions and two maps survive from the earliest years of the colony to guide an archaeologist's shovels and trowels. Here are the salient facts about the writers of these documents:

*John Smith:* Arrived in Jamestown 1607. Yeoman farmer's son, mariner, and soldier, often at odds with his less-experienced and higher-born colleagues. From 1608 to 1631 he published varying accounts of his twenty-nine months in Virginia, as well as heavily edited reports written by other settlers who stayed on. His sometimes-inconsistent accounts sought to justify his actions at Jamestown as well as promote colonization.

*Gabriel Archer:* Arrived in Jamestown 1607. Mariner and explorer, trained in the law. As recording secretary for the Virginia governing council he described the earliest days of Jamestown in what appear to be official reports sent back to the Company in England. A devoted enemy of John Smith, he died during the "starving time" of 1609–10.

*George Percy:* Arrived in Jamestown 1607. Son of the earl of Northumberland, Percy was one of the highest-ranked of the colonists on the social scale. He served as stand-in governor during the "starving time" and was reappointed in 1611. Percy wrote an account of the 1606–7 voyage from England and a refutation of Smith's 1624 *Generall Historie,* which had put much of the blame for the "starving time" on Percy's shoulders.

*Ralph Hamor:* Arrived in Jamestown 1609. A stockholder in the Virginia Company, later a member of the governor's council in the 1620s, he published an apparent promotional report in 1615, describing a flourishing Jamestown in 1611–14, urging further investment and emigration.

*William Strachey:* Arrived in Jamestown 1609. Secretary of the colony. His letter of 1610 includes an account of the colony as he saw it in May–July 1610 and a summary of earlier events, which Percy apparently dictated to him. The most polished of the early reporters, he wrote the most exact description of James Fort, but his reliance on Percy casts some doubt on the accuracy of his account of Jamestown's first three years.

*"The Ancient Planters of Virginia":* Writing in the spring of 1623, these surviving original settlers thought the Crown should know about the mishandling of the colony under the leadership of the Virginia Company treasurer, Sir Thomas Smythe. Although cast to shed ill light on Smythe, the account includes details about Jamestown houses and hardships during the early years.

*Don Pedro de Zúñiga:* The Zúñiga map of Virginia was delivered to King Philip III of Spain in 1608 by his ambassador to England, Don Pedro de Zúñiga. This is believed by some to be a tracing of an early map by John Smith. The map includes a minuscule sketch of James Fort. Zúñiga repeatedly urged King Philip to wipe out the colony.

*Johannes Vingboons:* The Vingboons chart is a Dutch navigational chart showing structures on Jamestown Island as well as downriver forts, all in an area labeled "New Nederland."

## THE FORT

In May of 1607, Virginia looked like the Garden of Eden to Percy and probably to the English "gentlemen, artisans and laborers" seeking a place to settle in the name of King James I, and, more important, a place to reap profit for their investors, the Virginia Company of London. At this point, Virginia appeared to be what they expected: the ideal place to plant a permanent colony of English people, to find gold and a route to the rich Orient, and to convert the natives to Christianity. Little wonder that these pioneers saw a paradise: they had left home during the gray, chilly English winter and spent most of the next four and one-half months crossing the

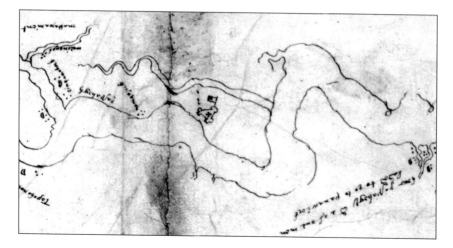

Known as the Zúñiga map (1608), this is the only known seventeenth-century rendering of James Fort. (Ministerio de Educación y Cultura de España, Archivo General de Simancas, MPD,19,163)

swelling Atlantic, cramped aboard three ships that were mere lifeboats by today's standards. It was spring in Virginia, a time when the gentle seductive breezes and lush first growth camouflage the inevitable deadly heat of the summer yet to come. The wildest dreams of a Utopian New World seemed to be reality. Surely a rich and genteel life would follow!

The Virginia Company officials had instructed the adventurers to settle at least one hundred miles from the ocean, in a place where a major river narrowed, offering defensive positions on either side of any attacking ship—which would surely be Spanish, avenging past English privateering raids. As an alternative, the colonists were advised to settle "some Island that is strong by nature."[2] As soon as they first spied land, the leader of the group and admiral of the fleet, Christopher Newport, allowed the opening of the sealed box containing a list of people preselected by the Company to rule the colony. The list named Edward Maria Wingfield, John Martin, George Kendall, Bartholomew Gosnold, John Ratcliffe, and John Smith, with Newport acting ex officio. These men voted Wingfield, the highest in social rank among them and the only original Virginia Company investor to actually go to Virginia, as their president. Wingfield then denied Smith a seat on this council, having had him held in chains since an alleged mutiny early in the Atlantic crossing. Led by Newport and Wingfield, and following their instructions, the three ships entered the largest river of the Chesapeake, which they named after their king. The party then sailed as far

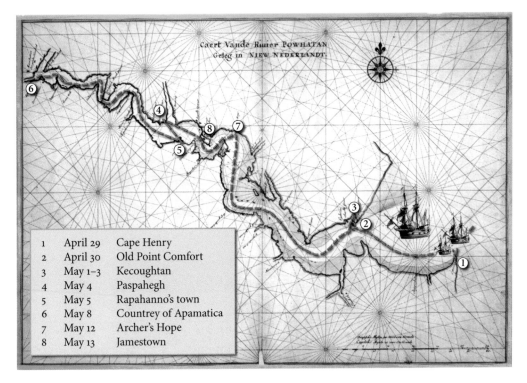

| 1 | April 29 | Cape Henry |
| 2 | April 30 | Old Point Comfort |
| 3 | May 1–3 | Kecoughtan |
| 4 | May 4 | Paspahegh |
| 5 | May 5 | Rapahanno's town |
| 6 | May 8 | Countrey of Apamatica |
| 7 | May 12 | Archer's Hope |
| 8 | May 13 | Jamestown |

Probable route of the Virginia Company adventurers as they searched the James River for the ideal place to establish Jamestown in 1607. The journey is shown on this map of the James River, probably drawn from a Dutch ship ten years after the landing at Jamestown. Caert [chart] Vande Riuer POWHATAN [James River] Geleg in Niew Nederlandt [Virginia] Atlas of the Dutch West India Company by Johannes Vingboons. (Adapted, courtesy of the National Archives, The Hague, The Netherlands)

as sixty-five miles northwest looking for that defendable narrow stretch of river. Reaching the Appomattox River without having found an uninhabited place with the right requirements, the colonists turned back toward the bay. Eventually they explored George Percy's paradise of "vivid and sundry color," later called Archer's Hope. Despite the otherwise perfect environment there, the deep water required for the easy landing of supplies was too far offshore. Timely landing of their heavy cannon was a necessity.

The next day, May 13, the group decided to settle a point of land that was actually an island at very high tide. Why there? Percy explained that, unlike Archer's Hope, here the channel was so close to the shore that ships could be tied to the trees.[3] Other considerations made Jamestown Island

Jamestown Island from the west.

the settlement site of choice. Again the Virginia Company's instructions came into play: the colonists were not to upset the Virginia Indians, especially by settling on land they already occupied. Jamestown Island was vacant. Although the island was a mere thirty-five miles from the open ocean, from which the Spanish could launch an attack, it still qualified as a naturally defensible place, with its narrow neck of land to guard against assault from the mainland Indians and its naturally hidden location in a sharp bend in the river. The several ridges at Jamestown Island provided ideal sites for a fort, particularly the third ridge from the west, the highest point of land on the north shore of the river bend. It is also possible that, although the Indians did not then occupy the land, they had been there in the not-too-distant past. By 1607 their cleared land might have evolved into a fair-sized grove of straight, tall, second-growth hardwood trees, ideal for building timber palisades and blockhouses.[4] These advantages apparently far outweighed the acres of low-lying marshland the colonists were warned to avoid and the lack of fresh water on the island. Smith deemed Jamestown Island "a very fit place for the erecting of a great cittie." Gosnold, on the other hand, viewed it with "some contention."[5]

So on May 14, 1607, after a voyage of more than five months, the colonists who had survived—104 of them, all men—filed ashore from the *Susan*

*Constant,* the *Godspeed,* and the *Discovery,* on to what the English adventurers decided to call Jamestown Island on the north shore of the James River.[6] That first landing day, Smith reports,

> now falleth every man to work . . . cut down trees . . . pitch tents . . . some provide clapboard to relade the ships . . . some make gardens, some nets . . . the council contrive [design] the fort . . . no exercise at arms or fortifications but the boughs of trees cast together in the form of a halfmoon . . . by Captain Kendall.[7]

The island was a busy place, with the men doing exactly what they needed to do for survival: clearing the land, establishing shelter, preparing to live off their own gardens and the native fish, and fortifying themselves despite Company instructions not to upset the Indians by doing so. Like Smith, Percy tells of throwing up a brush fort. Percy also writes of establishing a military guard "to watch and ward."[8] This exercise was wisely done. The settlers soon were challenged by the Paspahegh Indians from the nearest village.

At first two messengers arrived at the emerging settlement with news that their werowance, or chief, would be coming with a gift deer. Four days later, Percy reports, the werowance "came . . . to our quarter" as advertised, but instead of the deer he brought along "one hundred salvages armed," a message that the English soldiers were essentially outnumbered and surrounded. The leader also "made signs that he would give us as much land as we would desire."[9] Of course, Wingfield and the rest already knew they had ownership by the English king's patent of the whole of continental North America. Faced with this show of Indian military power, however, Wingfield must have rapidly accepted the offer, surely one that meant no more than the 1,600-acre Jamestown Island. But the deal seemed to go sour when one of the Indians grabbed a soldier's hatchet, prompting a scuffle in which a native was struck on the arm. The chief and his warriors left in anger.

The Indians seemed to be a forgiving lot, for two days later forty appeared at the Jamestown "quarter" with a deer. In addition, they offered to stay in the "fort" all night. Sensing ambush, the English denied the overnight and proceeded to flaunt their own military prowess. "One of our gentlemen" put on a demonstration to prove English weapons superior to the Indian arrows. He first set up a leather "target" (hand shield) for Indian target practice. An arrow penetrated a foot into the leather. Next a "steel target went up which shattered his arrow all to pieces."[10] This apparently ended the encounter and set the stage for open warfare one week later.

On May 27 Archer, who had become one of the captains, described the battle, "a very furious assault to our fort" by some 200 warriors. "They came up allmost into the fort, shott through the tentes." The battle "endured hott about an hower," hurting

> 11 men [Smith reported 17 casualties](whereof one dyed) and killed a Boy.
> . . . We killed divers of them . . . how many hurt we know not . . . Foure of
> the Counsell that stood in front were hurt in mayntaying the Forte, and our
> President, Master Wynckfield (who shewed himself a valiant Gentleman) had
> one shott clean through his beard . . . [a crossbar shot from the ship's cannon]
> caused the Indians to retire.[11]

This account not only forecasts the tragic future of Euro-American–Native American relations but also gives a snapshot of infant Jamestown itself. From this account it is clear that there was some sort of "fort" capable of repelling the attack for at least the hour it took for the ship's cannon fire to end the fight. Why it did take an hour for the sailors to shoot the cannon is more than a little mystifying, especially since during that time "they [the Indians] hurt us 11 men (whereof one dyed) and killed a Boy."[12] Wingfield seems to have escaped harm literally by a whisker, but the other four councilors in town, John Martin, John Ratcliffe, George Kendall, and Bartholomew Gosnold, were apparently not so lucky. However, the seriousness of their wounds drew no further comment from Archer. Captain John Smith, Newport, and others missed the attack, having left Jamestown soon after landing to explore the country in search of gold and a water passage to China, as instructed by the Company.

The assault turned out to be a wake-up call. Wingfield, who presumably now knew the men would need more than their beards, brush, and canvas to stay alive, ordered that the settlement be immediately and this time seriously fortified. The camp was to be enclosed with palisades (logs set side by side in the ground)—the men "labored pallozadoing our fort"—and the cannons were mounted.[13] These activities marked the beginning of James Fort. In only nineteen days, the enclosure stood complete. According to Percy, on June 15 "we had built and finished our fort, which was trianglewise, having three bulwarks at every corner like a half-moon, and four or five pieces of artillery mounted in them."[14]

Building the fort was no easy task for such small numbers in so short a time. If cutting and hauling logs, probably weighing 800 pounds apiece, and digging at least 900 feet of trenches to seat them was not enough of a challenge, almost daily the workmen had to dodge Indian arrows shot from the surrounding woods and marsh grasses.[15] One worker, Eustace Clovill, paid a dear price for "straggling without the fort." The snipers shot six arrows into him, causing his death in less than a week. The constant threat of incoming arrows, the heat of a developing Tidewater Virginia summer, and the stress of the fear-driven building schedule would eventually take its toll on the men. No wonder they almost mutinied: "the gentlemen and all the company [held] . . . a grudge against certain preposterous proceedings . . . [and] put up a petition to the council for reformation."[16] Newport somehow convinced the disheartened to push on, perhaps explaining that the eventual triangular design was the quickest and easiest way to protect them. It is unfortunate that these exhausted men could not know that they were in fact transforming the Paspahegh land grant into the exact spot of the genesis of the United States. Even if they could have known, however, they would soon have been in no condition to care:

This seventeenth-century Dutch image of soldiers and their tents on a river in the Low Countries is reminiscent of John Smith's 1607 description of the colonists' first day at Jamestown Island. (Courtesy Stiebner Verlag, Gmbh, Munich)

> [W]ithin ten days [June 25, 1607] scarce ten amongst us could either go or well stand, such extreme weakness and sickness oppressed us. . . . When they [the ships] departed, there remained but the common kettle [which amounted to] . . . half a pint of wheat, and as much barley . . . for a man a day, . . . and this contained as many worms as grains . . . our drink was [river?] water our lodgings castles in the air. . . . our extreme toil in bearing and planting palisadoes so strained and bruised us . . . in the extremity of the heat . . . made us . . . miserable.[17]

In the days that followed, Percy chronicled the deaths of twenty-five colonists, including the councilor Bartholomew Gosnold: "Our men were destroyed with cruel diseases as swellings, fluxs, burning fevers, and by wars, and some departed suddenly, but for the most part they died of mere famine."[18] Later Smith claims sixty-seven were dead by September, but finally "most of the soldiers recovered with the skillful diligence of master Thomas Wotton, our chirurgeon [surgeon] General."[19] Given all this stress, it is unlikely that any further work was done on the fort for some weeks after the June 15 "completion" date. When the popular Captain John Smith took over as the colony's manager in September—President Wingfield having been impeached for allegedly hoarding food—Smith oversaw the building of some thatched houses. In the fall of 1607, a number of emissaries from James River Indian tribes expressed intentions of peace, and every four or five days Pocahontas (the great chief Powhatan's daughter, who had befriended Smith) and her attendants brought the men provisions.[20] Despite these friendly actions, concern for security probably caused the new houses to be built inside the fort.

The exact form, size, and degree of sophistication of the council's fort cannot be determined from these early records, but it seems that much of the fort in its original configuration did not last long. In January 1608, after two supply ships and a hundred fresh men arrived from England, fire either seriously damaged or completely destroyed the fort. The new supply itself was to blame. Apparently something flammable in it, presumably gunpowder, set fire to "their quarters . . . the town . . . palisadoes . . . arms, bedding, apparel . . . much private provision . . . and [the reverend] Hunt lost all his library." On top of that disaster, the winter of 1608 was one of "extreme frost," and copper, one of the colonists' main means of exchange for food, had been rendered almost worthless by the ships' crewmembers' illegal Indian trade. That winter saw a rash of deaths in which, Smith reports, "more than half of us died." Despite these hardships, Smith reports a "rebuilding [of] James Towne," which included repairing the partially burned palisades, completely rebuilding the church, and reroofing the storehouse—a first reference to the existence of the latter. By summer Smith carried on with his voyages of discovery on Virginia's waterways away from Jamestown, with the presumption that the fort had been brought back in order.[21]

Yet whenever Smith returned to Jamestown from his explorations, once in July and again in September 1608, he wrote that he found the town in decay and the people "all sick, the rest some lame, some bruised—all unable to do anything but complain . . . many dead, the harvest rotting and nothing done." In September the council and company elected Smith president. Under his new leadership further construction and an apparent redesign of the fort were carried out. The fort was "invironed with a palizado of fourteen or fifteene feet, and each as much as three or four men could carrie . . . we had three Bulwarks, foure and twentie peece of ordinance upon convenient plat-forms . . . [the overall plan] reduced to the form of this ( ) [figure omitted but later called five-square]."[22]

Smith also restored discipline in the disorganized and disheartened militia: "the whole company every Saturday exercised in the plain by the west bulwark prepared for that purpose, we called Smithfield where sometimes more than an hundred savages would stand in amazement to behold how a file would batter a tree."[23]

Likely among the audience watching the troops perform were the first two immigrant women, Mistress Forest and her maid Anne Burras, and eight Germans and a Pole who had arrived with the second supply, the latter brought to make pitch, tar, glass, mills, and soap ashes. Nothing more is known about Mistress Forest, but Anne Burras soon met John Laydon, one of the few hearty survivors of the original 107 settlers. They married, presumably in Smith's recently repaired church. The mission of the Germans also was successful, for when Newport sailed back to England in late 1608, he carried among a cargo of clapboard and wainscot, Jamestown-made "trials of pitch, tar, glass . . . [and] soap-ashes."[24]

In 1608–9 the "five-square, James towne" seemed to prosper under Captain John Smith's strict leadership. That spring, although Smith apparently found enough unspoiled food in the store to make it to the fall harvest, he wrote that he instituted a "must work or no food" policy to make sure, among other things, that there would be a harvest. His work-for-food policy paid great dividends at the fort, where the men "quietly followed . . . [their] business that in three months produced . . . tar, pitch, and soap-ashes, . . . a trial of glass, made a well in the fort of excellent sweet water which was wanting, built twenty houses, recovered the church, provided nets and weirs for fishing and built a blockhouse in the neck of our isle."[25]

But again, by the summer of 1609, the corn in the store rotted while the men "digged and planted" thirty or forty acres under the direction of the fettered Paspahegh prisoners Kemps and Tassore, who were so "well used they did not desire to go from us." And the settlers caught more of the giant and nutritious sturgeon fish "than can be devoured by man and dog," which they transformed into bread. With that staple as well as various wild roots and fruits, according to Smith, "[w]e lived very well." But not for long. The same summer seven of a nine-ship supply flotilla made it in from England intending to revitalize the colony. Those ships also brought certain gentlemen who set out to murder Smith and "to supplant us rather than supply us." Over two hundred men took the new supplies away from Jamestown, going to live at the Falls of the James or downstream at the Nansemond River. When Smith sailed to the Falls in search of supplies in the late autumn, he returned with a life-threatening wound to his thigh caused by, as he put it, someone "accidentally" firing his powder bag. He soon decided to return to England, "seeing there was neither chirurgian nor chirurgery in the fort to cure his hurt." George Percy was named president.[26]

In reporting the condition of the colony at the time of his departure, Smith's *Generall Historie* offers one of the most complete state-of-the-fort descriptions—one that of course made his tenure as president look positive:

> Leaving us with . . . ten week's provision in the store, . . . twenty-four pieces of ordinance, three hundred muskets, snaphaunces and firelocks, shot, powder, and match sufficient, curats [cuirasses], pikes, swords, and morio[n]s [helmets] more than men, an hundred well-trained and expert soldiers, nets for fishing, tools of all sorts to work, apparel to supply our wants, six mares and a horse, five or six hundred swine, some goats, some sheep. . . . Jamestown was strongly palisadoed, containing more than fifty or sixty houses.[27]

But Smith also made clear his opinion that he was forced to leave behind the seeds of destruction, namely, "poor gentlemen, tradesmen, serving men, libertines [who were] ten times more fit to spoil a commonwealth than either to begin one or but help to maintain one."[28] The 1609–10 winter that followed became known as the "starving time." A flotilla of supply ships under the newly appointed lieutenant governor Sir Thomas Gates was shipwrecked in Bermuda. Indians besieged the fort.[29] The colonists' livestock was quickly eaten, including the horses, and some of their weapons were traded away for Indian corn. Only sixty of the 215 left at Jamestown survived.[30]

By spring, the *Deliverance* and the *Patience*, replacements for the governor's wrecked flagship, the *Sea Venture*, arrived from Bermuda to find "the palisades torn down, the ports open, the gates from off the[i]r hinges . . . and empty houses [some] rent up and burnt [for firewood]. . . . [T]he Indi-

*Above:* Thomas West, Third Lord De La Warre, first resident governor of Virginia, 1610–11. (From Alexander Brown's *Genesis of the United States* [Boston, 1890]) *Right:* Sir Thomas Gates, lieutenant governor of Virginia, 1610 and 1611–14. (From the original portrait by C. Jansen, in the possession of Sir Leonard Brassey, from Alexander Weddell's *A Memorial Volume of Virginia Historical Portraiture, 1585–1830,* 1930)

ans killed . . . our men [if they] stirred beyond the bounds of their blockhouse." Lieutenant Governor Gates was accompanied by William Strachey, who began his relatively precise record of Jamestown's events and appearance in 1610. The supplies brought in from Bermuda soon disappeared, and the expectation of resupply from the Indians proved to be wishful thinking. The situation declined so badly that Gates ordered an evacuation of the town. On June 7, 1610, "we . . . buryed our ordinances before the front gate which looked into the river."[31] With thirty days' supply, the survivors sailed downriver. According to one account, Gates planned to "stay some ten days at Cape Comfort . . . to wait the arrival of a supply ship."[32] More official accounts say that the party was in a head-long nonstop retreat back to England. In any event, Gates did not have to go that far or wait that long. Not far downriver the evacuees met an advance party from the incoming supply fleet of the new governor, Thomas West, Lord De La Warre. After only thirty hours' respite from Jamestown, the demoralized group had to backtrack and prepare for the new governor's arrival. Thereafter, the new leadership and especially the new supplies quickly seemed to rejuvenate the town.

Strachey's next description of the fort is considerably more positive than his first and remains the most exact we have. Only three days after his return to the abandoned town, Strachey observed,

> the fort growing since to more perfection, is now at this present in this manner: . . . about half an acre . . . is cast almost into the form of a triangle and so palisaded. The south side next the river (howbeit extended in a line or curtain sixscore foot more in length than the other two, by reason the advantage of the ground doth require) contains 140 yards, the west and east sides a hundred only. At every angle or corner, where the lines meet, a bulwark or watchtower is raised and in each bulwark a piece or two well mounted. . . . And thus enclosed, as I said, round with a palisade of planks and strong posts, four feet deep in the ground, of young oaks, walnuts, etc. . . . the fort is called, in honor of His Majesty's name, Jamestown.[33]

Percy's and Strachey's descriptions agree that James Fort was triangular with watchtowers and/or bulwarks at each of the three angles, where ordnance was mounted. This structure seems to be consistent with what appears to be a minuscule sketch of the fort on the map of Virginia delivered to King Philip III in 1608 by Don Pedro de Zúñiga.[34] Some believe this map to be a tracing of an early map sketched by John Smith. Each bulwark of the fort in the Zúñiga map has a different plan. Some of the plans may represent Strachey's watchtowers. While there were three sides, or curtains, between the bulwarks, only the south and east sides appear to be equal in length. These sides form a right angle with each other. This figure therefore certainly is "triangle-wise." The Zúñiga map also shows a much out-of-scale flag, which may be in reality a rectangular plan for an extension to the town or an enclosed garden area to the north.

In 1611, after De La Warre's illness forced him to leave Jamestown, there arrived yet another Company-appointed governor, Sir Thomas Dale. That year the optimistic settler Ralph Hamor described what seems to be a rather different Jamestown:

> The Towne . . . is reduced into a handsome forme, and hath in it two faire rowes of houses, all of framed Timber, two stories, and an upper Garret, or Corne loft high, besides the three large, and substantial Storehouses, joyned

together in a length some hundred and twenty foot, and in breadth forty, and this town hath been lately newly, and strongly impaled, and a faire platforme for Ordence in the west Bulwark raised.[35]

His glowing account of the "handsome forme" of the town and the "faire rowes of houses" paints a picture of a renovated and expanded fortified area. Hamor never really says the town plan expanded outside the limits of the original fort in any particular direction, but he does mention houses scattered beyond the town. This handsome town, whatever its form, did apparently include a governor's residence, built by and for Lieutenant Governor Gates presumably when he took office in the summer of 1611. This building was expanded by other governors as they saw fit. "The Governor's house in James Town first built by Sir Thomas Gates, Knight and the charges and by the servants of the Company since enlarged by others by the same means [is to] continue forever as the governor's house." The establishment of an official residence was a reflection of the 1609 Company charter, which vested both the commercial and the governmental affairs of the colony in the hands of the Company. Before then the governing council, directed ultimately by the king himself, carried on the affairs of the colony. Now that the resident governor had the power to govern, he presumably needed some building much more substantial than an "air castle" at Jamestown to reflect his authority.[36]

There are no more detailed descriptions of James Fort/town, but there are hints that its development was an on-again, off-again process through the decade. Governors Gates and Dale, even though they kept their main residence at Jamestown (1611–16), apparently let the fort slowly decay. Dale neglected Jamestown in favor of another fortified town he was building upriver at a place he called Henricus. Even before Dale's neglect, another document, if it states the truth, paints a Jamestown again in shambles by 1613. A Spanish prisoner held at Jamestown, Don Diego de Molina, smuggled a letter to the Spanish ambassador in London, urging a Spanish invasion of Virginia and a quick surrender of the disgruntled "slaves" at Jamestown, who were protected only by "fortifications . . . so fragile that a kick would destroy them . . . a fortification without skill and made by people who do not understand them."[37] Molina also said that the palisade walls were so full of gaps that the enemy outside was safer than the defenders inside.

Things were no better in 1617 when yet another new lieutenant governor arrived at Jamestown, Captain Samuel Argall. Planter John Rolfe's disparaging description of the town is almost an echo of Gates's discovery of Jamestown just after the "starving time":

> In James Towne he [Argall] found but five or six houses, the Church downe, the Palizado's broken, the Bridge [a wharf to the channel?] in pieces, the well of fresh water spoiled; the Store-house they used for the church, the market-place, and streets, and all other spare places planted with Tobacco, the Salvages [Indians] as frequent in their houses as themselves, . . . the Palizado's not sufficient to keepe out Hogs.[38]

Rolfe failed to mention that his own actions might have been in part responsible for Jamestown's decay. His development of a profitable tobacco strain that would thrive in Virginia soil had begun to drain the Jamestown population to hinterland tobacco plantations and diminished the settlers' interest in keeping up the fort—that is, except as they could grow tobacco in any vacant space there. Nevertheless, Argall set out to make things right by repairing the defective town. During his administration (1617–19) a 20' × 50' church was built.[39]

Also during Argall's tenure as governor, the Dutch were busy mapping Virginia, claiming it lay in "New Nederland." The area was so labeled on a circa-1617 detailed chart of the James River from its confluence with the Appomattox to the Chesapeake Bay. This chart, drawn from a ship as it sailed along, is one of 156 maps included in a worldwide *Atlas of the Dutch West India Company*. Known as the "Vingboons chart" for its maker, Johannes Vingboons, the map shows Jamestown Island, individual houses around modern Hopewell, and two other early Virginia forts: Fort Algernon at Point Comfort and Charles Fort at nearby Strawberry Bank. The downriver forts appear as attached gable-end buildings, three at Algernon and two at Charles Fort.[40] Jamestown is depicted in an identical way—attached buildings—and located about one-third of the way from the western end of the island. The Dutch charts, intended as navigational guides, usually show buildings as they would appear from a distant ship, not as mere symbolic structures. So either each of these forts had prominent multisection storehouses—"three large storehouses joined together in length"[41]—or the chart symbols depict blockhouses or watchtowers, the most visible features of forts from a distance. If they are defenses, then Jamestown and Fort Algernon appear almost identical—three blockhouses each—while Charles Fort had only two and perhaps a palisaded "yard."

In fact, the Jamestown Island buildings are labeled "Blockhouse Jamestown." If the triple houses mark the exact location of the town, as they almost certainly do, then the map locates the fort some distance from the now-eroded western end of the island. Allowing for distortion in scale, the storehouse or blockhouse symbol appears to be located precisely where the later church tower stands today.

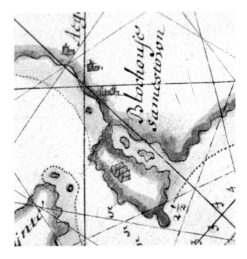

Detail of ca.-1617 Dutch chart of the James River showing Jamestown Island and vicinity. (National Archives, The Hague, The Netherlands)

Other documentary descriptions of James Fort's private and public buildings are vague but suggest that for months the town looked like a temporary army camp. First came the tents and the "castles in the air." As late as September 10, 1607, there were "no houses to cover us, our Tents were rotten and our [thatched roof] Cabbins worse than nought."[42] Three years later, however, things seemed to have improved some. Strachey described the houses in the fortified town:

> to every side, a proportioned distance from the palisade, is a settled street of houses that runs along so as each line of the angle hath his street. . . . The houses were all burnt by a casualty of fire the beginning of the second year . . . which since we have better rebuilded though as yet no great uniformity, either for fashion or beauty of the street. . . . The houses have wide and large country chimneys [wood, clay covered?] . . . [they] cover their houses now (as the Indians) with the barks of trees, as durable and good proof against storms and winter weather as the best tile . . . before in sultry weather would be like stoves, whilst they were, as at first, pargeted and plastered with bitumen or tough clay.[43]

Regardless of how improved these shelters became, it is clear that they were never intended to last long. According to Strachey:

> We dwell not here to build us bowers.
> And Halls for pleasure and good cheer:
> But halls we build for us and ours,
> To dwell in them whilst we live here.[44]

There was a constant repair and replacement program: "we were constrained every yeere to build and repaire our old cottages, which were always decaying in all places in the Countrie." These so-called "cottages" may have been prone to decay but they were not scarce. By summer 1608, "we had about fortie or fiftie severall houses warm and dry." The town houses increased to "some fiftie or sixtie" a year later. If the figure is not exaggerated, some of these houses had to stand outside the rather constrained space in the fort Strachey described.[45]

There is very little record of James Fort after the Dutch navigators produced the 1617 chart. A last-minute warning saved the fort from damage during the disastrous Indian uprising of 1622. A year and a half later, James Fort, other forts, and a number of the houses in Virginia were all very much at risk. By August or September 1623,

> James Citie . . . [and other parts of the colony] have been suffered by the Colony of late to grow to such decay that they are become of no strength or use
> . . . there are no places fortified for defense & safetie . . . the plantations are farr asunder & their houses stand scattered one from another, and are onlie made of wood few or none of them beeing framed houses but punches sett into the Ground And covered with Boarde so as a firebrand is sufficient to consume them all. . . . The fortifications antientlie used were by Trench and Pallizado and (which now are all gone to ruyne . . . [lined out] and diverse blockhouses made of timber . . . [lined out] great Tymber built uppon passages and for scouring the Pallizadoes: all which now are gone to ruin.[46]

The documentary evidence of the nature and extent of James Fort and the early town is often ambiguous. We know that much of this evidence could have been distorted for self-serving reasons. The 1623 document written by the ancient planters is significantly at odds with the earlier accounts. According to these surviving original settlers, in January 1608 the town only had forty occupants, most "at the point of death—all utterly destitute of houses, not one as yet built, so that they lodged in cabins and holes in the ground [and soon thereafter] . . . there were [only] some poor houses built."[47] They do, however, mention the houses Gates constructed, presumably in 1611, that constant repair left still standing when the ancient planters wrote in 1623.

Overall, a fairly consistent image emerges from these accounts. James Fort was some sort of triangular enclosure, between one and two acres in size, built on ground located on the James River shore near the southwestern end of Jamestown Island. James Fort became Jamestown soon in the literature; it included houses of varied quality, a church, a storehouse, and other buildings, and it grew in size. Many people died there from a number of causes, primarily disease, starvation, and battle with the Virginia Indians. The town had a number of episodes of neglect and decline, but each new governor's term brought the town back to serviceable condition or renovated and expanded it. The early fort fell into final decay and disappeared by 1624, when James I dissolved the Virginia Company and took over the colony for the crown.

## THE PEOPLE

The eyewitness accounts of Jamestown's first seventeen struggling years paint a picture not only of James Fort but also of the people involved in its founding—including the eyewitnesses themselves. Other available documentary evidence can tell us more of the events and people that affected the fabric of the developing Jamestown Island settlement. Demographic and biographical information can be gleaned from records of individual Englishmen who first landed there as well as of the people who came soon thereafter: the "diverse other" men and women. Their age, social standing, colonial and military experience, and place of origin in England all influenced how they reacted to the alien Virginia environment. Documents also tell of another people whose presence had a tremendous impact, both positively and negatively, on the siting and survival of Jamestown: the Virginia Indians. To a certain extent, they can be known individually, too. Finally, we can even come to know some of the story of the Spanish, whose constant threat of invasion influenced Jamestown's first development and whose failure to invade early on inadvertently let English roots take hold.

First, let us consider the Englishmen and their last hours ashore in England. It is technically false to state, as most history books do, that the first three ships disembarked for Virginia from London. Rather, the settlers last trod English soil at a place called Blackwall, slightly downriver from London, adjacent to the foreboding-sounding Isle of Dogs.[48] Blackwall in the early seventeenth century amounted to alehouses and churches supporting the docks of the emerging English maritime trade. Today, at the end of a street named Blackwall Way, is a place known traditionally as Blackwall Stairs, where the remnants of very old wooden stairs are visible at low tide. Local lore has it that the Virginia-bound legion of men and boys boarded the ships there in December of 1606. Until at least 1897, a Tudor half-timber structure stood nearby, called the Sir Walter Raleigh House by local historians—an inn where travelers, presumably once Sir Walter himself, awaited transport out of the Thames.[49] Conceivably this inn would have been the freshest memory of an English house that most of the future Jamestown settlers would carry with them during the tedious crossing to the New World. There must have been great longing to return to that rugged inn and the alehouses of Blackwall when the three outbound ships lay becalmed in bone-chilling weather near the mouth of the Thames for over a month—almost half of the anticipated length of the voyage.[50] Who were these shivering, frustrated would-be colonists—108 men and boys in all—waiting for the winds and their fortunes to change?

Certain biographical facts are commonly known about some of the Jamestown leaders. We know, for example, something of the members of the first council selected by the Virginia Company before the voyage, their identities revealed at the opening of that sealed box at the voyage's end: Edward Maria Wingfield, John Martin, Captain George Kendall, John Ratcliffe, Bartholomew Gosnold, and Captain John Smith.[51] They all had

Map of London area, dated 1610, showing Blackwall, the point of embarkation for the original Jamestown settlers. (By permission of the British Library)

military/combat experience acquired either in fighting the eighty-year wars in the
Netherlands, in privateering, or in establishing the English plantations in Ireland.
Captain John Smith had fought not only
in the Netherlands, but also in France and
Transylvania. Gosnold led the capture of a
Spanish galleon and took a colonizing party to settle briefly off Cape Cod in 1602. Except for Smith, they all were gentry, some
urban and some rural.

What is not so well known are their ages,
which ranged from twenty-seven (Smith)
to fifty-seven (Wingfield). The rest of the
council were in their forties, except Gosnold, who was thirty-six, and Kendall,
thirty-seven. At a time when fifty-six was
the average life expectancy, these men were
primarily "seniors."[52] (Thus, in his youth as
well as in his lower social status, Smith did
not fit the norm of the leaders.) The rest of
the party for whom biographical data has been determined so far ranged in
age from the forty-six-year-old Christopher Newport of Harwich to nine-
year-old James Brumfield of Lincolnshire. The average age of the noncoun-
cil men was about twenty-five.[53]

The so-called Sir Walter Raleigh House (now demolished)
at Blackwall, near London,
traditionally known for housing hopeful settlers waiting
to board ships to America.
(Tower Hamlets Local History
Library and Archives, London)

The settlers' home parishes and probably their family seats were either the greater London area (including the Kent/Sussex counties to the
southeast and Essex), Suffolk, the greater Peterborough area, and John
Smith's Lincolnshire. Of the original colonists whose place of origin can
be determined, twelve came from the city of London, and an equal number came from the greater London area and East Anglia. Those from East
Anglia—the river port town areas of Suffolk, Norfolk, Lincolnshire, and
Cambridgeshire—were younger than those from the greater London area.
A small percentage came from other towns or counties but not from any
other single region in England. Fourteen came with relatives: cousins, fa-
thers, sons, and brothers. Six had some kinship with Gosnold.[54]

From these statistics, drawn from research still in progress, one might
begin to speculate how and why these men and boys wound up filing down

Map of southern England showing the places of origin of a number of the first Jamestown colonists.

NUMBER OF
INDIVIDUALS

- 0
- 1
- 2–3
- 4–7
- 8–12

**CORNWALL**
Robert Beheathland
George Kendall
Richard Simmons

**ESSEX**
Henry Adling
Gabriel Archer
Edward Browne
Robert Ford
Matthew Fitch
George Martin
John Martin
Eustace Clovill
Edward Morris
Christopher Newport
Kenelme Throck-
morton

**HEREFORDSHIRE**
Richard Crofts

**HERTFORDSHIRE**
Roger Cooke

**HUNTINGDONSHIRE**
Edward Harrington
Nicholas Scot
John Stevenson
William Love
Edward M. Wingfield

**KENT**
Edward Pising
Thomas Wotton

**LANCASHIRE**
Robert Pennington

**LINCOLNSHIRE**
John Smith
John Herd
William Laxton
Robert Fenton
James Brumfield
Richard Dixon
John Dods
Nathaniel Pecock

**LONDON**
John Capper
Thomas Emery
Richard Frith
James Read
Thomas Gore (Gower)
William Garrett
George Cassen
Thomas Cassen
William Cassen
Richard Mutton
William Roods
Thomas Sands

**NORTHAMPTONSHIRE**
Jereme Alicock

**SHROPSHIRE**
Ellis Kinistone
(Kingston)

**STAFFORDSHIRE**
Edward Brinto
William Smethes
George Walker

**SUFFOLK**
William Brewster
Anthony Gosnold
(brother)
Anthony Gosnold
(cousin)
Bartholemew Gosnold
George Goulding
Thomas Webb
Thomas Cowper
Edward Brookes
Anas Todkill
William Unger

**SUSSEX**
George Percy
Drew Pickayes

**WILTSHIRE**
John Martin Jr.

**YORKSHIRE**
Lancelot Booker

those Blackwall stairs to begin their Virginia adventure. Finding gold was considered to be a realistic expectation, as was the assignment of land in Virginia to planters or adventurers.[55] It is logical to assume that many of the immigrants were the younger sons of gentry, with little prospect of inheriting the family lands in England. Insofar as we can now determine, at least six of the gentlemen were younger sons; the gentleman Bartholomew Gosnold, for example, had an older brother. Prospects for acquiring land in Virginia must have been appealing to these younger gentlemen, as to other immigrants well into the seventeenth century.[56] But land could not have been the primary consideration for many others. At least three other gentlemen, including Wingfield and Martin, were the eldest sons in their families.[57] Clearly, they were gentlemen with other motives, perhaps just the adventure of it all.

How did word of the voyage get out in an age when only one in ten could read and where the roads were hardly passable? The distribution patterns of geographic origins suggest that the principal leaders may have been the principal sources of information as well.[58] It is logical to assume that the settlers from London learned of the venture through the promotional program of the Virginia Company based there. Thomas Smythe, the London merchant, "whose wealth and influence played so large a part in the formation of the first Virginia Company," and who may have had a personal hand in collecting the London recruits himself, was Bartholomew Gosnold's cousin-in-law.[59]

Born in 1571 near Ipswich, Suffolk, Gosnold with his brother, Anthony, and sisters Elizabeth and Margaret attended school at his uncle John's moated manor, Otley Hall. Through his uncle, secretary to the earl of Essex, Gosnold became a daring mariner, venturing to the Azores in 1597 and accumulating booty by privateering against the Spanish. Essex intended to fund a New World voyage to include Gosnold, but Essex's implication in the 1601 Essex Rebellion and his ultimate execution left Gosnold no support for the trip. The following year the earl of Southampton—cousin of Edward Wingfield—stepped forward to fund the Cuttyhunk colony near Cape Cod, of which Gosnold was appointed admiral. Although the colony lasted only a month, Gosnold became known as an outstanding mariner and immediately began planning to sail to the southern coast of America.

Gosnold gathered the leaders and many of the other first settlers from among his East Anglian friends, neighbors, and relatives. He must have been a particularly effective promoter, since, like few others, he could

*Left:* Otley Hall, Suffolk, England, the moated manor house of Bartholomew Gosnold's uncle, and possibly the meeting place where Gosnold, Edward Maria Wingfield, Christopher Newport, John Smith, and Richard Hakluyt planned the Jamestown voyage and settlement. *Right:* Otley High House, Suffolk, the manor of Bartholomew Gosnold's father, Anthony.

describe firsthand the Atlantic voyage and at least part of the area then known as "Virginia." Gosnold would have been able to assure his listeners that the new Virginia adventure would be different. He had learned from the Norumbrian (New England) shortcomings and successes. He could well have said with conviction that the south of Virginia was a paradise in comparison to the northern latitudes.[60] John Smith credited Gosnold with being the principal promoter of the Virginia venture.[61]

By 1605 the plans for a southern colony led by Gosnold were much advanced, and by then included Wingfield, Gosnold's cousin Thomas Smythe, and Gosnold's friend, the soldier and traveler John Smith. In on the planning as well was Richard Hakluyt, the vicar of nearby All Saints Church, Weatheringsett, and the king's official geographer. It was Hakluyt who put into print the most vivid accounts of the English explorations in the New World and the most forceful and convincing arguments for founding English colonies. Otley Hall may have been used as the forum for the planning meetings of these promoter/friends and as a base for recruiting men from the vicinity. Judging from the way the East Anglian hometowns cluster on the map of southeastern England, it is logical to assume that Gosnold was an accomplished recruiter for the Virginia venture from the environs of Otley.

When the fleet sailed, however, Christopher Newport became the commanding admiral, and Wingfield, a chief stockholder in the Virginia Company, an aspiring president. As second-in-command despite his experience as a mariner, Gosnold must have watched helplessly as the fleet floundered in the mouth of the Thames for almost the entire first month of the voyage. Gosnold must also have been frustrated enduring Newport's long southern route to Virginia via the Canary and West Indian Islands when he already knew the benefit of the faster northern route. It was, in fact, at their first stop in the Canary Islands that Gosnold's friends, John Smith and Stephen Calthrope, along with John Robinson, were implicated in a mutiny. Smith was "restrained," probably in chains. By the time the fleet got to Nevis in the Virgin Islands, Newport ordered gallows to be constructed to hang him. The hanging never happened, possibly because Gosnold intervened.

We pick up the Jamestown story again in Virginia. After an unspecified illness of three weeks, the talented Gosnold died on August 22, 1607, and was buried in or near James Fort with full military honors. By the fall of 1607, according to Smith, sixty-seven of the original 107 settlers had died, and George Percy recorded the deaths of twenty-four gentlemen, one laborer, and two others during the months of August and September 1607.[62] The greatest number of the gentlemen, eleven of the sixteen who were reported by Percy as having died, came from London.[63] Others who died during the rest of the summer came from just about every other region in England. It is perhaps significant, however, that the men Captain John Smith took with him during his two voyages of "discovery" that summer, one to the Falls of the James and the other into the Chesapeake, included the men and boys from his home area of Lincolnshire and Norfolk. They were among those who apparently survived the summer death toll (or at least were not included in George Percy's list of the dead). Of course they were away from Jamestown Island during the real heat of the summer, sailing on the open water, which gives more credence to the assumption that Jamestown Island with its marshes and lack of fresh spring water may have been responsible for the quick demise of so many. On the other hand, perhaps Smith chose the strongest and healthiest of the group to go with him, thus culling out the people who might have survived had they stayed at the fort.

The story of Jamestown traditionally focuses on Smith and other leaders, so much so that a number of people whose actions immeasurably affected the settlement become invisible. John Smith listed 213 settlers' names among those who made the first few Jamestown voyages, dismissing the rest as mere "diverse others."[64] These anonymous "diverse others" should not be so quickly dismissed. Contributing just as significantly to the Jamestown story were hundreds of other unnamed colonists, both men and women, the Virginia Indians, and even the Spanish.

The Virginia Indians' first significant impact was on the siting of Jamestown itself. Historians have long maligned the choice of the Jamestown site, owing to the unhealthy nature of the low-lying marshy island and the danger posed by the island's location deep within Powhatan's territory. The island is so low-lying today that 80 percent is below the water level of storm flooding.[65] The lack of springs meant that only brackish river water or shallow wells could serve the colony, a fact often listed as contributing to Jamestown's high death rates. So why choose this place? Percy explained the choice by the proximity of the channel, but it is clear that the experienced military leaders saw the highest ground and the surrounding water as a natural defense against the expected enemies: the Virginia Indians and the Spanish.

To the natives themselves, "Virginia Indians" were neither "Virginian" nor "Indians." Those were their English names. In 1612 William Strachey, author of that precise James Fort description, wrote, "The severall terrytoryes and provinces which are in chief commaunded by their great king Powhatan, are comprehended under the donomynation of Tsenacommacoh, of which we may the more by experience speak being the place wherein our abode and habitation hath now well neere six years consisted."[66] Tsenacomacah was the native name of the territory under the control of their leader, Powhatan, or at least that part of the territory explored and first settled by the English. It follows that the native people could be called Tsenacomacans. But to the English, the people they met along the banks of the rivers were variously called savages, salvages, naturals, natives, barbarians, heathens, or Indians. (Today most people, including modern descendants, refer to the Virginia Indians of Powhatan's chiefdom in Tidewater Virginia simply as Powhatans.) In the same way, the Powhatan River became the James River, named for King James I.[67] In the eyes of many of the English, the land was vacant, the "savages" only another form of wildlife on the "untamed" landscape. In fact, the replacement of Tsenacomacan terms by English names was a first phase of the establishment of an English population to rule or replace the Tsenacomacans themselves. The king had claimed all of Tsenacomacah and beyond to the western sea and north to

John Smith's map of Virginia, which essentially delineates the boundaries of Powhatan's geographic influence, an area the Indians called Tsenacomacah. (First published in 1612; courtesy of the Library of Virginia)

modern New Jersey, as long as no other "Christian" nations had any settlements there. To rename places with English names meant conquest.

The Tsenacomacans had their own names for themselves, their villages, their rivers, and even the new English arrivals, Tassantassas (King James and his people).[68] We can know this, ironically, only from English accounts, biased as these observations of a foreign culture are. Nonetheless, these depictions of Tsenacomacans provide a profile of a significant group of players in the Jamestown story, telling of a nation with a sophisticated language, customs, government, and economy.

The southernmost river in Tsenacomacah was the Powhatan (modern James River), named for the long-time native leader of the united chiefdom that greeted the English colonists in 1607. Who was he? Some speculate

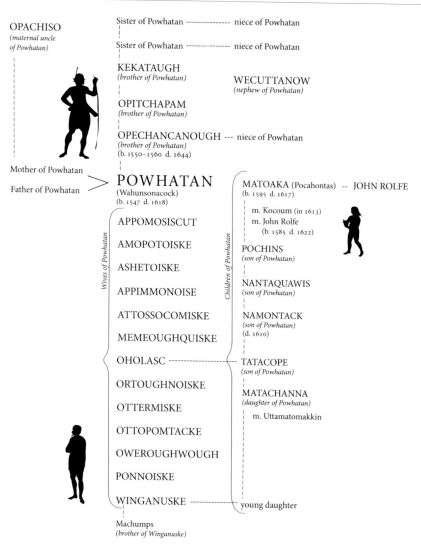

A hypothetical Powhatan family genealogical chart, based on English sources.

he was the cousin of Don Luis, who met the Jesuit settlers of the Chesapeake in 1570.[69] It was Don Luis who went to Spain with the Jesuits and upon returning led a massacre of the missionaries. Whether or not the speculation is correct, Powhatan is almost invariably characterized by the English as the single most powerful chief among the Virginia Indians: "He is of parsonage a tall well proportioned man, with a sower looke, his head somewhat gray, his beard so thinne that it seemeth none at al, his age near 60; of a very able and hardy body to endure any labor."[70]

Powhatan, also known as Wahunsonacock, was the head of a huge family whose genealogy we can know in some measure. A variety of records, mainly Smith's *Generall Historie* and Strachey's *Historie of Travell Into Virginia Britania,* list the names of thirty of Powhatan's relatives and in-laws.[71] Of his three named brothers, the most can be known of Opechancanough, werowance of the principal village on what the Tsenacomacans called the Pamunky River (modern York River). Upon Powhatan's death in 1618, Opechancanough became ruler either after or along with another brother, Opitchapam. Opechancanough led two devastating assaults against the English in 1622 and 1644. When he was over ninety years old, he was shot and killed at Jamestown, where he had been imprisoned after the 1644 attacks on the English settlements.[72]

One source claims Powhatan had "many more than one hundred" wives. The names of at least a dozen of them are recorded.[73] One wife, Oholasc, served as queen of Quiyoughcohannock. The names of seven children of Powhatan's five sons and two daughters are also on record. Three sons were werowances and the fourth, Nantaquawis, was described by Captain John Smith as the "manliest, comliest and the boldest spirit I ever saw in a salvage." Matachanna, one of Powhatan's two daughters, married Uttamatomakkin (Tomocomo), a priest who traveled with her more famous sister, Pocahontas, and her English husband, John Rolfe, to England in 1616–17.[74] Tomocomo was not impressed with the land of the strange Tassantassas— but apparently Pocahontas was.

Pocahontas, the favored daughter of Powhatan who befriended John Smith, was kidnapped and christianized by the English. She married John Rolfe in 1613, ushering in a period of peace between the settlers and the Indians. She also went to England, was received by the king, and shortly thereafter started for home. Lord Carew, in a letter to Sir Thomas Roe in 1616/1617, wrote that she waited "reluctantly" for favorable winds for her return voyage, sorely against her will. In the end, she died before sailing to

Virginia.[75] She is presumably buried in the chancel of St. George's Church, Gravesend, rebuilt after it burned in the early eighteenth century. Because of that fire and the rebuilding Pocahontas's exact burial spot remains a challenging puzzle for archaeologists and interested direct descendants of the Jamestown colony.[76]

Besides Uttamatomakkin and Pocahontas, a number of individual Tsenacomacans are recorded to have spent time with the English. Kemps, an Indian prisoner in the fort, taught the colonists to raise corn, and while he was a slave of George Percy, he guided the English during raids on the "Pasbeheans and the Chiconamians."[77] Pepasschicher also guided the English. Mantiuas, also called Nantaquawis, a son of Powhatan, traveled with them, and Machumps was "sometyme in England." Powhatan had Amarice killed for staying in the fort without his permission.[78]

Painting from an engraving from life of Pocahontas, the favored daughter of Powhatan, made shortly before she died in England. She was buried at Gravesend, east of London, in 1617. (Oil on tapestry, by Mary Ellen Howe, from an engraving by Simon de Passe; on loan to the Virginia Historical Society, Richmond)

It is a fact that Pocahontas married John Rolfe in 1613. Her first husband was an Indian named Kocoum. In asking permission from Sir Thomas Dale to marry Pocahontas, Rolfe seemed to be saying indirectly that such an intercultural marriage would be frowned upon by the English or at least be unusual. Other evidence suggests that intermarriage was officially scorned. Unofficially, however, there are strong reasons to suspect considerable mixing of the two cultures: the all-male population of the settlement during the first sixteen months would have spurred such mixing; and in 1612 the Spanish reported that as many as "40 or 50 of the men had married with the salvages."[79]

Despite the suggestion that Tsenacomacans had considerable access to the English and to Jamestown itself, serious animosity between the Indians and the English almost wiped the colony out during the "starving time" of 1609–10. Some Virginia Indians besieged the fort that winter, and the siege was so effective that "it is true that the Indians killed as fast without, if our men stirred but beyond their bounds of their blockhouse, as famine and pestilence did within."[80] The Indians withheld even their occasional food deliveries. One explanation for the trouble may be the arrival at Jamestown of twenty women and children on the *Blessing* in the fall of 1609; perhaps the siege was a result of these newcomers' presence. It certainly must have sent a strong signal across Tsenacomacah that what might have been perceived as a small, perhaps temporary all-male trading post was growing into something quite different: a permanent settlement of families.[81] Extermination of the invaders may have appeared to be the only course of action.

Whatever the effect the immigration of women and children on Tsenacomacan foreign policy, these newcomers certainly constitute another group of anonymous "diverse others" who influenced the developing "new England." We already know that the first English women, Mistress Forest and Anne Burras, came to the colony in the fall of 1608. They were not the only English women in town for long, however. According to the Spanish ambassador to England (and spy) Pedro de Zúñiga, one hundred women joined the four or five hundred men in the Gates 1609 flotilla to the colony.[82] The *Blessing* women accounted for twenty of these. Perhaps half the remaining eighty arrived as the remains of the fleet limped into the Jamestown port during the summer of 1609, and with the Bermuda ships *Deliverance* and *Patience* that arrived at Jamestown in May 1610.[83] The names of the women who arrived on the *Blessing* are not known, but Temperance Flowerdew, wife of the future governor, Sir George Yeardley, came in 1609, as did Thomasine Cawsey, Elizabeth Joones, and Amtyte Waine, in time for them, along with the women from the *Blessing,* to experience the "starving" winter of 1609–10. The list of named women grows to thirty-five by 1618, if the dates and the census of 1624–25 are reliable.[84] When Sir Thomas Gates returned to Virginia in 1611, he brought along his daughters, Margaret and Elizabeth.[85] There must have been hundreds of anonymous "diverse other" women who braved the crossing and the "seasoning time" of a Virginia summer as well. The three female burials uncovered by archaeologists beneath the third and fourth Statehouse foundations on the western edge of the town site may be evidence that few women survived at Jamestown for long. All three were dead before the age of thirty-four.[86]

The siege of James Fort almost ended the colony. The two Bermuda-built ships that arrived in 1610 came not only with women, but also with far too few provisions for a starving colony and the new arrivals. By June 1610 Gates decided to move the survivors out of Jamestown and set sail for England. Thanks to what has been characterized as last-second divine intervention, an advance vessel, followed by the arrival of Governor De La Warre and abundant fresh supplies, turned the deserters back to Jamestown in what seemed to be the nick of time. A more careful reading of one account of that so-called chance meeting, however, reveals that Gates knew De La Warre was on his way and was going to wait for him for "ten days at Cape [Point] Comfort" at the mouth of the James. After that time he was "otherwise so to go for England" with whatever he had left on board of his thirty-day rations.[87] This waiting period made good sense. Upon his arrival in the James from Bermuda two months earlier, Gates had found thirty people with Percy at Point Comfort, literally healthy as clams, living off the seafood there. They had thrived while their fellow colonists held the fort and died like "dogges." The wait for De La Warre was not a desperate measure, then, but a chance to be revived by the Point Comfort seafood before risking a voyage home with meager supplies, in the event that De La Warre's flotilla did not arrive. The notion that chance alone saved a failed Jamestown might well be an exaggeration.

Just as the Virginia Indians and the population of English women presented challenges as well as benefits to Jamestown, so did another group: the Spanish. The Jamestown colonists always had to prepare to defend against invasion by the ships and the troops of the Catholic Spanish. The threat was not entirely external: the first president, Edward Maria Wingfield, and perhaps other Englishmen had strong Catholic backgrounds, and the arrest and execution of Captain George Kendall seems to have been carried out because he was a suspected agent of the Spanish. The Spanish king, Philip III, received a steady stream of secret information directly from a "confidential person on His Majestie's [English] Council" concerning Jamestown events and details.[88]

The settlement was in a precarious place indeed, according to the Spanish. A letter from the Spanish ambassador in London, Don Pedro de Zúñiga, reporting to Philip details of Zúñiga's conference with James I, claimed that King James himself had said that if the Spanish wanted to "punish" (remove) the Jamestown colonists, "neither he nor they could complain." In fact, according to Zúñiga, King James called the Jamestown colonists "terrible people." Zúñiga was almost certainly exaggerating, trying to maneuver Philip to send troops to wipe out the colony, for in all his surviving

*Left:* King James I of England, artist unknown. (Colonial Williamsburg Foundation) *Right:* King Philip III of Spain, by Diego Velázquez, ca. 1634/35. (Museo Nacional del Prado, Madrid)

letters he consistently urges Philip III to do this. Regardless of what James I might have said or thought of Jamestown, clearly the Spanish desired to erase it from their "Indies." On January 17, 1608, Philip III endorsed a plan proposed by his Council of War whereby he "command[ed] that there should be prepared whatever was necessary to drive out the people who are in Virginia . . . [and] not to let anyone hear what is being done."[89] Presumably the plan was to send a fleet then lying in preparation at the Windward Islands to annihilate Jamestown. But there also seems to have been another proposal to the king for the colony's destruction, involving a double agent at Jamestown.

In a March 1609 letter to King Philip, Zúñiga refers to his dealings with Baron Arundel, a disgruntled English Catholic, who proposed to aid the Spanish by sailing on the pretext of a voyage of discovery, choosing a man in Puerto Rico to be planted as a spy at Jamestown. The man would be taken to Jamestown and instructed about the geography of the James River region and the nature of the English forts there so that he could relate to King Philip "by what means those people can be driven out without violence in arms."[90] What "means" the baron had in mind to erase Jamestown

The Somerset House Conference, 1604, artist unknown. This historic meeting between Spanish and English diplomats ended twenty years of fighting among the English, the Spanish, and the Dutch. The resulting peace treaty removed some of the threat of Spanish sea power from the challenges of English North American colonization. (National Portrait Gallery, London)

without firing a shot is a mystery. One theory is that a Spanish agent might have been sent to secretly lace the common kettle with arsenic. Such a poisoning might explain the periodic mass deaths at Jamestown, although it cannot account for deaths that occurred before March 1609 (sixty-six in the summer of 1607, and at least thirteen in 1608).[91] Alternatively, it is more likely that Arundel knew that the population of the colony had had enough of Virginia, and any offer to be ferried back to England might look far better than an impending winter without Smith's negotiating talents with the Indians.[92] Or maybe he thought it possible to gain enough of Powhatan's trust to persuade him to stage a more concerted siege of the fort. Then Jamestown would indeed be wiped out without resorting to Spanish arms.

In any case, Arundel's plan most likely would not have been executed. Once approved by the king—in itself a two-month process with the passage of letters to and from Spain—the series of voyages, the training period for the chosen spy, and the devising and execution of the plan would have required many more months. Apart from the question of time, after reading of the proposed Arundel scheme, Philip III did not approve of dealing with Arundel. He urged Zúñiga to act with "great caution with the Baron of Arundel." Over the next two years, the king merely kept asking for inside information about the colony without giving the green light to crush it.[93]

The fact that the Windward Island fleet never sailed to Virginia and that the Spanish let Jamestown take root by neglect, chance, or design has turned out to be one of the greatest diplomatic success stories in the history of the English nation. Thanks to what these "diverse other" Spanish did not do, Jamestown survived.

# REDISCOVERING JAMESTOWN

*James Fort: The Documentary Evidence*

Imagining what James Fort really looked like from documents alone can be frustrating. For example, according to Percy, the overall configuration of James Fort was "triangle-wise." What does that mean? Was it or was it not a triangle? Or was it "triangle-wise" because it was not a equilateral triangle? Or was it "sort of" a triangle, meaning Percy saw more than three sides, perhaps a short fourth wall? If the fort had three joining walls, then it was not "like" a triangle but in fact *was* a triangle. Percy also reported that the fort had "three bulwarks at every corner like a half moon." So were there as many as three protruding bulwarks at every corner, making a total of nine, or only three bulwarks total, one bulwark where each of three walls connected? Can a triangle even have corners? They actually have angles. Does the word *corner* suggest a fourth side? Is each of the three bulwarks a half moon, or demi-lune, a military architectural term for a corner defense shaped like a wedge with an inner curved wall, or do the three points at each corner together form a half moon? When Percy refers to "four or five pieces of artillery in them" (the bulwarks or the half moons), does he mean four to five guns total or four or five in each of three bulwarks, totaling twelve to fifteen mounted guns?

The Zúñiga map, likely a 1608 tracing of a draft version of Smith's *Map of Virginia,* seems to settle the question about the number of walls in the fort—three—but the shapes of the corner bulwarks, if they are architecturally correct, do not look anything like traditional half moons (see p. 12). Are these supposed to be circular bulwarks and rectangular gates on the river side, with a larger single circular bulwark on the land side? Is what looks like a flag on a flagpole really a flag at all, or is it a plan of a palisade connecting to a rectangular outer enclosure? Is the slightly off-center *X* a designation for the church? And what about scale? As drawn, the fort encompasses at least fifty acres and winds up near but not directly on the western end of the island. Surely the size does not reflect reality, although the relative location might. Almost certainly the asymmetrical shape of the triangle suggests that this symbol is no mere generic fort icon, intended only to locate the building in relation to the ocean and rivers for the guidance of future invading Spanish ships. Yet the church does not deserve even a sketch-plan view. Can the map details, or some of them, be taken literally? If only some qualify as truth, then which ones?

The other map of Jamestown Island made during the Virginia Company period, the Vingboons chart of the Powhatan (James) River, likely dating to 1617–20, shows only a triple-gabled building to designate "Blockhouse Jamestown" (see p. 13). Is this chart intended to show everything a ship's captain might recognize as he finds his way upriver? If so, had the fort walls already disappeared by the time the chart was drawn, leaving only the fort's most prominent building? Or was the chart maker selective, leaving out the palisades in favor of the clearest landmark for navigators?

Aerial view of James Fort site with superimposed reconstruction of James Fort, 2005.

Eyewitness documents provide no clearer guide to the location and appearance of James Fort. In July 1610 William Strachey described a very precise one-half-acre triangle and stated the dimensions of the three curtains (technically, walls between bulwarks): river side 140 yards, land sides 100 yards each. But his dimensions describe a fort interior at least twice the size of his one-half-acre estimate (1.1–1.75 acres). So can his measurements of the walls be trusted?

Even more puzzlingly, in a description of the fort in 1608, almost two years before Strachey wrote, Captain John Smith reported that the fort was "reduced" to a five-sided form. Does "reduced" in this sense mean "made smaller," or does it mean "changed" or even "enlarged," as it might have meant in seventeenth-century usage? Philip Barbour, modern editor of Smith's complete works, admits that only in the 1624 version does Smith state the pentagonal shape, while in two earlier versions of the same document the exact form was not specified. So was the fort really five-sided, or did Smith's memory dim during his fifteen-year absence? Our understanding of the fort's design is further confused by colonist Ralph Hamor's description of a "town" again "reduced," this time into a "handsome form" with two "faire" rows of timber-framed two-and-a-half-story houses. What is a "handsome form"? Does this phrase describe a linear form outside of the original triangle, as most scholars have decided, or does it imply that the timber houses paralleled the palisades in the original triangular fort? Did the 1617 Dutch chart maker perhaps record one of these rowhouses in sketching the triple-gable icon? Do these seemingly conflicting details reflect architectural change as Jamestown-the-fort evolved into Jamestown–the-town?

For all their numbers and other seemingly objective facts, these documents raise as many questions as they answer. Add to these records the obviously subjective testimonial descriptions of Jamestown penned in 1623–24 by eyewitness settlers criticizing or defending Thomas Smythe's twelve-year reign as treasurer, and envisioning Jamestown during the Company period becomes even more impossible.[1] Any attempt to make a composite from these various sources would likely leave us with the proverbial camel designed by committee. More documents might help, but after a century of historical research, the odds of finding new evidence of Jamestown's fort in the library or the attic are small. The archaeologist's recourse is to seek out more substantial evidence in the form of physical remains. In the case of Jamestown, however, few scholars held out hope for this form of research.

Philip Barbour said it best. After reading the negative report of National Park Service archaeology he concluded, "[A]rchaeological evidence can prove nothing [about the Fort design], for the undoubted site has been washed away into the James River."[2] The planners of the 350th anniversary of Jamestown's founding must have shared this belief: in 1957 they supported a document-based reconstruction of the fort in a historical theme park completely off the island.

## FINDING JAMES FORT: THE CHALLENGES

By 1994 most people agreed with Barbour that the site was "washed away into the James." There was little reason to think otherwise. As early as 1837, when William Randolph visited the Jamestown site, his eyewitness account of the fort's erosion lent credence to the belief that the site was now submerged with the island's western end, marked by a lone cypress tree some one hundred yards offshore.[3] Since that eroded section was the only part of the island once close to the deep-water channel—the mooring spot that Percy described in 1607—belief in the demise of all traces of the fort made perfect sense. That is, if the fort and the landing point were on the same site. But what if they were not?

The Association for the Preservation of Virginia Antiquities decided to ask that question. Beginning in 1994 the APVA sponsored archaeology "to locate and then uncover any remains of that first Jamestown settlement, especially traces of the Fort as it was originally constructed, and determine how it evolved to accommodate a growing population during the Virginia Company years, 1607–1624."[4] The effort might have seemed predestined to failure. Not only did the weight of evidence, both historical and archaeological, suggest that the fort had melted before centuries of wave action, but there were twenty-two and a half acres of relatively unknown ground to search.

Other built-in challenges presented themselves as well. Given the long and widely shared assumption that the first colonists located the fort on the doomed west end of the island, proof to the contrary would have to be extraordinarily conclusive. Any evidence found of a fort design would have to correspond to the seventeenth-century eyewitness descriptions, at least demonstrating some sort of triangular shape. In particular, in order to be sure that the site of the first fort had been located, any artifacts unearthed had to be found in undisturbed deposits that were old enough and military

View of Jamestown Island showing extent of agricultural fields, ca. 1930.
(National Park Service, Colonial National Historical Park)

enough to relate directly to that early fort era, 1607–10. The discovery of
wall fragments here and there, scattered building remains, and a few objects of a military nature dating to the 1607 period would not be enough
to prove anything. After all, those remains could be evidence of an outer
fortified area, such as Smith's five-sided town, that grew up somewhat later
than the original 1607 palisaded structure.

What happened on the Jamestown site in the centuries after 1699, when
the capital moved to Williamsburg and most occupants abandoned the
town, promised both to help and to hinder the archaeological process of
excavation. During those years the land slowly reverted to agricultural
fields. On the one hand, that was good news for future archaeology. With
the exception of the construction of a Confederate earthen fort in 1861, no
extensive ground-disturbing construction took place to destroy the buried
evidence of occupation. No modern town grew into and over the original town site to obliterate and conceal seventeenth-century remains, such
as had happened at Plymouth, Massachusetts, for example. On the other
hand, the eventual plowing of the western end of the Jamestown site between circa 1750, when the church was dismantled, and 1893, when the
APVA acquired the land, was bad news for archaeologists. Plowing the

land for farming would have blended the upper foot or so of the hereto-fore-intact layers of seventeenth-century town remains. Objects left on the site through the seventeenth century would have been mixed together in the plowzone as one layer, making precise dating difficult. In addition, plowing would have destroyed some evidence of soil levels deposited one on top of the other. As a consequence, surviving bits of James Fort and other seventeenth-century features would be exposed all at once, regardless of the sequence in which they had been created. A hole dug in 1607 that held a wall post and a filled-in drainage ditch that once marked a 1680 property line could appear archaeologically to be from the same moment in time.

Not all was lost, however. The plow would only have gone so deep, usu-ally a foot or so. This level could be shoveled off and screened for artifacts relatively quickly. Once a large area could be exposed in this manner, then relationships among any traces of the fort, such as the alignment or lack of alignment of a wall line and a building foundation, could help determine which things had existed at the same time. Three or more postholes form-ing a straight line would likely be the anchor points of a standing structure, probably a long-vanished timber fence line. A set of these holes in a rectan-gular pattern would quite likely form the footprint of a building once sup-

Not long after the Virginia government center moved to Williamsburg, much of the Jamestown site reverted to agricultural fields. Constant cultivation churned through the shallowest remains of the town, leaving undisturbed deeper seventeenth-century building postholes (*left*), ditches (*right*), cellars, pits, graves, and wells.

ported by posts anchored in the ground. Any other building foundation found to be aligned with a series of these post lines or post-line rectangles could confidently be assumed to have been built or planned at the same time.

Obviously, determining these significant relationships in space and time would require uncovering large continuous parcels of ground. Unfortunately, extremely large parcels could not be uncovered all at once, nor were there any clues as to which parcel might hold the evidence of such aligned structures. So the best possible excavation process at Jamestown was the "quilt" method. Once the digging lifted the plowzone, the excavation would progress by adding one completed ten-foot square at a time to an overall plan, revealing the pattern of the original town design, the direction of walls, plan of buildings, direction of ditches, and location of pits and graves. This quilting process would follow a trail of the Jamestown remains. If the excavated angles of walls and buildings datable to the first quarter of the seventeenth century took on a triangular form, a "triangular-wise" palisaded fort with half-moon bastions could be identified. In other words, archaeological proof of the fort could only be mustered by a deliberate, ever-expanding excavation strategy, moving from one excavated area to an adjoining area, wherever the apparent pattern of fort-period fragments led. Bit by bit, James Fort could emerge from its earthen shroud.

But twenty-two and a half acres—the size of the APVA property on Jamestown Island—was no small shroud. Excavated by the quilt method, that area would amount to 9,900 ten-foot squares. Before we began digging, therefore, it was critically important to narrow the boundaries of the site. Three factors helped us make the best educated guess where the center of the fort might lie.

The first factor was our knowledge of the site of seventeenth-century Jamestown's church. The foundations of the church had been uncovered in 1893–1903 by Mary Jeffery Galt, who excavated a number of burials and two superimposed church foundations next to the brick church tower—still the only remnant of the original town standing above ground. According to William Strachey the church was in "the midst" (middle?) of the triangle.[5] So if local lore was correct, and the fort site was "undoubtedly" submerged off shore to the west, then the church in the fort also had to be gone. In that case, the present foundations and tower were evidence of a seventeenth-century relocation campaign, in which the church was rebuilt a quarter mile to the east of its original site. Although it was known that the first substantial church, originally erected in 1608, was rebuilt in 1617 and again in 1639–46, there was no record that the church was relocated. In fact, churches rarely ever moved from their original locations, sanctified by prayer and the human burials in and around them. Why should the church at James Fort be any exception? It followed that the early fort likely surrounded the enduring church foundations and tower. If so, initial digging between the shore of the river and the church tower would intersect the fort's south wall line.

Second, it made sense that archaeological ground should be broken at a place where military and industrial objects datable to the first quarter of the seventeenth century had already turned up. In fact, such artifacts had been found in and about the church remains at various times during the first sixty years of APVA ownership, beginning with APVA founder Mary Jeffery Galt's excavation efforts. The two superimposed church foundations she uncovered established what she thought was

The brick church tower is the only above-ground remnant of seventeenth-century Jamestown.

the footing of the 1608 church building. Also, during the installation of an underground utility line in 1939, workmen unearthed a stray "pot." Fortunately, the location of the find was recorded, and the relic itself was saved in a collection of other objects serendipitously discovered on the APVA property over the years. Researchers studying the collections recognized the vessel as an intact crucible with a fragment of a second crucible, originally used in its intact form as a lid for the first vessel, fused to it by molten glass.[6] Smith's records of a successful trial run of glassmaking in 1608 suggest that these objects might have been left in James Fort during that first glassmaking operation.[7]

In the 1950s, in an endeavor titled Project 100, National Park Service (NPS) test excavations found a number of apparently random old ditches and trenches in and around the Civil War earthwork. An early seventeenth-century deposit of artifacts associated with a blacksmithing/gun-repairing operation were also uncovered, hinting at some sort of fort connection.

Crucibles (one fragmented and capping the other) likely used for the making of glass in 1608, found during the installation of utility lines "near the Pocahontas statue," ca. 1939.

Nevertheless, the archaeologists heading this research effort concluded that "in all probability it [the fort] stood on ground that has been washed into the James River."[8]

The third factor in our decision was speculation that the fort site might be recoverable. In the early 1960s British archaeologist Ivor Noël Hume conducted a survey of the reports, history, and collections of a number of past excavations of colonial sites in Virginia. Noting the church burials found by APVA under Galt and the possible "starving time" burial ground found by the NPS in the 1950s, Noël Hume concluded: "[T]ogether the two graveyards provide brackets between which the fort site probably existed." The site he indicated was located in the vicinity of the Confederate earthwork, which seemed to be a logical assumption. But by the early 1980s he completely changed his mind. He came to believe that the fort had indeed eroded away, not on the western but rather on the extreme eastern end of Jamestown Island. Virginia Harrington, an NPS Jamestown historian, took strong exception to this eastern-end erosion theory and called for excavations in the area of the church and the Confederate fort, if only to prove the area barren.[9]

Twenty-five years after the NPS archaeologists decided that the site of James Fort did not survive, the Project 100 records and artifacts were reviewed by a new generation of archaeologists building on the excavations and theories of the recent past and armed with decades of firsthand experience in excavation of outlying seventeenth-century fortified settlements in the Chesapeake region. Study of the random field tests that had uncovered apparently disconnected fragments of ditches and a trash pit could not confirm or deny that these were parts of James Fort. But an evaluation of the artifacts from primarily undisturbed or underrecorded deposits proved more promising. Lessons learned from fieldwork on other James River early plantation sites and new interpretation of the early seventeenth-century artifacts by museum scholars made possible more precise identification of

South churchyard, ca. 1940, with original location of Pocahontas statue and hence the place where workmen found the 1608 crucibles. For that and other reasons, this appeared to be the most likely place to start the search for James Fort in 1994.

these objects. It was now clear that the arms and armor in the Project 100 collection dated to the first quarter of the seventeenth century, thus testifying strongly to the existence of an underlying James Fort in the vicinity of the Confederate earthwork. Some of the ceramics found were types that might date to the James Fort period as well. Consequently, the study led to the "strong recommendation that an area excavation be conducted . . . on the interior, surroundings of, and, wherever possible beneath the Confederate earthwork."[10] At the least, these excavations might detect some architectural pattern in the assorted ditches and trenches exposed by Project 100, connecting the random-appearing dots; at best, the excavations might find James Fort.

Once the most promising area to search for the fort was determined, a final pre-digging exercise focused the search even more. The Zúñiga map of 1608, as out of scale as it is, provided enough data to create a hypothetical fort plan. This model could be transposed onto the modern churchyard landscape, thus giving some guidance for the initial digging. The measurements recorded by William Strachey set the scale for the model. Strachey's measurements were taken to be the length of the fort's curtain, not including the corner bulwarks.[11] The bulwarks were assumed to be at least large enough to accommodate cannons the size of demi-culverins (or at

Jamestown Rediscovery excavations begin, April 4, 1994.

least fifty feet in diameter). Given these assumptions, the hypothetical fort became 1.75 acres in size. The central church tower served to anchor the model of the fort to the modern landscape. If fragments of the actual fort appeared as the dig was carried out, the fort model could migrate and perhaps change scale based on the reality of the discoveries. In other words, ongoing archaeological discoveries would correct and recorrect the hypothetical fort model until it fit precisely onto the modern landscape.

That was the plan as I, a crew of one, put the first shovel into the ground on April 4, 1994, at a spot predetermined by blending fact, artifact, theory, and hope—at a place surrounded by all the promising signposts: the church, the Confederate earthwork, and the James River shoreline. The decision where exactly to shovel first came down to a discussion I had with Ivor Noël Hume, the project's first advisor. Since offering his theory that the fort had washed away to the east in the 1980s, Noël Hume's discovery of the glassmaking crucible in the APVA collections had brought him to the yard between the church and the river. As we stood there, however, we were still uncertain where to start. Finally we both eyed a slight depression in the lawn next to an active gravel service road, a clear sign that that place must have been disturbed some time in the past. Since it did not seem like a good idea politically to dig into and therefore to cut off a major useful Park Service road with the very first trench—at least until we could prove there was something under it—the roadside depression seemed as good a starting place as any. With much finger-crossing, the first real digging into the depression began the next day. There is no way to describe the elation when that digging almost immediately produced fragments of early seventeenth-century ceramics. The incredible chain of discoveries that followed, literally connecting the dots, unfolded like a mystery novel over the course of eleven electrifying years, 1994 to 2005.

## JAMES FORT: CONNECTING THE DOTS

### South Palisade

As spring turned to the summer of 1994, the crew of one had the great fortune to be augmented by a number of professional archaeologists experienced in seventeenth-century British colonial sites. Consequently a number of ten-foot squares could be opened up at the same time. Some of them revealed a distinct black streak angling through the undisturbed yellow clay. Parallel to that streak, a number of individual dark stains appeared at regular intervals. Careful scraping of the surface within the boundaries of the discolored streak showed patterns of soil color, a line of circular dark areas of loam within the light-yellow clay. There was little doubt that such soil stains were archaeological evidence of a palisade wall: marks of decayed circular or split timbers once standing side by side and held upright by solid packed clay in a narrow, straight-sided, flat-bottomed trench. Transformed by time into rich loam, the dark stains retained the exact shape of the vanished logs they had replaced. Carefully excavated, they left an exact mold of the timber, five inches to one foot in diameter. These stains appeared in a regular pattern as one progressed along the line: large, medium, and small. This pattern likely meant that, originally, each felled tree was tall enough to produce three palisades of diminishing width—the narrowest timber from the top of the tree, the widest from the bottom—and the three timbers from each tree were erected in sequence. At three places along and just inside the line, postholes and post soil marks appeared, undoubtedly signs of larger support or buttressing posts for the outer wall. This pattern strongly suggests that the palisade was a high, heavy structure, consistent with James Fort's reported wall height of eleven to fifteen feet. The precisely dug straight-sided and flat-bottomed trench, probably two and one-half feet deep originally, would have met the requirement for firmly supporting palisades. This was no misshaped and erosion-scarred drainage ditch. The line ran 17 degrees south of a compass east-west alignment for over fifty feet from a point where it had been destroyed by a later seventeenth-century drainage ditch on the east and the construction trench of a seawall

Excavations during the first season discovered a palisade line and the source of the utility line crucibles: a number of pits containing thousands of other discarded early seventeenth-century artifacts.

on the west. Establishing this line as the south wall of James Fort would provide a key interpretive tool for the future, presenting the possibility that other structural evidence that might align with it in some meaningful and mathematical way could identify other pieces of the James Fort puzzle.

The form of the wall trench and the soil stains left by decayed posts therein clearly marked a palisade. Whether or not this could be identified as the wall of James Fort depended on establishing its date of construction and how long it had stood. Finding datable artifacts in fill deposited during construction and destruction was the key to uncovering the age. If, for example, the clay fill around the postmolds held only prehistoric Virginia Indian pottery while the postmolds contained a few European artifacts, including perhaps a coin minted in 1606, then it would be certain that the palisade went up sometime after 1606. Archaeologists term this date the *terminus post quem* (date after which, or TPQ for short) of a given deposit—in this case, the palisade construction fill. The actual TPQ date determined for the wall, 1607, derived from the fact that this form of the palisade appeared to be remains of European construction, the earliest of which is documented to that year. It is important to note, however, that the 1607 date was indeed only the date *after* which construction could happen. The TPQ alone could not tell us, for instance, that the palisade was part of the fort completed in June 1607. The wall might belong, instead, to one of the later possible renovations: Smith's in 1608–9, De La Warre's in 1610, or Argall's in 1617.

The actual excavation of the postmolds' backfill, made up of the decayed post and the clay deposited as the posts were raised, did strongly suggest, however, a connection to the fort period (that is, prior to 1623–24, by which time, according to eyewitness documents, James Fort was a ruin). A sample digging of the sixty-six identifiable postmolds found relatively few datable objects but enough to establish a circa-1610 TPQ for the termination of the wall. A tobacco pipe crudely made of local clay and a ceramic crucible base found in the fill of one of the related wall-support posts were so similar to those found at a 1585 minerals lab workshop site at Fort Raleigh, North Carolina, that they likely dated to the early James Fort years.[12] A fifteenth- to early seventeenth-century Venetian glass Nueva Cadiz trade bead, a late sixteenth-century Scottish snaphaunce pistol lock, and a Hans Krauwinckel (1586–1635) casting counter (German calculating token) were found where some of the palisade timbers once stood as well. The TPQ period suggested by these late sixteenth-century to early seventeenth-century objects fits quite nicely into the fort era—good news for the fort-seeking hopeful. The soil that had been packed around these objects during construction provided further evidence. This construction fill held only a few bits of prehistoric pottery, suggesting that only pre-1607 Virginia Indians—and not English settlers—had ever been on the site before palisade construction began that year. The palisade we had discovered was definitely old enough to be part of James Fort.

A line of individual postholes paralleling the palisade and spaced at nine-foot intervals helped date the wall and offered some hints of how the south palisade had changed through time. This series of posts could have supported timbers upholding a raised plank platform or roof tied into the palisade. Such a structure would have provided some covered space, a luxury in the fort's earliest years, and might have doubled as an elevated platform to give musketeers an improved field of fire. But was this structure part of the original fort plan or an improvement?

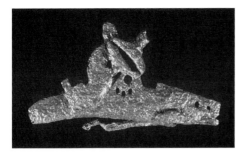

Late sixteenth-century Scottish snaphaunce pistol lock found in the fill of the south palisade line.

A sixteenth-century German coin-like jetton (originally made for calculating) and a sixteenth-to seventeenth-century glass trade bead found in the south palisade line.

The answer once again depended on careful excavation, artifact recovery, and analysis. Like the palisade postholes, the discolored holes left from the platform-supporting posts held construction fill (in this case dirt put back into the hole to seat a post), and decayed timber postmolds held destruction fill. The holes turned out to contain a number of European artifacts, most significantly a distinctive type of window-glass waste. This glass was also found in great profusion in a nearby cellar/pit with a TPQ of circa 1610.

But the fact most crucial to establishing the date of the platform's construction in relation to the construction of the palisade was the presence of European artifacts in the construction fill. The construction fill of the palisade trench contained only prehistoric Indian artifacts. So if the palisade trench dated to the James Fort construction of May 28–June 15, 1607, then the platform addition was an improvement, or possibly a slight change in the original design. At any rate, the palisade trench and the related postholes seemed to be strong evidence that we had found one wall of the fort. Could there be other footprints?

## South Bulwark

Expansion by more ten-foot squares moving east from the riverside fort wall eventually uncovered another possible palisade trench, but one with a distinctively different plan. Instead of striking off in a linear pattern, this wall line formed an arc about twenty-five feet long. Starting at the base of an APVA granite monument, the trench extended toward the riverbank, gradually becoming shallower until it disappeared. A larger and deeper ditch mirrored the curve of the smaller trench, nine feet to the north and east. The parallel trenches—presumably contemporaneous—immediately brought to mind the circular bulwark of the 1608 Zúñiga map. The outer trench might have been a defensive ditch or dry moat protecting the wall shown in the map. The narrower curving trench did have the required shape of palisade construction—straight sides and flat bottom—and held fourteen clearly visible post stains. But compared with the south wall line, this bulwark palisade barely penetrated the subsoil, hardly deep enough to support upright timbers. The trench ranged from five inches deep, where it was cut by the foundation of the monument base, to one-half-inch deep, where grading—possibly during the Civil War—had wiped it away. Close to the river, considerable original soil was missing, probably at least two and a half feet. All along the south edge of the bulwark palisade trench the plowed soil covering it had become progressively deeper, while along the section of the curved palisade trench to the north, what appeared to be old unplowed topsoil survived below the plowed soil. This indicated that some sort of grading had removed the original pre-1607 topsoil to the south, but it had survived to the north. The palisade trench cut through the surviving topsoil, indicating that this was indeed the original topsoil, whose upper surface would have been close to the original pre-fort ground surface when the palisade was constructed. The palisade trench itself again held only Indian pottery, further evidence that this trench was dug in historically virgin ground, establishing a TPQ of 1607. By 1996 the discovery of the south palisade trench, the curved bulwark trench with its accompanying ditch, and the early dates and military nature of the associated artifacts became early compelling signs that we were finding the "lost" remains of James Fort.

The form of the wider and deeper ditch, or dry moat, and the artifacts associated with it strongly suggested that the ditch was part of James Fort. The moat trench was banana-shaped, with an abrupt terminus on the northwest end (near the granite monument) where one could predict the curved palisade ended at a gate location. The moat was deepest near the monument and contained various layers of dirt that told the story of its life. At the bottom, rain-washed clay and decayed plant material had slumped in from the rampart side as top layers of clay on the bank washed back in. Then organic topsoil-like fill, alternating with mixed soil containing small lumps of subsoil clay, filled the top of the bulwark ditch, the mixture of dirt resulting from the partial leveling of the rampart when the fort was abandoned. (Natural washed clay would not produce lumps, but shoveled soil would.) As the natural erosion levels built up, glassmakers evidently poured a layer of hot slag (waste produced during glass production) at the

Discovery in 1996 of the south palisade wall trench (1), curved bulwark palisade, and accompanying ditch (2), together suggested that James Fort had been found.

northwest end of the bulwark ditch. The glass waste spilled into the ditch from the north, presumably coming from a manufacturing site inside the fort, carted through the aforementioned gate, then tipped into the partially open ditch. We know that glassmakers arrived in 1608 and sent a "trial of glass" back to England before the end of the year. So the presence of the slag deposit shows that the entrenchment had been open long enough to receive the glass waste and accumulate some eroded silt between May 1607 and 1608.[13] Other evidence in the bulwark backfill showed that glassmakers worked in the vicinity: fine river sand and high-fired stoneware crucibles with glass adhering to their bowls, possibly leftover raw material from the glassmaking process, filled the top of the center section of the entrenchment.

The excavation of the fill along the bulwark ditch exposed two occurrences of digging and backfilling: a right-angle trench to the east and a later extension of the bulwark ditch to the south. But the fill sequence could still indicate that both of the earlier ditches could well have stood open and then been abandoned and backfilled at about the same time. Or perhaps different crews were digging parts of the bulwark ditch at the same time and eventually met slightly out of line with each other. It is possible, too, that the backfilling took place slightly later, even though all were open at the same time and therefore part of the same bulwark. In any case, it should be obvious from the number of differing possible explanations of the trench-digging and filling sequence that reading the archaeological pages of the earth might be more an art than a science!

The moat location and the apparent extra-thick plowzone and survival of old topsoil next to it provide more information about the bulwark design. They suggest that an earth wall or rampart once stood over and along the curved palisade. The builders would have used the dirt removed from the entrenchment to build this wall. This dirt would also have created the two and one-half feet or so depth of soil necessary to support the palisade logs. Digging an entrenchment and piling up a rampart were standard procedure in fort construction, requiring an attacking enemy to struggle through the entrenchment, then scale the rampart before getting to the palisade. The dirt embankment can also explain the survival of original topsoil below the depth of the James Fort earthwork because it kept later

Artifacts associated with signs in the ground of the fort configuration proved old and military enough to establish construction as early as 1607: a late sixteenth- to seventeenth-century English Borderware jug and an iron breastplate from a suit of armor.

plow blades always above the topsoil, even as the plowing gradually leveled the earthwork. In other words, the subsequent plowing, perhaps as much as 150 years in duration, gradually took down the embankment until it reached the old topsoil level and the last few inches of the palisade trench.

Fortunately, acquisition of the property by the APVA in 1893 ended cultivation, or this bulwark footprint would never have survived. Still to be explained, however, is why grading erased not only the topsoil but also the palisade trenches along the riverbank.

Captain William Allen owned and farmed Jamestown Island during the middle of the nineteenth century. His slaves built much of the earthwork that the Confederate Army planned to use to stop Union ships from sailing up the James River and capturing Richmond. The surviving earthen shore battery once stood as high as six feet above the original prebattery grade. Where did the dirt come from for this construction?

The answer is obvious: from the immediately surrounding area, from the digging of moats, and from scouring inside and along the nearby riverbank. Some of the James Fort dirt, then, is in the embankment mounds of the Confederate fort. In fact, there are reports that during the fort construction, the builders found old burials and seventeenth-century armor. It would have made sense militarily to grade down the adjacent elevated shoreline to water level as well, effectively eliminating cover for any Union amphibious landings. Post–Civil War drawings of the church tower shoreline area do clearly show dirt mounds and the cliff.

The theory that such grading was done during the Civil War is made all the more plausible by the shallowness of the postholes scattered about within the arc of the palisade trench, which were much too shallow to have supported the upright timbers. So dirt is indeed missing. It is possible that the posts formed a wooden retaining wall holding an earthen cannon platform.

The right-angled ditch extension east of the curved palisade trench and the bulwark ditch suggest a more complicated bulwark design than a simple circle. The ditch strays from the circular pattern to become simply a straight line for thirty feet, where it makes about a 90-degree turn toward the river. Following this early seventeenth-century fort footprint was challenging. Most of the ditch existed beneath the remains of a burned building postdating the existence of the fort by at least two decades. That building's construction made a significant impact on the fort remains, complicating our efforts. The 46' × 30' structure, which once stood on a deep foundation

Overhead view from under a protective tent of the bulwark ditch found beneath the John White building foundation, view facing south.

of stone, had a basement and included two massive exterior brick chimneys, one each in the two twenty-three-foot-wide basement rooms. Original construction of the basement and one of the chimneys cut into the bulwark ditch extension, which had already been backfilled. Fortunately, the ditch had been dug two feet deeper than the cellar floor of the building, so it survived that later construction. Since the building was an integral part of the seventeenth-century Jamestown story, however, everything that was removed from it in order to record the earlier fort footprint had to itself be recorded and interpreted. What turned out to be the ruins of the 1640s house/warehouse of merchant/politician John White required months of excavation.[14]

Eventual digging beneath the basement floor of the White building determined that the bulwark ditch was originally at least four feet below the estimated original fort-period ground surface and perhaps six feet wide. The dirt removed by the colonists to create the ditch undoubtedly wound up piled to one side of it, creating an earthwork to strengthen the

Circular pit inside southeast bulwark; possibly a place to store powder near the bulwark gun platform.

curved palisade wall. But because the ditch extended to the eroded shoreline and was therefore lost at that point, its precise design must remain somewhat conjectural. In light of the shape of the south and west James Fort bulwarks as shown on the Zúñiga map, it would make sense to speculate that the advance earthwork and palisades mounted on it formed three sides of a square bulwark (perhaps one of two such bulwarks) for cannon. This rectangular shape does not sound like the bulwarks Percy saw as "like a half-moon," a military term for circular work with chevron-shaped forward projections.[15] But the extended bulwark is probably an addition to the curved ditch and so not part of the original construction that Percy described as standing in June 1607. These rectangular bulwarks may well have reworked a simple earlier circular-walled bulwark.

More soil layers and another feature found inside the confines of the bulwark also suggested that the design of the bulwark changed over time. A number of significant deposits that had escaped the Civil War grading added more insight into the defense's design and its evolution. In addition to the circa-1640 White building ruin, the bulwark area excavation revealed that layers from the building's occupation and destruction spilled south and west from the foundation. Those levels also accumulated on top of a deposit of sand and domestic trash that increased in depth toward the river. This deposit appeared to be an attempt to extend the shoreline behind some type of bulkhead perhaps lost during the 1901 construction of the concrete seawall. A ten-foot-wide doorway in the center of the White building on the river side as well as the presence of exterior postholes suggested that this area was used as a loading dock, perhaps the reason for the seventeenth-century shore reclamation effort. In any case, the White building debris and the shoreline material extended southwest until they rested upon a circular pit, filled with washed-in clay and dark organic soil holding scores of artifacts dating circa 1610. This collection included a number of gun parts, 1602 Irish halfpennies, an ornate horse bit, and a medical instrument known as a spatula mundani, which was used to treat constipation. The medical implement turned out to be quite precisely datable to 1609, as there was record of it being sent to the colony with a chest of other medical instruments in that year.

The pit itself may have originally functioned as a relatively safe place to store gunpowder for the bulwark cannons. How it fit into the overall scheme of the curvilinear bulwark is problematic. It is located in a position that would have been in the path of the circular palisade if it had originally completed the circular form suggested by the surviving palisade trench. Consequently, both the magazine and the later rectangular bulwarks could not have been original to the first fort design but rather part of changes made later. Also, since the aforementioned bulwark ditch was apparently dug in two sections, the probable powder magazine may have come along as part of the rectangular bulwarks, a form at least partially suggested by the Zúñiga map. The only problem with that scenario is that the magazine

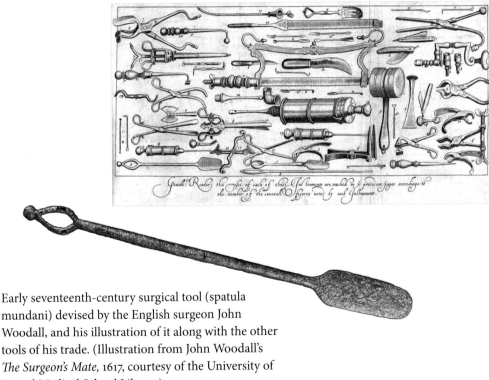

Early seventeenth-century surgical tool (spatula mundani) devised by the English surgeon John Woodall, and his illustration of it along with the other tools of his trade. (Illustration from John Woodall's *The Surgeon's Mate,* 1617, courtesy of the University of Bristol Medical School Library)

would then be located where one would expect the cannon to be mounted. The only solution to such crowded quarters would be a raised timber gun platform above the magazine. Could these changes all be examples of "[the fort] growing . . . to more perfection," as reported by Strachey in 1610? The dates of the reworked bulwark ditch and the magazine could certainly fit that explanation, but the Zúñiga map, on which these shapes seem to appear, was made two years earlier. Here it seems no explanation fits all.

This evidence of construction and remodeling, however difficult to understand completely, does bear witness to the military prowess of the Jamestown leaders. Wingfield, Gosnold, and the other captains "contrived" (designed) the fort in May/June of 1607. Since the colonists were constantly under fire from the Virginia Indians during construction, a secured fortified area had to be constructed as quickly as possible. A triangle requiring only three walls could be built in the shortest period of time. Circular bulwark walls, strengthened by advance moats and mounds, reflect the battle experience these leaders brought with them from their service in the Netherlands and Ireland. Such English designs, while archaic in comparison to what the Spanish were building in Europe, were good enough to repel the Virginia Indians, an enemy without muskets and cannons. The designers admitted, "We have made ourselves sufficiently strong for [attacks from] these savages."

This construction may not have been considered "sufficient," however, to repel cannon-wielding Spanish ships at undermanned Jamestown. The rectangular-shaped advance batteries would be a necessary addition as time and arrow-free days would allow. Given the months of off-and-on siege and starvation at the fort for the next three years, it is likely that any improvements more in keeping with European standards had to wait until Lord De La Warre's rescue mission in the summer of 1610 and his "perfection" of the fort.[16]

### East Wall

Once the southeastern bulwark and south wall lines appeared to be established archaeologically, finding any surviving evidence of an east wall became the focus. As the bulwark began to take shape, a relatively faint linear soil stain angling off to the north, which had been found during the very first season of excavation, acquired added significance. It was already known that the stain was old enough to be from the fort period, because it had been severed by the digging of a circa-1620s drainage ditch. As there were no signs of the telltale rotted palisade posts, however, the feature had been written off as a small drainage ditch. Tracing the stain back toward the bulwark area for some fifteen feet established that it was straight as an arrow, it had the required straight sides and flat bottom of a palisade trench, and it terminated directly opposite the path of the curved bulwark palisade five feet from the monument base, which stood between the two paths. The bulwark line did not emerge from the statue base and thus connect directly with the east line, but this gap probably indicated that there had been a gateway between the two.

Once it was clear that the trench was part of the fort design and likely the east wall of the triangle, four spaced trenches were dug at intervals along the projected line. These trenches all uncovered more of the east line, defining it for one hundred feet. No upright timber postmolds were found, though. While the 45- to 46-degree angle between the east and south wall trenches would fit a triangle of Strachey's overall dimensions, this lack of evidence that timbers stood in the trench would make it hard to prove that this line was part of the fort at all. At the same time, however, Virginia Indian artifacts, found in testing the trench, along with the absence of any European artifacts, suggested that this indeed was an original and early part of the fortification.

Trenches near the church determined that, unlike all of the other areas excavated in the James Fort vicinity, this area had never been plowed. Certainly, plowing near the church tower, the only remnant of Jamestown still above ground, or in the adjacent graveyard would have been considered off limits. While plowed soil can indeed have its advantages archaeologically, the discovery of uncultivated ground was promising in its own way. Unplowed land preserves soil layers in their original context from the time of their deposition up to the present. In theory, then, the entire depth of the original palisade trench might have been left undisturbed along some of the east line, offering the possibility of viewing a complete palisade cross-section.

The excavation process to that point had approached the palisade lines literally from top to bottom. On the south, that method was logical, allowing each stain left by the timbers to be removed individually. On the east line, however, no postmolds were visible at the surface to dig out. So an attempt was made to examine the east line by digging, not from top to bottom, but from the side of the trench, which had a good chance of revealing any deeper evidence of posts. This process proved only partially successful.

Primarily, the side view revealed backfilled gouges, which turned out to be signs of holes dug to remove the posts. The removal of the posts accounted for their invisibility at the top of the trench. In other words, most of the original upright timbers did not rot in place but were dug out and removed, leaving no rotted timber molds. One mold *was* found, however, at the end of the section that had been dug out and removed, proving that there actually were posts in the line at one time.

The question then became: What time? The fill was devoid of any artifacts capable of establishing the date of the palisade construction or removal. All that was found were some fragments of animal bone, shell, and stone worked by natives years or even centuries before the construction of the fort. This slight evidence could argue for a palisade built and then removed in or soon after 1607, when no historical artifacts would be lying around to become mixed in the wall destruction holes. It was tempting to suggest that the wall came down soon after some of the palisades burned in January 1608.[17] That explanation had several problems, however. There was no obvious sign of fire in the palisade fill, nor was there evidence that the wall was rebuilt before Strachey would have written about it in 1610. And since the artifacts unearthed did no more than establish a TPQ of 1607, they could only tell us that a palisade, if any had been built here, had disappeared after prehistoric Indian times; they offered no more precise guidance in establishing the rise and fall of James Fort.

A test trench on the side of the Confederate earthwork along the projected line of the east palisade suggested the same palisade removal scenario. Nothing more than a ditch filled with mixed soil, in alignment with the other sections of the east line, was found—still no post stains. Nonetheless, except where a large shallow 1680s-era pit (dated by wine-bottle fragments found there) and nineteenth-century road grading wiped it out, the line could now be clearly identified for at least 240 feet from the riverside bulwark to the Civil War earthwork. It was also clear from the nature of the soil layers above the backfilled palisade trench that the Civil War earthwork was constructed from dirt redeposited as soldiers or slaves dug through the 1607 fort soil to create a moat next to it. Such a process of construction explained why not one but two soil layers held seventeenth-century artifacts on top of the palisade slot: one layer would have been the plowzone created after the fort's demise, and the other the redeposited level of seventeenth-century earth. Subsequent excavations into the same earthen wall nearer the church also revealed these reversed-in-time soil levels. Excavations beyond the earthwork to the north, along the projected line and distance suggested by Strachey, found that the east line disappeared somewhere in between. Although the east line might have been discovered, there was no sign of a north bulwark.

## The North Bulwark

Until the summer of 2003 our excavations to the north, based on our model and Strachey's measurements that produced a 1.75-acre fort, were leading nowhere. So far, digging precisely in the places suggested by those dimensions had uncovered only a single but straight palisade trench identified by the horizontal digging process used on the east wall. A vertical excavation, providing a side view, exposed individual postmolds in a typical squarely dug and narrow palisade trench. But this trench made no sense as part of the missing bulwark: it ran straight north for at least 130 feet, then entered a surviving branch of a swamp known as the "pitch and tar" swamp. A bulwark wall would not take that course: by definition it had to form a securely closed-in space with a wide range for cannons. Once again, however, the Zúñiga map offered a possible explanation. One curious aspect of the map was a rectangular shape connected to one of the bulwarks of the triangular fort by a short line—a shape that looked like a flag set on a flagpole. Could what had been taken for a flagpole actually be a wall connecting the circular fort bulwark to a flag-shaped enclosure, possibly an enclosed garden? In that case, the straight palisade trench running to the north might be that wall (see p. 12). Another characteristic of the single line made this interpretation of the apparent flagpole symbol all the more plausible: the line terminated at the fort end in a curious hook shape near where our model would place the curved bulwark wall. The proximity of this line to the curved bulwark suggested that the two might have once been connected. The deeply graded nineteenth-century roadway, a few feet from the hook, would have gouged away all signs of both the link and the bulwark. As for the north bulwark itself, that corner of the triangle seemed lost.

But there was another possibility: finding an end to the east palisade should reveal the starting point of the adjoining bulwark. That end of the line had to lie in the last place left to look, under the corner of the Civil War fort. Why? Simply a process of elimination. Previous skipping ahead beyond the earthwork corner, digging directly along the projected line, had come up empty, and trenches on the other side of the earthwork corner along the line exposed a continuing wall line. Perhaps the elusive end of the line was in between, under the earthwork corner. So it was—and more.

Upon removal of the buried seventeenth-century plowzone, here ten feet beneath the earthwork corner, the east line was found to terminate. As a bonus, the end joined two other palisade trenches, one a section of the curved bulwark wall and the other an additional line, in all likelihood part of an eastern expansion of the palisaded area. At long last the triangle was two-dimensional.

A measurement of the full length of the east wall, from the riverward to the landward end, produced the true curtain wall dimension, 266 feet. This figure did not jibe with the one-hundred-yard curtain reported by Strachey. Had he miscalculated? At that point a miscalculation by Strachey seemed to be the most plausible explanation of the discrepancy.

At least we now knew that our fort model, based on a curtain of one hundred yards, was clearly too big. On and off for years, that model had led the search for the north bulwark astray, literally on the wrong side of the road. And while finding the junction of the three palisades—east wall, bulwark, and later extension—had revealed more of the fort plan, the road grading and the earth scouring conducted during construction of the Civil War earthwork left the size of the actual bulwark for conjecture. The few feet of the bulwark palisade that survived this destruction appeared to curve enough for us to project a regular wall with a sixty-foot diameter. Such a wall would be slightly larger than the projected circular form to the south. This shape certainly tended to corroborate the Zúñiga map, which shows a larger bulwark to the north, a smaller one to the south and west. The map also shows that the north bulwark was more oval than the other two. In addition, the map's flagpole image—what we had tentatively identified with the single north-running palisade—connects directly to the bulwark wall at about 45 degrees west of a center line through the triangle. The trench we had uncovered did not join the theoretical bulwark circle but ended before joining the conjectured bulwark. There was a small space of relatively undisturbed ground between the northern trenches' terminal hook and the hypothetical course of the bulwark circle in the graded road. A gap might reflect the location of a gate, although such a gate, being outside the projected circle, would not open into the bulwark. This gate might be instead a passageway from the marsh side of the island into a space bounded by the river and the rectangular enclosure represented by the Zúñiga flag. Gate or not, if the palisade marked by the trench did connect to the bulwark, it would do so some 15 degrees west of the triangle center line, not 45 degrees

Excavation below the Jamestown Civil War earthen fortification (*background*) revealed junction of the James Fort east palisade wall trench with the north bulwark and another slightly later palisade protecting the "town" to the east.

west. Allowing for the sketchy nature of the Zúñiga map, however, both the compass direction of the map and the reality of the palisade on the ground extending west of center suffice to justify the conclusion that the "flagpole" was a palisade—and that the Zúñiga map reliably depicted the design of James Fort.

What does not appear on the map but did materialize on the ground was a third palisade found attached to both the dug-out east wall and the north bulwark trenches. That extra palisade trench was deeper than the other two and had visible postmolds. This palisade was clearly a later addition to the fort triangle, serving to expand the area enclosed by the fort. As a later construction, it would logically not have appeared on the 1608 map. An expansion of the fort area could also explain removal of the east wall. If the expanded area to the east was completely enclosed by additional palisades, then the east wall would have become obsolete, an unnecessary barrier inside the fortified area. Discovery of yet another related palisade trench going east and a closer look at seventeenth-century eyewitness descriptions of the town's defenses together proved that James Fort changed its shape through the years, and that these additions would continue to complicate our search for the original triangle. Nevertheless, the search for that original third side—the west wall—continued.

## West Wall

Although the length of the east wall had begun to cast some doubt on the dimensions of Strachey's fort model, it still seemed a good plan to excavate inside the Civil War earthwork, where our model indicated the missing west wall line should be. A digging season there proved discouraging. There was no topsoil, plowzone, or palisade line. It seemed that all evidence of the wall if it had ever been there had been destroyed in the construction of the 1861 fort. By early 2003, not finding traces of the elusive west wall began to cast some doubt about the relationship of the palisade trenches and apparent bulwarks on the south and east. A fort at least had to be a triangle.

However, the digging in the Civil War fort was far from wasted. The scouring in 1861 could not destroy ground features that were deep enough—a well, for example, which would be far deeper than a palisade trench. Sure enough, a few feet outside of the missing hypothetical west wall, a well datable to the fort period appeared inches below the surface. This discovery proved to be a time capsule full of James Fort artifacts. *Where* the well turned up was puzzling, however. It did not seem to make sense that a water source for the fort would lie beyond the safety of its palisade; a fort under siege with no water could not hold out for long. Could this fort-period well have once actually stood inside the fort, perhaps conveniently near its center, and not outside? Could the palisade wall we sought be missing, not because it had been graded away, but because we were looking for it in the wrong place? If the fort was much larger than we had projected it, the palisade might actually be far to the west of the well. In other words, the model that had guided the digging might be too small. If the well indeed marked the middle of the fort, then the fort would have been at least twice as large as predicted.

Had Strachey miscalculated more seriously than we had suspected when the one-hundred-yard curtain wall he specified seemed to be only 266 feet long as found? That was a possibility. But a test trench dug during the NPS excavations in 1955 cut across much of the area where an enlarged model suggested the west wall should be. No palisade trench was there. Perhaps, instead, Strachey's dimensions were accurate after all, and this well was only one of many later water sources. In that case, at least one of those wells remained to be found within the border of the fort's palisades. The west wall, too, remained unfound.

Knowing just how deep the Civil War scouring had gone in 1861 might show whether or not it could have wiped away the palisade. The key to determining this depth would be establishing the pre-1861 grade close enough to the well to gauge accurately how much dirt was missing. If the pre-1861 soil level was more than two feet higher than the present surface inside the earthwork, then any evidence there of the west wall would certainly be gone. The only place to find this all-telling soil would be under the Civil War earthwork itself. We knew from our probing for the north bulwark and from the first archaeological excavation underneath the earthwork forty-five years earlier that seventeenth-century layers did in fact lie unscathed there.

We had always considered disturbing the Civil War landscape to be a last re-sort. That landscape was itself a visible piece of Jamestown Island history. The question of the relative significance of these two historical records had been put to Civil War preservationists at the beginning of the Jamestown Rediscovery project. They concluded that this earthwork, because it had never seen battle, could be sacrificed to some degree for the James Fort search, providing that the excavation only disturb as much as necessary and record the earthwork in sufficient detail to make possible an accurate reconstruction. Fair enough. However, the thought of having to dig through four to twelve feet of soil deposited from 1861 to the present was daunting. Almost as daunting if not mocking was the 1907 statue of Captain John Smith that stood overlooking the area we proposed to test. Just before the Jamestown Rediscovery project began, Dr. John Cotter, the distinguished

A brick-lined well in the original parade ground, Smithfield, known to be just west of James Fort (*left*), beside an apparent Civil War storage shaft (*right*).

View of west palisade wall trench and apparent west bulwark trench at the point where the river erosion was cut off by a concrete wall in 1901.

Jamestown archaeologist of the 1950s excavation beneath the Civil War fort mounds, jokingly mused that John Smith was gazing at the vanished fort, far out in the river.[18] In other words, Take heed, future archaeologists: the fort is truly gone. If truth be known, until the missing third leg of the triangle could be found, there was still some chance that Cotter was right.

As it would turn out, however, the John Smith statue peered from a secure place within the fort. The search trench designed to prove why the hypothetical wall was missing to the west did exactly that, and in a surprising way. The wall was not found near the well, because it had never been there in the first place. The true wall location—the last, vital side of the triangle—turned up, quite by chance, in the search trench instead. The fateful test trench, about forty feet west of the well, exposed a five-foot-long dark palisade stain right at the base of Civil War fill. Postmolds survived, and the profile fit the regular palisade form. James Fort was found!

From that point, multiple excavation trenches were dug along the extended line, tracing it to the bank of the river where the seawall construction had ended the shoreline erosion in 1901. At that place, the eroded Civil War earthwork on top of the early seventeenth-century fort left a cliff of sorts. The palisade trench appeared in the face of the cliff in a natural cross-section next to an associated pit or ditch filled in with an artifact-rich dark loam. Digging continued intermittently away from the river on each side of a Civil War mound, exposing sections of the palisade trench for a total of two hundred feet. Once this last essential piece of the three-sided fort revealed its alignment on the ground, the entire triangle came into clear focus. Projection of each line came to an intersection with each of the two others, revealing at long last the true dimensions of the fort: 304± feet on each land side (100 yards) and 425± feet (140 yards) along the river, forming a 1.1-acre enclosure. The continued presence of James Fort on Jamestown Island was a fact.

Strachey had told us that his 100 yards, 100 yards, and 140 yards measurements were of the curtain walls. Again, in standard military terms, a fort curtain is the length of the wall between bulwarks. Our model, with its hypothetical circular bulwarks, had been based on the belief that Strachey meant a traditional curtain. What we found on the ground yielded the Strachey measurements—but only if the measurements were made from points where the walls intersected. These intersections actually occurred inside the bulwarks that we had found archaeologically. Strachey had given accurate measurements, but from different reference points: he was technically not measuring a curtain wall. Rather he had described the distance between the points where the lines of the walls intersected. Few if any reading his account had ever understood it that way, despite the qualification offered in his next sentence, locating the bulwarks and a watchtower "where the lines meet." This episode is a rare instance of signs in the earth enabling us to verify and even correct a written account. The power of this physical evidence to help us decipher a firsthand account should also be a sobering reminder of how easily seemingly straightforward eyewitness accounts can be misunderstood. Strachey's measurements of James Fort were accurate—he just had his own definition of "curtain."

In misreading Strachey, we had also developed a hypothetical model of James Fort that was more than a half acre larger than the actual fort. Does it matter that the fort was actually about a third smaller than its traditionally understood size? Undoubtedly, what counts most is what we can learn from the initial enduring English presence in America. Yet to recapture the landscape of colonization accurately is to understand colonization in context. The bigger picture depends upon that context.

So the site of James Fort, once considered completely lost on eroded land, exists almost intact on uneroded land. Shoreline erosion dissolved only the west bulwark, probably half of the south bulwark and about three quarters of the south wall, leaving about 90 percent of the overall fort intact on land. This discovery was a real gift for Jamestown as it approached its 400th anniversary. But there were to be other birthday presents. Our excavations also revealed the expansion of the original fort design and began to define the evolving plan of the early town.

## FIVE-SQUARE FORM

James Fort became known as Jamestown rather quickly in eyewitness accounts. This change in terms suggested that the form and substance of the settlement was evolving from strictly a fortification to a town-like setting. Documentary accounts have given us some idea of the changing town design and the types of houses and public buildings within and about the fort. Archaeological remains bring the design and structures of Jamestown into clearer focus.

Signs of the developing Jamestown had appeared early on in the excavations. Removal of plowed soil beyond the south bulwark uncovered an add-on palisade trench. This trench forged a right angle with the east wall line but left a gate-width gap between them. The palisade had run for sixty feet until it ended next to what soil stains hinted was the remains of a backfilled cellar under a post-supported building. Excavation a few inches below the plowzone along the length of the palisade revealed the clearest stains of decayed upright timbers yet found. Testing with the side-view method of excavation revealed clear earthen molds of decayed timbers anchored side by side in two-foot-deep trenches. While the extended plan was clear, the chronology—when this line became an addition to the triangle—could not be precisely established. Once again, only prehistoric Indian artifacts appeared in the fill.

But the writings of Smith, Strachey, and Ralph Hamor seem to leave little doubt that the triangular James Fort did not encompass all of Jamestown for long.[19] Their descriptions, read in light of the extended palisade, may also explain both the removal of the east wall of the original triangular fort and the eventual location of the Jamestown church where its tower and reconstruction stand today, directly on and outside the east wall. After Smith was appointed president (September 10, 1608), he wrote that "James towne being burnt, we rebuilt it [the overall plan] reduced to the form of this ( ) figure [omitted but later called "five-square"]." The word *reduced* is the key

Skillful removal of clay originally tamped around the town palisade posts to hold them upright leaves a perfect soil cast of each wall timber along the extended fort wall line.

to understanding what Smith describes. To repeat, today the word clearly means "made smaller," but in seventeenth-century usage the word might mean "changed," "restored back," or maybe even "made larger." To Smith, "reduced" could well mean "changed" and "enlarged," because he reports that by the summer of 1608, Jamestown consisted of forty or fifty houses. If this is no exaggeration, there were far too many structures here to fit into the now established and relatively small 1.1-acre triangle.[20] Another palisaded enclosure, probably rectangular in shape, might well have been attached to the original triangle, resulting perhaps in Smith's pentagon. The curious third palisade discovered at the north bulwark might have extended out to a connecting wall to form this "five square" as well. The dimensions of this presumed eastern enclosure would only add about one-half acre to the triangle, still probably too small for all these new houses. Perhaps the palisade at right angles to the east wall, possibly more substantial than the earlier palisades, was one of the walls Strachey described as either added or reconstructed/repaired by Sir Thomas Gates and his men after Lord De La Warre arrived in 1610.[21]

These extra palisades would have secured the land east of the original triangle, the Smith five-sided housing development, and possibly even the 1611 town of Hamor's description, "reduced into a handsome form [with] two faire rows of houses . . . newly and strongly impaled."[22] If the extended eastward line were evidence of the new town of Smith, Strachey, and Hamor, however, a palisade in that direction right next to the south bulwark might seem to prevent the bulwark's use for flanking cannon-fire—although, since the palisade apparently ended at the post building whose cellar had been found, the field of fire was only partially blocked by palisade growth in that direction. Perhaps, as the fort grew east, the bulwark was abandoned altogether in favor of a new design, which may have included a blockhouse and yet another appended palisade wall. Excavation of the south bulwark ditch also uncovered a section of a palisade trench postdating the square-shaped bulwark and extending toward the river. This trench may be evidence of fort expansion that would possibly render the south bulwark obsolete in time.

Could the addition of the palisade, and the possible obsolescence of the south bulwark, be part of more changes wrought by De La Warre in 1610? The date of this additional palisade is unclear. We can know, however, from its position beneath the floor of the later stone-based John White building that the ditch predates at least 1634, the date of the Charles I shilling found in the floor. This dating might suggest that the puzzling palisade was an addition to the fort during its last years, the 1620s. In fact, there is a curious indirect reference that might mean the fort lasted longer than anyone has heretofore imagined. In 1631 a reference is made to the existence of a captain of the fort. What fort is this? There is only the documentation of a turf or earthen fort appearing in 1642. So if the captain's fort is some form of the original James Fort, then it had a longer life span indeed. In fact, letting the fort rot down in the 1620s, as the records suggest, flies in the face of the tragedy of the Indian massacre of 1622, which led to legislation requiring all settlements to build palisades to protect themselves thereafter. In any case, maybe the Jamestown fort's apparent decay described in 1623 set off yet another face-lifting effort soon thereafter.

These archaeological signs of a changing palisade configuration may at least suggest why the east wall of the triangular fort was eventually dismantled: the wall wound up inside the expanded palisaded area and therefore no longer served as a barrier to attacks from outside the compound. It too had become obsolete. Again, the dates of these events remain uncertain: we know only that the triangular configuration must have existed until July of 1610, when Strachey so accurately measured it. The additions and renewals so far discussed must have occurred, then, after that date—possibly soon after, as part of De La Warre's renovations.

The enlargement of the fortified town also explains why the church tower would have come to straddle the site of the fort's original east wall. The discovery of the outlines of James Fort had revealed to us that Jamestown's church must have moved after all, despite the aforementioned rarity of such a move and the absence of records attesting to the relocation. As time passed and James Fort grew, the church must have needed to be recentered as the hub of the larger community. According to Strachey in 1610, the original church of 1608, central within the triangular fort, was in shambles. Strachey also wrote, however, that De La Warre ordered it repaired, meaning that it was upgraded in place. So the resiting of the church, from the center of the triangular fort/town to the center of the expanded town, apparently occurred in 1617, when Samuel Argall ordered construction of a new and smaller church, 50' × 20' compared to the 1608 size of 60' × 24'. During the Galt-Tyler church excavations of 1901, however, a cobble foundation of the dimensions of the 1608 church was found on a site that would lie beyond what we now know to have been James Fort's original east wall.[23] This location suggests that the construction of the church under Argall in

1617 might be a second occasion for the church's recentering. Clearly, future excavation of the brick church site and tower needs to be done.

The new town walls must have gone up before that, but exactly when is in some doubt. There were no artifacts in the various expansion palisades to date construction. Still, it stands to reason that by De La Warre's time the new five-square fortified area beyond the triangle continued to grow. So it makes sense to date the dismantling of the east wall and the redesign and expansion of the fort to some time between late 1610, after Strachey saw the complete triangle, and 1617, when Argall built his church. If that church provides evidence for identifying the new center of town, we can perhaps make a good estimate of the town's size in 1617. Supposing the expansion to be rectangular, the new town would have been three times the size of the original triangle, a total of three to four acres. Archaeological remains of what could be the new east wall—a relatively vague palisade trench aligned with the post building and traceable, except where later graves cut through it, for over one hundred feet north—suggest that this estimate of acreage might be generous. In order to delimit a significantly larger fort, capable of enclosing more houses, the line found would have to make a turn to the east, then continue to encompass more space in that direction. A trench of this sort remains undiscovered.

## JAMES FORT'S BUILDINGS

The size of the area required to contain the buildings of John Smith's or Ralph Hamor's descriptions depends upon just what actually did constitute James Fort houses: holes in the ground? castles in the air? cabins? two-story timber buildings? A study of the buildings of James Fort can address not only these questions but others as well: How were English ideas of building adapted to the Virginia environment? What evidence can be found for a town plan? What can we know about the use of individual buildings? And what can the buildings tell us of the historic events we know to have transpired in Jamestown?

At least two of these questions are related: If what people lived in at James Fort were whimsical "air castles" or nothing more than flimsy tents, then the archaeological search for a town plan could have been doomed. Such structures probably left few archaeological signs in the earth. (It is possible, however, that four pits found paralleling the west wall of the fort, all dating to the first three years of settlement, are signs of crude quarters supported by lean-to roofs attached directly to the palisade.) Most other types of more permanent construction, however, could leave solid archaeological traces, such as cellars, postholes, and masonry foundations. Fortunately, all these building signs were present. Excavations located clear evidence of five James Fort–period buildings: four inside the fort (hereafter, for reference purposes only, called the barracks, the quarter, and the rowhouses or rows) and a fifth in the east extension (the factory, a building outside the fort for storage and trade with the Virginia Indians). The barracks, quarter, and rows each aligned with each of the three walls of the triangle, and the factory paralleled the east fort wall in the fort extension. This arrangement certainly suggests the plan described by Strachey: rows of settled houses along each palisade wall. Three structures—barracks, quarter, and factory—are of strikingly similar design, while the rows are something quite different (as will be discussed below). The almost identical archaeological remnants of the first three are a cellar and a number of slightly irregularly aligned postholes. It is possible that each of the buildings began as a cellar hole with a crude roof covering it. Over time the larger post-supported buildings were added, incorporating the original cellar. (The four possible lean-to cellar buildings along the west wall, on the other hand, never evolved to the post-building stage.) The spacing of the postholes, in which vertical support timbers would once have been seated, reveals rectangular floor plans. All three similar buildings are one room wide and multiple rooms in length, and all retained their cellars at one end.

What people in these buildings lost or threw away is as important to the Jamestown story as the remains of the buildings themselves. Such objects become accidental and impartial records of life that went on in each structure. Recovery and interpretation of what seems to be lowly trash gives unusually clear insight into the past. The cellars of the barracks, quarter, and factory generally contained the same sequence of artifact-rich fill layers. An initial accumulation of tracked-in or washed-in fill built up on each of the dirt cellar floors, containing objects that were left there while the cellar was in use. Above these time-capsule-like occupation zones, a distinctly similar deposit of dark humus mixed with lumps of clay subsoil and nails appeared. This rather strange mixed-soil layer filled all the cellars to a depth that would have rendered them unusable. Thus it became reasonable to conclude that the fill was a result of the collapse of the building above— the falling of earthen walls. Above these layers, the cellars were filled with garbage and trash-laden deposits, filling the cellar holes up to what later

Crude pit-like cellars and small, almost random postholes found at
Jamestown along the west palisade wall trench suggest that lean-to
structures, like those shown here on the set of the Jamestown movie
*The New World,* once stood along the west and likely the east James Fort
palisade walls. (*The New World,* copyright MMVI, New Line Productions,
Inc. All rights reserved. Photo courtesy of New Line Productions, Inc.)

became a plowzone. All this material can now reveal what went on (and when) inside and outside of the cellars; it can provide insight as well into the superstructure and purpose of each building; and it can tell us something, too, of the lifespan, destruction, and afterlife of the buildings and their sites.

## The Barracks

Archaeological remains of the barracks floor plan consisted of twenty-six imprecisely aligned, irregularly spaced postholes of random depth, forming a 55' × 18' rectangle divided into at least two rooms with a cellar and a fireplace. Relatively small postmolds survived in most of the post-

This silver English halfpenny bearing the Tudor rose and thistle of James I, king of England and Scotland, and minted from 1606 to 1608, was found in one of the cellars, indicating a likely 1607–8 date for these makeshift quarters.

holes, indicating a light timber framing. The rather random and insubstantial nature of these remains, especially in light of the fallen earth-wall layer in the cellar, provides clues to how it was built.

The small circular posts, one as undersized as three inches in diameter, and the varying depth of their seating postholes suggest that the building frame was supported by what John Smith called "cratchets," basically nothing more than forked sticks. Smith wrote that the 1608 church was "a homely thing like a barn, set upon cratchets covered with rafts, sedge, and earth; so also was the walls." He added that the "the best of our houses [are] of the like curiosity but the most part much worse workmanship."[24] Cratchets work almost like crutches: the wall plate timber rests in the V-shaped fork exactly as an arm rests on top of a crutch. No intricate carpentry is needed to hold the plate timber in place. Such a structure also would not require holes dug to any uniform depth; the depths might vary according to the random natural length of the cratchets themselves. The misalignment of the cratchet poles from side to side means the building probably had no crossing ceiling beams, with the exception of the west-end room, where the posts do line up crosswise. Without ceiling beams to tie them together, the walls of such a house would seem hardly capable of supporting a roof. However, if the walls were made of thick earth—as they might have been, given Smith's reference to hard mixed clay, along with the presence of a mixed loam and clay deposit in the building cellars—supporting a roof might be possible.

The zigzag post line provides a clue that the barracks roof might have been very lightly framed, maybe even light enough to be lifted ready-made on the cratchets during the setting of the posts. If a roof frame was made of saplings, the irregular natural curves of these light roof members along the eaves would result in an equally irregular post line where the cratchets were set into the ground.

These building details of the Jamestown barracks point to a particular English building tradition known as "mud and stud," a style common in the postmedieval East Midlands region of England—especially the eastern half of the county of Lincolnshire, where over three hundred buildings in this style still stand today. Construction of such buildings begins with a framework of slight timbers either seated in the ground or based on stone pads. Between the uprights, crosspieces are added to the upright frames, and vertical slats or studs are nailed to the crosspieces. The resulting interior skeleton-like frame gives support to the wet mud walls until they can dry enough to stand on their own. Some walls are as thick as a foot or more. On the outside of the mud wall, fabric presents a smooth,

Buildings with cellars like this found beneath the factory all contained (*from bottom to top*) occupation, collapsed mud walls, and garbage and trash deposits.

uninterrupted clay surface that requires frequent recoating, often with a thin covering of lime plaster. Roofs of these buildings are traditionally of a light framework, with natural pole rafters lashed together to form a hip or half-hipped roof. Lincolnshire mud-and-stud wall lines tend to zigzag to conform to the natural curves of pole roof framing.[25] Should one of these Lincolnshire buildings with earthfast frame collapse and become an archaeological site, the remains in many respects would match the James Fort barracks. The major difference, of course, would be that the uprights in Lincolnshire are heavier and therefore, unlike cratchets, need to be held together by joinery.

Not surprisingly, the chief designers/ builders of the early houses at Jamestown were most likely from Lincolnshire. Captain John Smith of Alford, Lincolnshire, reported that he directed the building of houses. William Laxton, a Lincolnshire carpenter who was among the original settlers, must have been familiar with the mud-and-stud tradition.[26] In light of the abundant wooded land of Jamestown Island and the perfectly adhesive nature of the underlying clay, this building style, so familiar to Smith and Laxton, should have instantly dictated the housing process. But the barracks site shows that while the materials at hand fit the Lincolnshire building process to a T, the Virginia climate did not. Evidence of the builders' solution for this problem lay among the barracks' remains.

Pattern of support postholes (*right*) and the cellar and pit complex remains of the barracks.

Excavations of the barracks showed one support timber cutting into another along each wall line at the west end of the building, evidence that the west end was built twice. Other signs of rebuilding included fragments of fire-hardened clay walls, or daub, in the later posthole fill. These findings are consistent with the trustworthy Strachey's reports that the original buildings, presumably the ones that burned, had clay walls, chimneys, and (as illogical as it seems) roofs, all three likely sources of the daub fragments.

Another reason (besides fire) for the presence of daub in the posthole fill would be an upgrade of the buildings, which, according to Strachey, entailed adopting Virginia Indian building techniques and materials, such as replacing the clay walls and roofs with tree bark to form a better barrier from the relentless Virginia summer sun. This then would be an early sign of the adaptation of English building methods to the reality of the New World, creating the first Anglo-American buildings.

Does the burned daub that was found confirm that all or part of the building was destroyed by fire—perhaps the 1608 fire Smith describes as having burned the quarters in the town and some of the palisades "8 or 10 yards distant?"[27] Smith's description does not fit the location of the barracks and the other post buildings, which were actually ten feet away from the palisades, not ten yards. Was this figure one of Smith's exaggerations? Strachey also attests to a rebuilding after the 1608 fire, although his was not an eyewitness account as he did not arrive in the colony until 1610. His description of the Jamestown of 1610, however, is consistent with the alignment between the fort walls and the buildings we had found: "To every side [of the fort,] a proportioned distance from the palisade, is a settled street of houses that runs along, so as each line of the angle hath his street."[28] Only the lean-to cellar buildings along the west fort wall are too near the palisade for a "street" of any kind to have existed there. So the lean-tos must have been abandoned and filled in to create the street "to every side" of the triangle by the time Strachey penned his description.

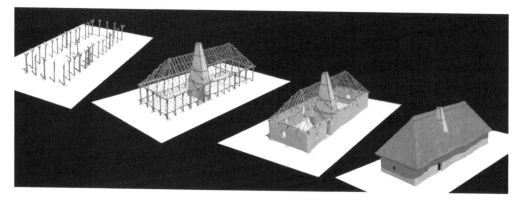

Stages in the construction of the mud-and-stud barracks, based on the pattern of its support postholes, the fill in the cellar, and what is known of the English architectural tradition. (Architect, Earl Mark; Virginia Polytechnic Institute and State University)

The cellar/pit in the end of the barracks included an original clearly cut cellar hole that experienced a number of earth-removing and filling episodes. The original cellar was about five feet wide, aligned along the south wall of the easternmost room of the building. This cellar accumulated fill and some discarded objects before it was disturbed by the digging of more randomly shaped holes that culminated in a small seven-foot-deep square shaft. It is unclear whether these later holes were dug when the building was still standing or after it ceased to exist. If dug while the building was still standing, the excavation must have been intended to expand the cellar. If the digging took place after the barracks had come down, its purpose is more difficult to figure out.

Whitt Cottage, Thimbleby, Lincolnshire, England, a classic example of a surviving postmedieval mud-and-stud building, which exhibits a traditional building technique likely transported to early Jamestown.

In fact, any pit or irregular hole in the ground presents interpretation problems for the archaeologist. Why did people dig these holes in the ground near their houses? To get dirt to fill something else in? To quarry clay for other uses, such as brickmaking or preparing daub? To create the hole itself—perhaps to serve as a mix-basin for brick or daub clay, or perhaps to serve no higher calling than becoming a lowly trash dump? The purposes of the barracks cellar/pit seem to be almost all of the above. To make the hole, colonists had to dig through some particularly fine-grained clay, a type that would have been ideal for building material such as brickmaking or daub. At the bottom of the pit, this same clay was mixed with decayed hand-cut marsh reeds—strong evidence that the cavity did in fact become a mixing bowl. Daub requires some sort of tempering material, and marsh reeds would make the resulting daub more workable wet and more permanent dry. So it is possible that, after the barracks went down, the pit became a "pug mill" for the mixing of the wet clay with the reeds. Finally, layers above the raw daub clearly show that after its use as a pug mill, the rest of the pit became a place to dump garbage.

The cellar/pit helps us to date the barracks itself. Before the cellar filled with refuse, someone left an artifact on the floor that establishes an early seventeenth-century TPQ date for the building's use. A single tiny clay tobacco pipe bowl with a teardrop-shaped heel design lay on the earthen floor surface. Fortunately, the sizes and shapes of colonial-period pipe bowls can indicate when the pipe was made and when it was in general use. The earliest pipe bowls had a very small capacity, probably owing to the scarcity and price of tobacco when Europeans began using it. We know this from viewing datable seventeenth-century Dutch paintings depicting pipe-smokers and from the shapes of pipes found on other dated archaeological sites. Bowls began small, growing in size and evolving in shape as time passed. The pipe bowl in the pit appears to match the bowls shown in the earliest such paintings, suggesting a manufacture/use date of 1590–1610. This same pipe bowl shape appears at Jamestown with regularity in other deposits where late sixteenth- to early seventeenth-century coins and other precisely datable objects have been found. Pipes from other New World sites set the date of their use more precisely. Bowls with the same shape and teardrop heel have been discovered at the site of Fort Saint George in Maine, which only existed for one year in 1607–8, and at the wreck site of the *Sea Venture*, the Jamestown supply ship that sank in 1609.[29] In the barracks, a sizable section of a broken Virginia Indian–made bowl decorated with impression marks of wrapped cord—a type known to be in use when the colonists first arrived—rested in the cellar fill with the circa-1607–10 pipe bowl. This suggests a very early seventeenth-century date for use of the cellar, and probably for the construction and occupation date of the barracks itself. It also reflects English reliance on Indian corn, perhaps delivered in these earthen bowls, further evidence, like the shift away from clay to bark as a building material, of the impact of Indian neighbors upon the colonists.

The consistently early dates and the military nature of the vast quantity of the over 44,000 artifacts found within the remaining series of related pits reveal that the barracks was indeed part of the James Fort enterprise. Precisely datable artifacts included three coins ranging in date from 1590 to 1602, casting counters or jettons (small copper coin-like discs used in mathematical calculations) dating as early as 1580, Elizabethan lead tokens from the 1570s, and a lead cloth seal that dates no later than 1603.[30] Thousands of European pottery fragments were also found—English, Dutch, French, German, and even Spanish types—all of manufacturing dates within the period. Triangular stone-hard vessels known as crucibles were among the ceramics from the barracks pit as well. One fragment from the pit proved to fit onto the broken, glass-coated pair of inverted crucibles from the aforementioned 1930s utility trench. The crucibles, along with

The shapes and sizes of tobacco pipe bowls from early Jamestown have proven to be consistent evidence in determining the date ranges of a number of key components of the Jamestown archaeological record. *From the top:* 1580–1610 (from the barracks cellar/pit), 1610–30 (a rowhouse builder's trench), 1610–30 (a Statehouse burial), 1630–40 (Berkeley Row), and a faceted stone pipe bowl of ca. 1620 (from the Smithfield well).

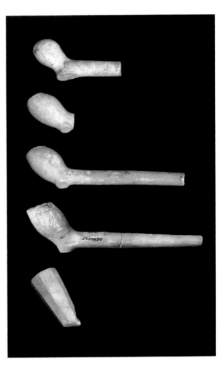

thousands of fragments of broken English window glass (cullet) found in the pit trash layers and similar debris related to glass-melting from nearby deposits, suggest the fallout from glass-making, undoubtedly debris from the "trials of glass" Smith referred to in 1608. Military arms and armor of the late sixteenth to early seventeenth century also found their way into the pits, including an intact cabasset-type helmet, sections of body armor, gorgets (neck guards), a couter (elbow protector), and tassetts (leg armor). The armor, firing mechanisms from muskets (matchlocks), and lead shot are undeniable evidence of a military post. All this support for a date of 1607–10 tells us that the barracks is the remains of one of the earliest Anglo-American buildings yet found in North America.

A vast quantity of discarded food remains and animal bones was found in the cellar/pit as well, giving vivid testimony to the struggle for survival at Jamestown during those first precarious years, 1607–circa 1610.[31] This approximate date for the bones is suggested by the objects found with them, but an even more precise date is established by interpreting the bones in the context of the documentary record. According to Strachey's report, when he and the shipwrecked Bermuda contingent of Governor Gates's original flotilla arrived at Jamestown in May 1610, they brought with them some food gathered during their nine-month shipbuilding stay in Bermuda. Among the easiest to gather was the cahow, a Bermudan bird that failed to understand the importance of flying away from hunters. The shipwrecked colonists quickly recognized this free lunch and almost certainly kept the cahow in some preserved state as naval provisions. Among the

A German stoneware bottle know as a Bartmann (bearded man) with decorative coat of arms (Italian), made ca. 1610, from the barracks cellar/pit.

bones found in the barracks cellar/pit were those of the cahow. The cellar also held Bermudan conch shells, a number of tropical fish common only to Bermuda, and some pieces of Bermudan limestone. There is no record of supplies coming from Bermuda to early Jamestown at any time other than May of 1610. These uniquely Bermudan foods and other supplies must have been brought to Jamestown by the ex–*Sea Venture* passengers, eventually to be cooked and eaten by them and the surviving settlers of the "starving time" at Jamestown. The bones wound up in the barracks cellar some time afterward.

These relics of transported Bermuda supplies tell us something more. The number of these bones and shells is small in comparison to the remnants of what must have been the colonists' provisions from the Virginia woods and rivers. To understand the full meaning of the meager Bermudan supply, it is necessary to revisit estimates of Jamestown's population after the "starving time."

Smith's publication, *The Generall Historie,* reports that only sixty of the five hundred people at Jamestown survived the "starving time."[32] A combination of numbers from several eyewitness accounts, however, suggests that while the death rate at Jamestown was appalling, it has been exaggerated. By adding and subtracting population estimates, using accounts of individual and group deaths and reports of numbers arriving on various ships, one can estimate that by the fall of 1609—the beginning of the "starving time"—215 people were living at Jamestown and thirty more in its environs.[33] At the time the group arrived from Bermuda, according to Strachey's figures, ninety were left alive in the colony, with sixty of these living in the town. So the number of deaths during that time was less than half the total reported by Strachey (155 compared to 440). However, with the influx of the estimated 135 *Sea Venture* survivors, the total population at Jamestown would have jumped to 195.

In this context, the few remains of Bermudan foods fill out the harrowing story told in documents. The Bermudan contingent would not have carried many extra supplies on their trip to Jamestown, as they had no way of knowing that they would find a starving colony; nor would they know that their own arrival would amount to a dangerous explosion in Jamestown's already stressed population. The ensuing events, however, showed that the Bermuda contingent, instead of saving the colony, imposed a new burden on Jamestown.

Taking over leadership of the colony from George Percy, Sir Thomas Gates immediately saw the need to assess the ratio of population to provisions. Gates at first concluded that the Bermudan food supplies should be kept in reserve for a possible retreat voyage back to England. In the meantime, he would send parties out to forage among the Powhatan, hoping to gather enough food to get the colony back on its feet. Having no luck with that plan, Gates figured that enough food was left to supply the colonists at Jamestown for sixteen days if he rationed two cakes (possibly a type of dried fish cake) per person per day.[34] If no supplies could be found during that period, the colony would be abandoned.

We have already heard the rest of this story: after sixteen days, no food materialized. The colonists would have to leave. They buried the ordnance and whatever else might be reclaimable if they ever came back, gathered up everything else that was of saleable value, then headed down river toward the open ocean. Their interim destination

Late sixteenth- to seventeenth-century iron helmet (cabasset) found in the barracks cellar/pit and the conserved breastplate from the bulwark ditch.

was the Grand Fishing Banks off Newfoundland. It should be stressed again that Gates and the retreating Jamestown settlers could have planned to stop at the Charles and Algernon Fort area and wait at least ten days for possible English supplies to arrive.[35] There, the settlers knew, they could live off shellfish for the short term, as Percy's party had done while awaiting Gates's arrival from Bermuda two months earlier. Just over a day after the settlers

Collection of discarded food bones and shells from the barracks cellar/pit. Some, like the butchered bones of horses, rats, and poisonous snakes, are grim reminders of "starving time" diets, 1607–10.

had left Jamestown under Gates's direction, an advance boat arrived from Lord De La Warre's ship, announcing the imminent arrival of the latest new governor. Luckily, De La Warre brought with him enough supplies to save the colony. With the addition of the De La Warre entourage, the Jamestown population could well have been 345. If De La Warre actually brought provisions to support the total population for a year, as reported, his ships must have been heavily laden indeed.

While the bones from Bermuda in the barracks cellar/pit reveal the pressure put upon the weakened colony by the arrival of Gates's contingent, the other discarded food remains found there graphically depict the sufferings of those who had tried to hold the fort during the "starving time," the winter and spring of 1609–10. The presence in the pit of poisonous snake vertebrae and musk turtle gives some indication that life at Jamestown had reached crisis proportions. Butchered horse bones, and the bones of the black rat, dogs, and cats also powerfully demonstrate how desperate conditions must have become. Fifteen bones or bone fragments of a large dog or dogs were recovered from the fill in the nearby dry moat. These did not show signs of butchering, but their proximity to other bones that did may indicate that, while these animals were brought to Virginia as hunters or weapons of war, they might eventually have become a food source.

X-rays of skull fragments show that dogs at Jamestown lived hard lives even before they may have ended up on the dinner table. One radiograph shows a small piece of lead shot embedded in a dog's skull. This injury was not the cause of death: the x-ray also shows that the bone had healed around the shot. The injury may have resulted from combat after the Indians acquired muskets (as early as 1608, according to John Smith).[36] Documentary sources indicate that the Indians realized the strategic importance of the colonists' dogs. Gabriel Archer reports that a Virginia Indian attack on the Jamestown settlers in May 1607 resulted in the killing of "our dogs." Of course, the Indians may have had nothing to do with the wounding of the dog, which could also have resulted from a stray hunting shot. There is some evidence that the injured dog did belong to the colonists rather than the Indians: a rendering of one local Indian dog suggests that such dogs were relatively small with very distinctive skull shapes. (Some believe that relatives of these Indian dogs, the American dingo, still roam free in the backwoods of coastal North Carolina.)[37] While the exact breed of the dog with the head wound is not known, it has characteristics of a mastiff.[38] There is no question that this dog was relatively large, perhaps in the forty-five- to fifty-five-pound range. According to records, greyhounds and mastiffs were at Jamestown.

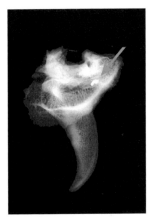

X-ray of dog (possibly a mastiff) jawbone showing lead shot in a healed wound.

Resorting to killing and eating one of their key means to hunt and so to live off the wild surely demonstrates the extremity of the hunger of the Jamestown colonists in the "starving time." But once the settlers were confined to their "blockhouse" as Strachey reports, domesticated animals, such as dogs and cats, and even indoor animals like rats would have become the only source of food for the besieged colonists. Percy apparently was not exaggerating when he wrote, during the "starving time," "Then having fed upon horses and other beasts as long as they lasted, we were glad to make shift with vermin, as dogs, cats, rats and mice."[39]

## Quarter
Building remains of the quarter closely resemble those of the barracks: the cellars of the two buildings were similar in size and in location (at one end of the building), and they contained similar fill. The width of each building was seventeen feet, and the framing holes were spaced with similar randomness. It can be concluded that the quarter had been another mud-and-stud building. In the period postdating the fort, however, the quarter site had suffered considerable damage, probably starting with the growth of a nearby oak tree. Grading during the creation of the adjacent Civil War

Excavated site of the quarter building showing wall posts and cellar of another example of likely mud-and-stud construction.

earthwork in 1861 took a sizable bite out of the site. Finally, the building remains were unmercifully shaved and punctured by the grading of a road in the late nineteenth century and the installation of a commemorative fence around the church, which was reconstructed in 1907. It is amazing that any trace of the quarter survived all these earth-shattering impacts. Excavation of what trace remained was limited by the church tower, which had been constructed on the quarter's southern end, preventing a determination of the building's length.

Even the deepest disturbance, however—the nineteenth-century road—left a few inches of the northwest corner posthole intact. The rest of the building footprint fared still better. Building remains nearer the seventeenth-century church tower were within the aforementioned no-plowzone, where soil was left untilled, presumably out of respect for the church graveyard. This unplowed portion of overburden presented a unique chance to determine the original depth of postholes and the cellars of this and possibly the other mud-and-stud structures. The unplowed building surface stood four feet above the cellar floor. This establishes its undisturbed original depth. As much as two feet of the original seventeenth-century surface in and around the west side of the barracks were missing. But by the same token, at least that much earth is probably missing all across the fort site except in the immediate vicinity of the church tower.

The cellar's occupation zone—a six-inch-deep deposit accumulated during the time the cellar was in use, now covered by the fallen mud-wall level—lay on top of a group of artifacts whose position suggested that they had all been abandoned there at the same moment, creating an accidental time capsule. In one corner, charred wood and clay marked where a cooking fire once burned, and beside it, a Virginia Indian pot was found, still containing traces of turtle bone. A butchered hip-bone of a pig and a butchered turtle shell lay nearby, suggesting that pork, or a combination of pork and turtle, comprised the menu. Near the pot lay a large Venetian trade bead. So was the cook a Virginia Indian—perhaps a woman? Might she have been one of the forty or fifty Indian wives of English settlers, according to the Spanish claim?[40]

The Indian (?) cook had been surrounded by weapons. A sheathed dagger was found within arm's reach of the cooking fire, and behind it lay a musketeer's bag of gunflints, lead balls, and powder. Iron shovel blades were on the floor as well. The shovels and weapons in a cellar were no real surprise: cellars would be likely places to store such objects. The fire, however, is hard to explain. How and why would someone burn a fire on the floor of a mud-and-stud building's cellar, when the ceiling—the floor above— would presumably have been made of wood? A possible answer is offered by evidence that the cellar had originally had a lightly constructed, wooden

*From foreground to background:* Butchered turtle, crushed Virginia Indian pot containing remains of cooked turtle, large trade bead, butchered pig bone, sheathed dagger, and charred wood on scorched clay cellar floor—a moment in time at the quarter.

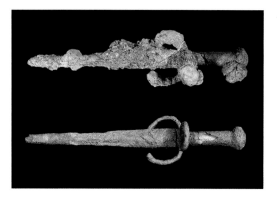

Late sixteenth-century dagger, from the quarter cellar, before and after conservation.

Musketeer's "kit" on the quarter cellar floor, includes musket balls, a gun flint, a single-charge powder bandolier, and the copper pouch base.

dividing wall. This wall might speak to an earlier tent-pit structure, perhaps one of the mere hole-in-the-ground shelters settlers first lived in, according to that negative report of "the ancient planters" in 1623.[41] In this earlier structure, a fire might have blazed away on the pit floor without danger. The artifacts and documents together could suggest, then, that the mud-and-stud superstructure was an evolution from an earlier crude cellar/house. In any case, the dagger, Virginia Indian pottery, a large, glass Indian trade bead, and copper objects date the cellar to the first few years of settlement. The building's association with the east wall of the triangular James Fort, superseded by later renovations, further suggests this dating. The quarter, too, then, is an example of the very beginnings of house construction in Anglo-America.

**Factory**

The most complex floor plan of the mud-and-stud buildings appeared in the factory, whose architectural details and artifacts could reveal something of its use during the first three years of the settlement, 1607–10. The factory was eventually found to be the largest of the mud buildings, seventy-two feet long, and there was clear evidence that it was divided into at least three and perhaps four rooms. The southernmost room was built over a comparatively enormous, partially wood-lined cellar, constructed in two phases under a superstructure that was supported by the now-familiar irregularly spaced upright posts. The fort's palisade wall was connected to the building at what appeared to have been its original southwest corner post. At some point the cellar was expanded into an L shape by digging beneath the building's superstructure.

A series of entrance steps descended from the west at the head of the cellar, fanning toward the south as they entered the subterranean room. Although the cellars of the barracks and the quarter had been unlined, this cellar showed clear signs of decayed timbers on the east and north walls. Cavities in these walls left molds of these timber supports. The east wall of the factory held back a mixed clay liner, presumably packed behind the timber to waterproof this wall, which was closest to the edge of the building above. The west wall did not have such a lining, presumably because it was well away from the outside wall line of the building. The original south wall would also not have required waterproofing clay, as it too was well underneath the superstructure.

Natural subsoil clay in the L addition made up the cellar floor, but a mixture of sandy clay leveled the floor in the north half of the room. In that section, the floor held two barrels buried upright, which apparently served as sumps whenever the cellar took on water. Judging from the lower few inches of washed sand on the floor and in the barrel, flooding was not uncommon. No barrel wood survived, but the dark stain left where the wood had decayed formed a perfect mold in the sandy fill around and in it. These washed layers and the installation of the barrel also suggest that the cellar had had a reasonably long life.

Another fire had burned in this cellar along the west wall. Charcoal on the floor and clay heated enough to turn red pinpointed a fire "place." There was no evidence along the clay cellar wall above the fire area that there had ever been a flue. Here again was a puzzle: how could a fire exist in a basement below what had to be a wooden floor without setting it on fire? Had the factory, like the quarter, possibly been a pit house before it was transformed into a mud-and-stud building? Documents suggest a more intriguing explanation.

In addition to the stairs, walls, and floor, excavations uncovered a line of small postholes cutting into the subsoil below the dirt floor just south of the stairs. These holes suggested the presence of some sort of partition there before the floor level had been raised. A wall in that location would not make much sense unless there was need, as in a prison, to secure the cellar space at times from access via the stairs. Perhaps that barrier and the fire are both explained by one of John Smith's tales. Smith wrote about putting one of two Powhatan brothers in a "dungeon" until the other brother returned a stolen pistol by sun-up.[42] Failure to comply would result in the execution of the prisoner. That night, taking pity on his prisoner, Smith

Archaeological remains of the factory attached to James Fort by palisade, showing wall postholes and three rooms: cellar with stairs and drainage barrels (*foreground*), central room, and "workshop" (*background*) with three brick hearths.

allowed him to burn a charcoal fire. The fire, apparently flueless, naturally would have produced poisonous carbon monoxide. No wonder the prisoner was unconscious by the time the brother returned the pistol. Thinking him dead, the brother loudly and justifiably cried foul, at which time Smith told him that if he promised to end the thievery of arms forever, Smith would bring his brother back to life. The brother agreed. A stiff shot of "aqua vitae" (strong alcohol) did the trick, and, according to Smith, he thereafter had little trouble getting his way with the Indians. He had the power to raise the dead, or so they thought.

So a flueless charcoal fire, which perhaps burned only once, and an inner security wall at the base of the cellar steps might identify the site as Smith's dungeon. Jail or not, it is clear that the cellar did serve as part of the Jamestown defense system. Shelves cut into the north and south walls could have been built there to serve musketeers. These shelves would have given an elevated firing position through a ground-level opening. The value of the cellar for such defensive purposes is suggested by its position: the superstructure of the factory extended so far beyond the palisade wall that it could act as a bastion. In that case, a musketeer could provide flanking fire toward anyone assaulting the palisade.

Like the other two fort-period cellars, the factory cellar held several distinct types of fill, laid in this sequence: washed sandy clay at the bottom; above that, the aforementioned fill that washed in along the floor from the south and into the barrel sump; on top of that, a deposit of what has to be the collapsing of mud-and-stud walls; then a rich vein of trash and garbage spilling in from the south and east. Finally, brown loam filled the resulting depression, presumably to enable easy plowing of the cellar-building site. Three of these layers represent the end of the life of the cellar: the wall collapse, the trash and garbage, and the leveling loam. The same sequence is observable in all three mud-and-stud buildings, with the exception of the trash layer, which is missing in the quarter. Such a deposit may have been wiped away in the quarter with all the nineteenth-century earthmoving.

What these layers tell is the same story of construction, use, and demise that can be discerned in the barracks and the quarter. First, the builders dug a cellar, presumably stockpiling the mixed topsoil and clay and maybe even living in the cellar for a time. Then the light cratchets went up as a frame above the cellar and beyond. As a network of lighter studs lined the walls between the major upright poles, the stockpile fill was spread (pargeted) onto the frames. A light sapling roof frame was built separately and then

"C. Smith taketh the King of Pamaunkee prisoner, 1608." (Plate 45, *The American Drawings of John White*, vol. 2; copyright The Trustees of the British Museum)

raised up as forked-pole wall posts went into place. The light roof was hipped for strength. When the mud walls were dry and stable enough, thatch was added to complete the roof. The cellar then was used for a concentrated period of time, likely during the stressful first three years, 1607–10. Some time after that, the mud walls collapsed into the cellar as the building disappeared. Last of all, a rich layer of trash went into most of the remaining cellar space.

That topmost layer of trash is rich not only in its abundance and variety, but in its capacity to illuminate the early history of Jamestown's fortifications. This capacity derives, first of all, from one distinctive characteristic of the trash deposits in the cellars of the barracks, quarter, and factory, and, for that matter, all of the rest of the early fort trash deposits (the fort moat and the circular magazine at the south bastion, and the west bulwark ditch): all these deposits were apparently created at one and the same time.

How do we know this? All of the deposits contained pieces of some of the same ceramic vessels: that is, in archaeological terms, there could be some cross-mending. If broken pots found at different deposits across a site mend together—that is, if the pieces of the same pot found in different deposits fit together—then it is possible that the deposits were made soon after the pot broke. Therefore, ceramic cross-mending among the cellars and other features theoretically suggests a massive deposition all across the site at about the same time. Not only did such cross-mending characterize these trash deposits, but all held almost identical artifacts: scrap copper, jettons (copper coin-like calculating tokens), armor, weapon parts, the same types of broken pottery (especially Delft drug jars), and food remains. Another similarity in the trash layers is that the most recent artifacts in all of them date to no later than 1610; therefore, all four cellars seemed to have a similar backfilling date.

Why so much was thrown away at the same time after 1610 remains an important question. One possible answer might be called "the De La Warre cleanup." In June 1610, when Lord De La Warre with his fresh troops, supplies, and settlers arrived to save the day after the "starving time" of 1609–10, the trusted William Strachey wrote that the new governor "brought the fort to more perfection" and, among other things, "cleansed the town."[43] What exactly was perfected, what was cleansed, is not very clear. Cleansing likely meant clearing the grounds of accumulated litter, repairing or removing shabby buildings, and repairing and/or perhaps redesigning palisade lines. These activities might possibly account for the great number of contemporary 1607–10 trash deposits. But if all the cellars, moat, and bulwark trenches were filled by De La Warre in 1610, what was left of the original

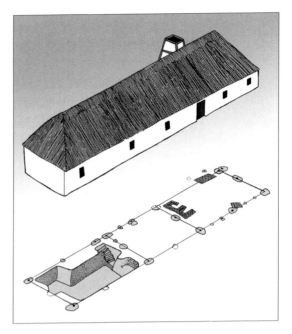

Archaeological plan (*below*) and mud-and-stud conjectured reconstruction of the factory.

James Fort thereafter? The fort cannot have disappeared, since Strachey described its form as triangular, just as Percy and Smith had described it earlier, with two 300-foot sides on the east and west and a 420-foot side on the south made of "planks and strong posts."[44] And these are exactly the dimensions of the one and only fort found archaeologically.

Another explanation for the trash layer may lie in Strachey's earlier description of the town, written about what he saw on May 20, 1610, the day he arrived with the previously shipwrecked party from Bermuda. Strachey made a strong point that the town was in shambles, with the main gate off its hinges and the houses and palisade torn down and cut into firewood. Although we have explained the dismantling of the fort's east wall as part of an intentional expansion, some of the removal could have resulted from a desperate gathering of firewood. If this east palisade had not yet become an interior wall, its removal would have explained why, as Strachey remarked, the Indians could kill anyone who ventured from the "blockhouse" (to which the survivors may have been confined because it was the only place secure enough to provide protection).[45] Razing a palisade, even in part, would have left the whole settlement wide open to attacks from the Powhatan.

The "blockhouse" could mean, of course, the blockhouse built near the isthmus at the extreme western end of the island, or the blockhouse on Back River. But it is also possible that some settlers were seeking safety in the factory or other fort buildings, all of which would have become, in a sense, blockhouses as soon as some palisades were gone. Strachey also noted that the surviving settlers were suffering from pestilence within the blockhouse. If they were in fact trapped inside the buildings for their own safety, then it is not beyond the realm of possibility that their garbage and trash could wind up in the cellars below them. Under siege by the Indians, who would risk an appearance beyond the protection of the blockhouse walls just to get rid of rubbish?

Some of the trash found in the cellars, however, does not fit this explanation. The debris included industrial waste from glassmaking, pipemaking, metallurgy, and the reworking of armor. Starving and trapped settlers would hardly bide their time busily manufacturing things and dropping the waste in the cellar below. The siege explanation also does not account for what appears to be the collapsed walls found below this industrial waste in the factory. This redeposited clay layer can only be the consequence of wall destruction. So a blockhouse confinement, brought on by an Indian siege, cannot convincingly explain the cellar garbage.

A third possible explanation for the layers of contemporaneously deposited trash could be called the ghost-town theory. This means what it implies: the fort may have been abandoned early on, in favor of the improved two streets of "faire" houses described by Hamor in 1611. That being the case, the fort would begin to decay from disuse and neglect as the colony experienced a long period of peace with Spain back in Europe and with the Indians in Virginia. During this time of semidesertion, the fort and its smaller extension might have begun to erase itself, any holes and ditches such as moats and cellars eroding, and, finally, in the case of buildings, the mud walls caving into the cellars. Descriptions of the fort during those years of peace give the distinct impression of such a ghost town.[46] Mud-and-stud houses would fall in if not constantly repaired, which fits with the deposit of mixed clay above a relatively thin occupation zone. As the fort reached a hopeless state of decay, and the settlers adopted a disastrous, false sense of security (right before the 1622 Indian uprising), the useless fort would have been totally abandoned. The cellars would become convenient trash dumps for refuse lying about from the early occupation years. The consistently early dates of the trash (1607–10) and the fact that so many of the fragments from the same vessels are scattered among the various deposits, suggest that this trash came from a common source. All of the pieces from broken and discarded objects would have originally been thrown together, only to get scattered in the backfilled cellars later. Such a scattering would have left the objects in a layer on top of the collapsed mud walls.

This scenario would explain why all the artifacts are so consistently datable to the very early occupation years, although this redepositing may have occurred as late as the middle 1620s. But this scenario does not jibe with the early abandonment of the lean-tos along the west wall or with the discovery of the later rowhouses (see below) that replaced them. So De La Warre's arrival amounted to much more than a cleansing: it was a comprehensive redesign of the interior plan. Thus the De La Warre cleanup theory seems the most logical explanation for the accumulation across the fort of so many contemporary artifacts.

Since the artifact and food remains from the backfilling of the factory cellar could have been hauled in from anywhere on the fort site during the cleanup operation, they might have little to say about what human action took place in the immediate vicinity of the extension building. But some objects were found embedded in the factory cellar subfloor and in its relatively thin occupation layer, obviously dropped and lost right there as people used the space. For example, a Nuremberg 1580 jetton, a fragment of a French Martincamp ceramic flask, and a 1573 silver English sixpence all date to the late sixteenth century. These artifacts tell us that the cellar was being used as a cellar during the very early fort period—more evidence that the triangular fort expanded sooner than later in its early years, certainly by the time De La Warre completed his many "perfections." Together with the building floor plan, the artifacts also offer clues to the use of the building. In the northernmost rooms of the complex, over one hundred jettons were found in the plowzone as well as scattered across the top of or embedded in a thick clay floor. Again, being *in* the floor means they were dropped when the room was occupied. Perhaps most telling of all, a fragment of a glass alembic (a domed vessel used in distilling) was found in the floor, almost certainly broken off of the alembic recovered from the trash levels in the cellar under the southernmost room. There, a ceramic boiling vessel known as a cucurbit rested in the fill with the alembic. The alembic and the cucurbit are the two main components of a distilling operation. These objects and other specialized ceramic vessels found with them—including crucibles, a distilling dish, and a dipper—are all implements required for the detection and refinement of precious metals. These artifacts may also be the only clue to the purpose of the three brick fireplace hearths found in the north room, as no other evidence of industrial waste appeared in any of the fill from the occupation period.

The fire in the largest hearth—which showed evidence of two periods of construction—had been hot enough to partially melt the brick surfaces. Since distilling only requires enough heat to boil liquid, either something else was being heated there or the continuous fires took their toll on the surface of the brick. Distilling is still one of the most likely uses of the rooms. The process also requires a collection vessel at the end of the line, and French Martincamp flasks could have been used for that purpose.

Jettons would not have been used in distilling, so their presence in the northern room in such great numbers is rather puzzling. Their presence might suggest that the northern room was some type of accounting office, or perhaps occupied by the cape merchant, the man appointed by the Company to keep track of the supplies and any material that could be shipped home to turn a profit. If the space was an accounting office, then the James Fort cape merchants who were responsible for the Virginia Company "store" were based there in 1607–10.[47] It is also possible, and probably more likely, that jettons were used, not for their original purpose of calculation, but for a currency. Official coinage might not have been readily available that far away from England.[48] If that is the case, then what were the settlers buying there? And if the jettons had intrinsic value, why had they been lost and scattered on the floor in such great numbers? Perhaps the jettons were used to buy food from the Virginia Indians. It would make sense that such transactions should occur in a building that was somewhat secure, yet outside the actual triangular fort.

But plowing disturbances had made understanding the northern room(s) difficult. An even greater source of difficulty was the churchyard burial ground that extended across the building site. Over a dozen burial shafts pierced the earth floor, especially in the northern room, so that only segments of the original floor between the burial shafts remained intact. Fortunately, most of the hearths survived the burials. Also, the earthen floor that escaped the burial disruptions not only held the jettons but also two

Ceramic "boiler," known as a cucurbit, found in the factory cellar. This vessel is part of a still, indicating that scientists with the early settlers had the equipment to test for gold and other precious metals that ultimately eluded them.

curious artifact caches in small shallow holes. One such hole contained an English-made (Borderware) candlestick TPQ 1580, two Hans Krauwinkle TPQ 1580 jettons, and a very unusual 1577 Livonian silver coin. Stranger yet, next to the main hearth, someone had buried dozens of quartz pebbles, apparently in an early seventeenth-century case bottle sealed with a pewter stopper, but with the bottom of the bottle broken away. The artifacts were located between the eastern wall line of the factory and the chimney, suggesting they were buried in what must have been a lobby entrance, a small room between the front door and the chimneystack. Lobby entrances were common in lowland English houses of the postmedieval period; the room acted as a holding space for strangers, a place to decide whether or not they were eligible to venture into the more private main rooms. Small collections of objects placed in voids along chimneystacks and under floors have turned up in postmedieval houses in Suffolk as well. Some argue convincingly that these English caches were placed there by superstitious country people, believing that articles as personal as shoes would keep evil spirits, such as witches, from entering the house through the one opening that could not be closed, the chimney flue.[49] The caches in the factory's lobby floor could well be a sign that Suffolk superstition was alive and well at Jamestown.

A metallurgy shop? A store? A prison? A factory? These are questions and possible answers as to the use of the building. We can only speculate, also, about whether this extension building was set apart from but attached to the triangular walls of James Fort for any special reason. Whether or not the building stood after the period of architectural change introduced when De La Warre brought the Company governance from London to Jamestown is unknown. What is less questionable is that the factory, in common with the other mud-and-stud buildings, reflects a local vernacular tradition. What may be most intriguing are the hints that these remains, like the remains of the barracks and the quarter, offer of the colonists' complex interactions with the Virginia Indians: learning from their building techniques, relying on their food supply, entering into human relationships more complex than those of enemies or neighbors keeping at a well-regulated, cautious distance. Whatever we can or cannot know of the form and lifespan of the factory, we can be sure that negotiating these relationships formed one of the major challenges of these struggling years of the colony.

## Governor's Row

Remains of the third and fourth buildings inside the James Fort triangle, the rowhouses (hereafter rows) tell a different story architecturally. This story, in turn, offers new insight into the Virginia Company's steadfast commitment to making a success of their Virginia enterprise despite the obvious challenges to survival presented by nature and the Virginia Indians during the first two years. Excavations on the west side of the fort triangle beneath the Civil War earthwork and its underlying plowzone revealed remnants of cobblestone foundations, defining the limits of two enormous buildings paralleling the west wall line for over 170 feet.

Grading for the Civil War earthwork and plowing by farmers had again seriously disturbed portions of the buildings' remains, but enough escaped these disturbances to define the basic plans. The southernmost structure measured 90' × 18' and had three chimneys with back-to-back fireplaces in them. The double hearths make it probable that this structure had at least six rooms, one fireplace in each. There were no cellars. The solid cobble footings indicate the buildings were of box-frame construction, with sills protected from contact with the decaying effect of the wet clay beneath. These footings were built for permanence beyond that of their mud-and-stud predecessors. Inside the foundation, however, were signs that timber floor joists had been laid directly on the ground.

The foundation to the north measured 18' × 66' with one back-to-back brick chimney toward the northern end. There the Civil War grading was lighter than elsewhere, allowing more of the floor joists to survive. This row appears to have been divided by the chimney into a seventeen-foot-long room to the east and probably one heated and one unheated room to the south. Grading to the south, however, may have erased one or more chimneys. Although grading for the Civil War earthwork erased most of the west wall line, both of its corners were spared. The northern row has a brick addition of yet undiscovered design or dimensions. Discovering signs of such permanent buildings raised a number of significant questions: were they old enough to be a part of the town plan of the fort era, or did they belong to the post-fort town? What did they look like? What were they used for?

One fact proves that the rows date to the fort era: the distance that separates their foundation from the west wall of the fort is generally the same as that separating the barracks and quarter from their parallel palisades. Like these other buildings, then, the rows were part of the early, fortified Jamestown, standing on the opposite side of the "street" from the fort wall. Unlike these mud-and-stud buildings, however, the rows do not appear to have been part of the original 1607–9 house construction. A Bermuda limestone was used in the southernmost chimney foundation, the type of stone used as ballast in the Bermuda-built ships that arrived with Gates in 1610.[50] For that reason, the rows must date after June 1610. Archaeological test excavation of the trench dug and then filled around the cobblestones by the builders at the time of construction produced fragments of pottery and tobacco pipe bowls lost by the workers. One bowl shape dates it to after 1610, which corroborates the evidence of the limestone (see p. 89). Finally, it is significant that seventeen single and two double burials lay about and beneath a chimney and the wall of the southern row, all parallel or perpendicular to the west fort wall. Burying people inside the fort would have been out of the view of the native Indians, thus following the instructions of the Virginia Company: "Above all things do not advertise the killing of any of your men, that the country people [Virginia Indians] may know it, if they perceive that they are but common men . . . you should

Overview of the two building sites found in the fort with cobblestone foundations and back-to-back brick-chimney foundations (probable governor's residence [*foreground*] and the rowhouse [*background*]). Note also the west fort palisade trench (*upper right*), cellars/pits, and posthole from lean-tos along the wall, and postholes from what appear to be at this writing pre-governor's residence/rowhouse post-in-the-ground structures (1607–10?) to the left of the cobble line.

do well also not to let them see or know of your sick men."[51]

Excavation of the two double burials established that these were likely the graves of four of the twenty-five gentlemen Percy listed as dying in the first disastrous summer of 1607 or soon thereafter. Like the use of Bermuda stone, the 1607 date of the graves underlying the row is more evidence that the rows were not part of the very first years. What is more, the graves lay in aligned cemetery fashion in an area with no other indication of contemporary use of that space, while the lean-tos along the palisade—the earliest shelters—were built beyond the burial space limits. In other words, those who lived in the fort before the construction of the rows knew the graves were there and avoided building on or among them—while in later years, when this row was likely constructed, the probably unmarked graves were perhaps lost from memory.

Discovery of clay tobacco pipe bowl of a 1610–30 style in the builder's trench of the rowhouse corroborates the documentary construction date of 1611.

Could this substantially built rowhouse be one of the "faire . . . houses" Ralph Hamor crows about in his *True Discourse*? Could it even be the governor's residence built by Sir Thomas Gates in 1611?[52] The Hamor document is usually dismissed as propaganda, falsely hyping the colony as a great success in order to offset the gruesome stories of immigrant deaths that had been circulating in England. His description of "two faire rowes of houses, all of framed timber, two stories high, and an upper garret or corn loft" seems too good to be true of the heretofore-struggling Jamestown. In fact, Hamor's later indictment of the mismanaged town in a written attack on the Virginia Company treasurer, Thomas Smythe, gives an opposite account, depicting the houses as "mean and poor."[53] Hamor's extreme shift gives more reason not to trust his facts. Nevertheless, with their masonry footings and multiple chimneys, the rows could well be the buildings Hamor describes.

A late sixteenth-century London series of attached dwellings, likely a prototype of the James Fort rowhouse complex. (From John Thomas Smith's *Antiquities of London* [London, 1791]; copyright Museum of London)

These footings could support a two-and-one-half-story timber-framed building, perhaps of the scale of a London rowhouse of that time.[54] While practically all such buildings went up in smoke during the Great Fire of London in 1666, an engraving of a rowhouse built in 1577 for the support of poor widows seems to fit the Jamestown buildings' multichimney plan and Hamor's "faire" houses.[55] The division of the London house into apartments at every chimney might well be reflected in the Jamestown remains. Hamor's earlier document, then, adds to the evidence that the rows were constructed some time after July 15, 1610, when Strachey apparently describes the town without them, and 1611–14, when Hamor describes his houses and the Company mentions the governor's residence. As for the other of Hamor's two rows of houses, either this was an exaggeration, or he really meant two rowhouses, or their remains lie somewhere yet to be discovered. It is possible that the Dutch map of 1617 depicts the southern building, indicating that each of the three sets of two rooms defined by the back-to-back chimneys had its gable roof.

Excavation at about the geometrical center of the triangular fort found a line of three postholes, ten feet apart. Their size, depth, and postmolds indicate they once held massive structural timbers, apparently signs that one of the larger public buildings Strachey wrote about was located in the middle of the fort: the storehouse, guardhouse, or church. The holes are oriented along a line that would almost divide the fort triangle in two and thus be perpendicular with the south wall. This almost certainly indicates

Three oversized postholes in the center of the triangular James Fort mark the likely location of the Virginia Company storehouse. Later post-fort disturbances such as the construction of a brick-lined cellar in a mid-seventeenth-century house (*foreground*) may have erased more evidence of the earlier building.

the building was part of the James Fort design. Future excavations may discover whether or not these are the early signs of such significant structures, but there are also indications that postfort construction of a building with a sizable cellar and the digging of a deep moat around the 1861 Civil War earthwork may have destroyed more signs of these early buildings.

Another building site possibly related to the fort is among the Jamestown Rediscovery archaeological finds. Digging through the plowzone just north of the factory revealed a cellar-like pit. The artifacts inside suggest that the pit may have been one of the earliest parts of an expanded fortified town. It first appeared beneath the tilled soil as a circular discoloration about eight feet in diameter, possibly another backfilled well. The upper three feet of fill held trash-laden layers containing apothecary jars (one complete jar and many nearly complete), sheet-copper waste, jettons, fine glass buttons, a case bottle, fish hooks, ammunition and small powder flasks known as bandoliers, traces of cloth, a Scottish James VI coin of 1597, and a Groningen (Netherlands) token dated 1583. The fill also contained many Virginia Indian artifacts, including related (i.e., "mendable") pieces of pots, a section of reed matting, and arrow points accompanied by stone flakes from their manufacture.

Excavations have recovered over two hundred such projectile points inside the footprint of the fort, along the palisades, around and in the bulwark, and in the bulwark ditch. Their shapes and sizes date them primarily to two periods: the Archaic, 8000–1200 BC (30%) and the Late Woodland, 900–1600 AD (68%).[56] Of course, ancient Indians living or hunting on the island left the archaic 8000–1200 BC points. But the Woodland period points predominate and comprise a unique assortment of shapes, sizes, and stone types, suggesting that they came from a wide area of coastal Virginia and North Carolina. The great number found buried with 1607–10

A number of decorative Delft tiles found in the Civil War earthwork fill in the vicinity of the governor's residence, perhaps evidence of the fine quality of the building from the time of occupancy by Governors Argall and Yeardley.

European artifacts suggests that the arrow points were being used by Indians taken into the fort or else reused by the settlers themselves. Smith reports that in exchange for bells, the Massawomeks gave him "venison, beares flesh, fish, bowes, arrows, clubs, targets, and beares skinnes." Some of the arrows must have arrived in the fort during battle. A few of the points may even be from the rain of forty arrows Archer witnessed flying into the fort.[57]

What is most remarkable about the arrow points found in the pit north of the factory is that the stone type of one of them is identical to that of some of the numerous stone flakes found with it. This debatage, or stone flakes, tells us that the manufacturer—a Virginia Indian—was producing the points in the fort itself.[58] It is very doubtful that settlers took up that craft; after all, they had metal-pointed bolts for their crossbows, and they had guns.

Nor are the arrow points from this pit and elsewhere across the fort site the only signs of the Indians' presence. The reed matting found in the pit was of the sort mentioned by Smith and others as important objects in the material world of the Virginia Indians. Made of marsh grass held together with bark fiber cord, the mat survived because it had been buried immediately under copper waste and ammunition bandoliers. The copper salts had acted as a sterilant, fending off organisms that normally would decompose the reed fibers. Thanks to this chance layering of deposits, this object is the only surviving example of a Virginia Indian mat yet found—and a further witness to the close involvement of the Jamestown settlers with their Indian neighbors. The mat joins with the arrow points, with finds such as the quarter time capsule, and with evidence in the west bulwark ditch of the native manufacture of shell beads (raw materials, partially made beads,

Late Woodland Virginia Indian pot, digitally reconstructed. This type of pottery makes up an average of half the total quantity of pottery found in ca.-1607–11 deposits in and around the fort. This and evidence of the manufacturing of stone tools and shell beads indicate much cultural and perhaps social interdependence of the English and the natives.

Artifacts laid out by upper (*foreground*) to lower levels (*background*) of deposits in "town" house cellar. Fill taken together appears to comprise one of the earliest deposits yet found in the expanded fort/Jamestown site.

Some of the more than two hundred Virginia Indian stone projectile and knife points found in historical deposits at James Fort. There is evidence of the manufacture of points within the fort.

and shaping stone) to contradict the belief that the English and the Indians were un-compromising mortal enemies. Although Smith would report the native view that the English were all there to destroy them—"a people come from under the world to take their world from them"—it is improbable that any Indians who had believed that would have voluntarily lived in the fort and befriended the colonists.[59]

This is not to say that in the earliest weeks of the 1607 summer there was any love lost between the settlers and their immediate neighbors, the Paspahegh. Captain Gabriel Archer reported almost relentless attacks at the fort. On the day Archer counted the forty incoming arrows, he also reported the death of a dog at the hands of the Indians. On four other days, he mentioned that long grasses and reeds stood along the fort palisades and bulwarks, noting that the Indians would hide in them and take aim at the colonists. "Sunday [May 30, 1607] they [Indians] came lurking in the thickets and long grasses, and a gentleman one Eustace Clovall unarmed straggling without the fort, shot 6 arrowes into him." Clovill died a week later. Soon after, Archer wrote that "3 of the [Indians] had most adventurous-ly stollen under our bulwark and hiden themselves in the long grasses." Amazingly, it seems that the Indians themselves offered a solution to the long-grass sniper problem: "He [Indian] counselled us to Cutt Downe the long weedes rounde about our fforte."[60] Apparently, Powhatan's war policy of attrition was not a unanimous decision within his chiefdom. In any case, by August 1607, cutting grass must have become a low priority for the sick and dying soldiers.[61]

Below the top three feet of the object-rich fill, the shape of the pit north of the factory changed from circular to rectangular. Finally, beneath a concentration of oyster shells, the shaft bottomed out onto a fairly level earth "floor." Mere pits do not have floors, so this feature is likely yet another trash-filled cellar. The cellar would also have likely lain beneath yet another tented-over cellar structure or mud-and-stud-type building, constructed on the same axis as the factory, west of north. No other evidence survived, however, of a superstructure. Probably the many seventeenth- to eighteenth-century churchyard grave shafts surrounding the cellar had destroyed any related building postholes. In any event, through the artifacts it contained, the pit not only showed the important relationships between the colonists and the Virginia Indians, but it also revealed the presence of another early building just outside of the extended palisade. This location may tell us more about the meaning of these artifacts: might the cellar and the building above it have lain in an area reserved for Indians, thus keeping the triangular section of the town separate and more secure? Future excavation to the north of the pit may determine that this structure came to be inside the extended fort, attaching to an as-yet-undiscovered wall line turning east from the churchyard. If that was so, the close relationship between the English and some Virginia Indians would seem an even more indisputable fact.

Part of a native mat made of reeds fastened together with bark cord, preserved because of the presence of a fragment of copper above it.

## A Fort Well

Another important goal of Jamestown Rediscovery was to find the fort well. Why? First, the discovery of the well would offer an opportunity to understand more clearly why so many people died at Jamestown. On that subject documents disagree. Captain John Smith reported that the well he ordered dug in 1609 held "sweet water." The same reference implies that this well was the first to be dug at Jamestown, presumably ending the practice, during the preceding two years, of drinking the slimy and brackish water directly from the James River. Strachey, however, tells a completely different story of the well and its water. He blamed the rash of deaths in 1609–10 directly on the same well, which he claimed was "Six or seven fathom deep, fed by the brackish river oozing into it; from whence I belief the chief causes have proceeded of many diseases and sicknesses which have happened to our people who are indeed strangely afflicted with fluxes and agues and every particular infirmity."[62] Apparently Strachey would not have called those 1609–10 months the "starving time": he suspected another cause for the deaths of that winter. Which of the conflicting descriptions of the well should we believe? Was Smith's and Strachey's well "sweet" or "poison"? Finding and testing the fort well water could answer that question, a critical step toward recapturing the reality of Jamestown's health challenges.

Locating the fort well had other potential attractions. Wells can be particularly valuable archaeological finds. When objects accidentally fall into the shaft of a working well, the water cushions the impact; as a result, unbroken artifacts accumulate at the bottom. The water also acts as a preservation agent. Permanently wet environments inhibit the rusting of metallic objects and can preserve organic materials such as wood, leather, and plants in a waterlogged state. These objects rarely survive in the alternating wet and dry conditions characteristic of other archaeological deposits, such as pits and cellars. Also, once wells are abandoned, they often become a convenient place to get rid of garbage and trash, usually over a short period of time. So well excavation can present an opportunity to recover unusually preserved artifacts in a time-capsule-like state.

Excavations so far have indeed discovered a well as old as James Fort, in the plain known as Smithfield outside the west bulwark. Since this well was found fifty feet outside the protection of the west wall, it cannot be the well Smith built in the fort in 1608–9 or likely the contaminated well Strachey described in 1610. Nonetheless, the Smithfield well turned out to be the hoped-for time capsule. It also provided a chance to test the quality of well water at James Fort in the time of the Virginia Company settlers.

Located in an area heavily scoured by Civil War grading, the top of a brick-lined well shaft had been discovered during the misdirected search for the west wall. The well's brickwork was partially intact at ground level and enclosed within a larger surrounding backfilled hole made at the time of construction. Backfilling of this builder's basin was part of the construction process: courses of the original circular brick lining below ground, built with rectangular bricks and brick wedges, required the force of the exterior basin backfill to hold it together. Such construction physics was essential not only to building the shaft but also to keeping it open to the water table, reached at a depth of nine feet. The lining remained intact below the water table, where it finally rested on a wooden curb at fourteen feet below grade.

The presence of a curb and the shape of the builder's shaft together indicated how the well was constructed. Evidence shows that the settlers first dug the wide basin down from the colonial ground surface to a depth convenient to work in. Then builders narrowed the basin diameter, creating a step. They then continued digging downward another four feet until wet soil was reached at the groundwater table. At that point workers seated the wooden ring-like curb on the surface and built a chest-high cylinder of bricks. Their next step was to dig inside and under the curb, allowing the section of brick shaft to slide downward. Then the process was repeated: brick courses were built on the partially lowered shaft and the shaft was gradually lowered further by more undercutting, until a depth was reached at which enough water could accumulate to make the well operational.

Brick-lined well with surrounding construction shaft showing an early seventeenth-century iron breastplate as found in the abandoned well fill. Artifacts from the construction deposit dated the building of the well to the later fort period, ca. 1615.

This seemingly complicated process was necessary to hold back the soft, sandy clay sides of the hole while digging beneath the water table. Once the soft water-bearing walls below the water table were secure, the shaft could be built up, from above the water table to the ground surface. The levels at which brick fragments, dropped by the masons as they formed and implanted the small wedges, were found indicate that the shaft was built in chest-high increments, followed by the packing of backfill outside it, until it reached the seventeenth-century surface. Mortar-encrusted bricks in the shaft tell us that the well builders mortared the well head above ground, packing fill around the standing shaft in the builder's basin as they went. This top-down/water-table-up method of building wells was common in England and Virginia.[63]

Artifacts that inadvertently made their way into the fill in the builder's

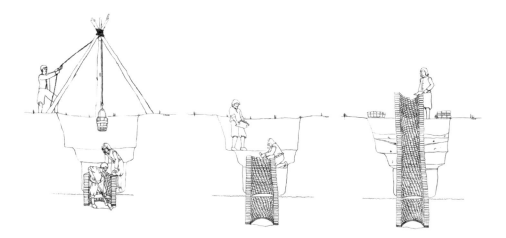

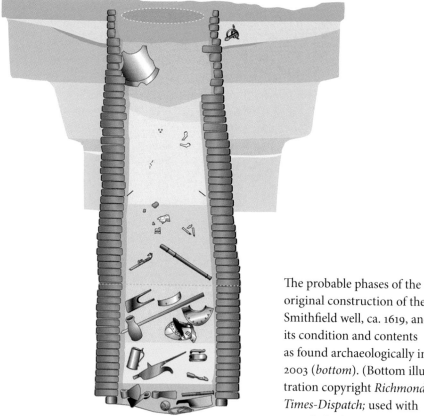

The probable phases of the original construction of the Smithfield well, ca. 1619, and its condition and contents as found archaeologically in 2003 (*bottom*). (Bottom illustration copyright *Richmond Times-Dispatch;* used with permission)

basin reveal that the Smithfield well was built during the first fifteen years or so of Jamestown settlement. Ceramics and pipe bowls in the collection are types known to have been made as early as the beginning of the seventeenth century, such as Spanish earthenware ceramic costrel (handled jug) fragments. Although remains of other such costrels found in Virginia have been dated no earlier than 1619, the Jamestown fragments do not necessarily share this TPQ, since no other site yet excavated in Virginia is as old as Jamestown, and Spanish costrels are known to date as early as 1600 in Europe.[64] Fragments from an Italian-made bowl, a type made as early as 1600, and pieces of a tobacco pipe thought to be made in Virginia, possibly by the 1608 immigrant pipemaker Robert Cotton, both suggest a fort-period construction date for this well. Another pipe with a distinctive octagonal bowl also wound up in the builder's fill (see p. 89). All that is known about this pipe's manufacture date is that an identical example was found on the mainland north of Jamestown Island, at a site believed to have been occupied in the first quarter of the seventeenth century. Taken together, these dates put the construction of the Smithfield well comfortably within the James Fort years. Documents narrow the well chronology even more.

After Strachey's indictment of the unhealthy well—possibly Smith's fort well gone bad—other references to Jamestown wells suggest dates but unclear locations. For instance, the strict martial laws put on the books by the new governor, Sir Thomas Gates, in 1611, include rules intended to keep certain well-polluting activities, such as washing dishes, away from "the olde well" and clear of the vicinity of the "new Pumpe" (a new well with a pump?). Undoubtedly the old well is the Smith-Strachey well and therefore located in the fort. But the location of the newer well is not specified.[65]

A further reference to this later well with its new pump may be Governor Sir Thomas Dale's report that when he came to Jamestown in May 1611, he put in a new well. The reason given for Dale's action was "the amending of the most unwholesome water which the old afforded."[66] It is possible that Dale's new well went into a central place in De La Warre's 1610 perfected Jamestown, and that the Smithfield well and Dale's new 1611 well are one and the same.

Another new governor, Captain Samuel Argall, arrived at Jamestown in 1617 to again find "the" well of fresh water "spoiled." As part of his many fort repairs, he either cleaned out the existing well or he replaced it altogether.[67] Is the Smithfield well the spoiled well possibly abandoned by Argall? The answer again lies in context and TPQ. If Argall did abandon the spoiled well, it typically would become a trashcan, quickly collecting artifacts in 1617–18. However, while the discards in this well contained no precisely dated object like a coin to set a solid TPQ, documents and contemporary artwork can help date certain artifacts in the trash—revealing them to be too late to have been rejects from Argall's time.

The shaft held nearly 1,400 objects in seven distinct layers: two near the bottom, almost certainly containing objects accidentally knocked into the water when the well was in use; five containing artifacts purposely thrown down the abandoned shaft during and after the lining had partially collapsed.[68] The objects from these layers can therefore provide dates for both the use of the well and its abandonment. Certain recovered drinking vessels, arms, apparently one full suit of armor, tools, and even a shoe together set the demise of the well in the fort's final years, 1622–25. An intact, lidded pewter drinking flagon found almost at the bottom of the shaft can be dated roughly by its style but perhaps more precisely by the monogram stamped on the lid thumb piece. The vessel shape appears in English illustrations predating 1620. Three initials on the thumb piece—R E under a P—may identify the owners as Richard and Elizabeth Pierce, a couple who arrived at Jamestown in 1618 and lived just off the island on a tract known as Neck of Land by 1625. If these are the Pierces' initials, it follows that the well was in use after 1618, the year of their arrival in Virginia. Another pewter vessel, a standard measure baluster form dating to the second half of the sixteenth century, although a rare find of the usually perishable pewter, is not a particular help in dating the well. But two broken German ceramic drinking jugs in the collection do help: a molded blue-and-gray stoneware baluster jug, bearing a molded scene telling the story of the Prodigal Son, and most of a brown stoneware jug known as a Bartmann. The paneled baluster jug with the biblical scene closely matches a museum piece dated 1618, suggesting that the jug was made at about the same time. A medallion embossed on the sides of the Bartmann included enough armorial symbols to suggest that it displayed the arms of three German principalities that existed as united states only during the period 1521–1609. The Bartmann may date later than that, however, because a similar jug was found on the 1629 wreck of the Dutch ship *Batavia*, but potters are suspected of using outdated molds to make the medallions.[69] It would be safe, however, to assume a 1609–29 date for the vessel—again well within the late fort period at Jamestown.

The well fill also contained a pole arm known as a "bill" and a breast-

Some of the hundreds of objects found in the Smithfield well before and some after conservation.

plate, with a very datable alteration, from a suit of body armor. After the Indian uprising in 1622, a thousand bills, deemed obsolete in England, were sent to the colonies, probably half to Virginia. The breastplate is of an early seventeenth-century style with ridged belly, made to accommodate the popular vests of that time known as doublets. This breastplate is also datable by a tab of armor attached to the right shoulder, a feature of two other breastplates found in Virginia, one at Jamestown and the other at an upriver site, Jordan's Point, first occupied 1620–35. Seven axes and two hoes found at the bottom of the well are of types dating to the early seventeenth century. Most of these artifacts were found in serviceable condition, so it is likely that they were accidentally lost as they broke free from their duty as makeshift counterweights for well buckets.[70] Such counterweights would have been unnecessary baggage, however, if the well bucket came equipped with the massive iron handle found near the bottom of the shaft. This handle would not only have acted as a swivel to keep the rope from untwisting

Video image of a pewter flagon at the moment of discovery.

Late sixteenth- to early seventeenth-century pewter drinking flagon from the Smithfield well after conservation. The thumb piece was monogrammed R E under P, possibly identifying the vessel as the property of Richard and Elizabeth Pierce of neighboring Neck-of-Land, located on the mainland north of Jamestown Island.

but would have tipped the bucket by its own weight. The handle's broken condition, however, suggests that the makeshift counterweight buckle became its replacement.

The most surprising find in the well fill was a full suit of armor—a helmet known as a burgonet, front and rear gorgets to protect the neck, a breastplate, and a number of tassetts or frontal hip and thigh protective plates—scattered through the well fill from top to almost bottom. The armor may have been discarded in favor of the lighter and less restraining "jackets"—an adaptation to the Virginia climate—or perhaps out of a false sense of security brought on by the years of peace with the Virginia Indians before the 1622 uprising. Finally, a child's shoe, of a style datable to the 1610s, was also found in the waterlogged well deposit.

Science had a chance to set the well date even more exactly. The waterlogged wooden curb, made of sections of red oak, did more than reveal the well's construction process; the wood was so well preserved that the growth rings of the tree it had come from were still visible. The width of yearly growth rings in trees usually depends upon the amount of rainfall: such rings are generally wider in wet years, narrower in dry years. Hence, comparison of the pattern of the curb rings with the known ring sequence for oak, in a process known as dendrochronology, can determine when the tree lived and when it was felled. Dendrochronological study indicates that there was a drought in Virginia from 1606 to 1613, the very years of struggle for the colonists. The red oak from the well showed a series of smaller growth rings over a period of about seven years. This finding raised expectations that the date the tree was felled, and thus the date the well was built, might be determinable. Not that easy. Only about fifty rings were visible in the well curb wood. To date oak with high reliability, a much longer sequence of rings is required. Disappointingly, no analysis even reached a 50/50 chance of reliability. One weak reading dated the sequence to the year 1600, another stronger reading to 1799—both of little help in dating our well. Nonetheless, the Jamestown wood ring is preserved, awaiting perhaps the future refinement of the dendrochronology process. In the meantime, the circa late-1610–20s construction date and a 1620s backfilling date based on documentary and artifact evidence stand to define the well's lifespan.[71]

Although this well was not the one that Smith and Strachey disagreed about, it did provide a chance to evaluate their different judgments of wells in 1609 and 1610. Strachey seems to have been correct in his estimate of the depth of Jamestown wells: the Smithfield well would appear to have been six ancient fathoms (eighteen feet), the figure Strachey gives.[72] The shaft only stood fourteen feet as found, but the missing four feet would probably have disappeared during the Civil War grading in 1861. Testing has shown, however, that Strachey's other assertions were more disputable.

Results of a groundwater test of the modern Jamestown water table might seem of limited relevance to the quality of water at James Fort in the early seventeenth century. One fact makes such a test useful, though: the groundwater at Jamestown today should be, if anything, more contaminated than it was in 1609–10. For example, today's water should be more highly saline than it was four centuries ago, given an estimated sea-level rise of four feet. Also, given modern industrial river pollution and over one hundred years' use of the APVA Jamestown septic system on the island, one could reasonably expect tests to find much higher levels of contamination, namely *E. coli,* in the water table than existed during the fort period.[73] Consequently, finding drinkable water today would presumably assure that James Fort's water supply was not a source of danger to the colonists.

As it turned out, the salt levels of today's water proved negligible. Moreover, the two-foot rise and fall of the tide has no effect on the water level in the Smithfield well, which is located less than one hundred feet from the modern river shore. In other words, the nearby brackish river and swampy wetlands do not seep into the well water at all. In fact, the testing found that

A section of the wooden curb at the base of the Smithfield well. The growth rings of this red-oak timber show variation and possibly indicate a drought time (series of narrow rings) during its lifetime.

the Jamestown water today is clean enough to meet modern drinking-water standards, after removing the contaminants introduced as a result of the modern excavation.

Why, then, was Strachey wrong about the Jamestown well-water salt content, as he seems to have been? Explanation may lie in the probable source of his facts. In his preface to *The Historie of Travell,* wherein he discusses the allegedly polluted well, Strachey credits Percy as his source, "from [whom] these Commentaries and observations, I must freely confess I have collected these passages and knowledges."[74] It is likely that Percy, who was acting governor of the settlement during the "starving time," would blame all the deaths on his watch on something other than shortage of food. Deaths by starvation might be taken as the worst possible commentary on his own abilities to negotiate for food. Percy may have also had an incentive to discredit his old Jamestown enemy, Captain John Smith, who had already reported digging the first well at Jamestown in 1609 and claimed it held only sweet water. Perhaps the sweet groundwater that was scientifically found at Jamestown may help historians ferret out just who was telling the truth in some of the seventeenth-century eyewitness accounts of the fort period. So far, the implication seems to be that Strachey relied unquestioningly on Percy's reports—and that at least some of Percy's information may have had what today might be called a positive spin on reality.

# THREE

# RECOVERING JAMESTOWNIANS

When an emergency rescue squad arrives at an accident scene, medics immediately search for signs of life in the victim. If the vital signs are not evident, the medics' job is over. The remains of the body become the responsibility of forensic scientists, legally required to identify the body, if unknown, and to determine the cause of death. In the course of their physical inspection of the remains and of biological tests, these scientists can find signs of life in a different sense: they can reconstruct much of a person's life story. Through such efforts, the dead inform the living.

Archaeologists, too, search for signs of life, although their subjects are only skeletal remains. At Jamestown, burial recovery, meticulous examination, and careful analysis have led to a richer understanding of the colony's population. Thanks to these methods, we need not be restricted to written facts and artifacts to come to know seventeenth-century Jamestown: we can actually come face to face with Jamestown people of the past, getting to know them personally from the signs of their lives still held in their skeletal remains.

Exploration of the mystery surrounding the remains of a young colonist who died of a gunshot wound has been especially revealing of the dangers of life in early Jamestown, bringing to light some possibly unrecorded events of the Jamestown saga while exemplifying ways in which technological advances have heightened our ability to see into the past. Uncovered burials in other unmarked graves inside the fort tell of the lives of several individual settlers: a woman laborer, some of the original gentlemen, and a captain found just outside the fort walls. And study of over seventy burials from an unmarked burial ground on the western end of the island introduces us to a cross-section of the population, offering further insight into the hardships of life at early Jamestown.

## JR102C

Excavations near James Fort's south wall, intended to help define the barracks and its yard, unexpectedly exposed a burial—the first found during the course of the Jamestown Rediscovery excavations. Even though this grave lay beneath a once well-traveled gravel road, the burial site eventually yielded traces of a decayed coffin and a fairly well-preserved skeleton. The greatest surprise of all, however, was the discovery that the remains included a lead bullet embedded in a severed lower leg.

The burial was possibly as old as the first months of James Fort. Not only was the grave located within the archaeological traces of the wooden palisade, but it also was aligned with that wall. Artifacts in the soil that had originally covered the coffin—a few fragments of Indian and European pottery and a Venetian trade bead—all dated either to the years just before English settlement or to 1607–10. Like the palisade trenches, this grave was apparently dug through ground that had only been trod by prehistoric Indians—or if by Europeans, only briefly and some time very soon after they arrived at Jamestown Island on May 13, 1607.

According to forensic anthropological study conducted on site and later at the Smithsonian Institution, the grave was that of a European male.[1] Some surviving nails and the shape of the dark soil left by the decayed wood showed that this man had been buried in a hexagonal coffin—meaning that he was someone of social standing, likely a "gentleman." Perhaps he was one of the eighty-some gentlemen who came to Jamestown May 1607–January 1608.[2] He died in his late teens to age twenty, a fact determined primarily by the stage of development of the wisdom teeth and the lack of complete fusion of the bone near certain joints. This young man also suffered from tooth decay, one tooth seriously abscessed. Judging from the bone formation where major muscles attached, this person was moderately muscular but not used to performing hard labor, more evidence that he had lived the life of a seventeenth-century gentleman. At a height of five feet, nine inches, he was slightly taller than the average Englishman of the period. There was also clear evidence of the cause of death: a massive gunshot wound to the lower right leg, inflicted by a .60-caliber lead ball and twenty-one smaller misshapen lead shot. The impact of the bullets caused a severe compound fracture of the two major bones of the lower leg, both the tibia and fibula. In effect, this man had had his lower leg blown off.

Piecing together, or "mending," the shattered leg bones helped forensic investigators reconstruct the trajectory of the lead ball and shot. The path of the lead musket ball began at the outside surface of the right knee, then broke completely through the leg bone just below the joint, finally coming to rest beneath the skin next to the knee. The smaller shot penetrated and shattered bone across a five-inch area centered on the knee. The angle of the bullet trajectory indicated that the individual was positioned level with the gun that fired the shot. The force and magnitude of the impact of the lead musket ball and shot likely severed an artery. There was no sign of healing. Little wonder: massive blood loss from such a wound would have caused this person to bleed out, resulting in death in a matter of minutes. There were no other signs of trauma before death. Fractures in the skull were apparently caused by the eventual collapse of the coffin.

A copper straight pin was found on the young man's left temple, and a copper stain, presumably from another pin, was found near the leg wound. These remains of copper suggested that the victim either was wrapped in a cloth shroud held together with pins, a typical burial practice of the time, or possibly had bandages on the leg wound and on his head. The position of the legs, spread apart at the knees, seemed to indicate that there was no shroud; alternatively, the shroud may have come undone when the body shifted in the

Burial (JR102C: hereafter referred to as JR) found near south bulwark in James Fort, a gunshot victim.

X-ray showing lead ball and fragments of lead shot found imbedded in JR's wound, the cause of death.

coffin on entering the grave. The burial was oriented approximately east-west with the head to the west, according to traditional Christian beliefs and practices of the time. Significantly, the burial's orientation was actually south of east, the same as the orientation of the nearby fort building and palisade, which helps to establish the early date of this burial. A test of the carbon decay in the bone indicated that this person could have died as early as 1607. Found in the third layer of the one hundred and second excavation unit dug since the Jamestown Rediscovery archaeological project began, this young man became thereafter known by his field record number: JR102C—JR for short.

Who was JR? Science may offer clues to his identity. Because the chemical composition of people's bones can reflect what they ate during their lives, and because what people ate in the seventeenth century derived mostly from local sources only, tests to recover certain bone chemistry can determine where people came from. Determining geographic region of origin, in turn, can help establish a person's identity. Of particular interest in the bone chemistry is the relative presence of two types of stable carbon isotopes: the $C_3$ isotope, found in the bones of people who primarily eat wheat, and the $C_4$ isotope, found in the bones of those who primarily eat corn. The bones of recent English immigrants in America, according to this theory, would show a wheat diet, while the bones of American Indians and seasoned English immigrants at Jamestown would show a corn diet.

The results of the stable isotope tests of JR were somewhat puzzling. While his readings were considerably lower than the readings for Europeans who ate wheat, he showed an almost too strong reading for the corn isotope.[3] Disregarding the rather unusual number, the test can be interpreted to mean that JR had indeed lived long enough in Virginia to build up the carbon signs of a corn diet, or it is possible, on the chance that he spent time in Italy or the Caribbean, that he acquired the unusual $C_4$ isotope from eating millet, a grassy plant common in those regions and carrying the same isotopic signature as corn. It stands to reason that if JR was European and died in 1607, his profile would have to be that of a recent immigrant, a wheat eater, and signs of the wheat isotope were not there. If so, then he likely did not recently come from England or Europe. But again the archaeological alignment of the burial within the fort and the artifacts in the grave shaft suggest burial during the first few years of settlement when every European was an immigrant. These conflicting results seem to call into question either the reliability of this isotopic test or the true archaeological circumstances of the burial, a classic example of the frustrating dual role of archaeology as inexact art and/or science.

Nevertheless, an additional isotopic test confirmed JR's identity as a European. If the assumption is made that he is English, the test can show more precisely where in England his original home was. This test detects elements carried in drinking water that become embedded in teeth as they form during an individual's younger years. Thus isotopic study can reflect facts about people literally from the cradle to the grave. Tests of one of JR's teeth for lead, strontium, and oxygen isotopes seemed to indicate that during his childhood JR once resided in southwest England or Wales.[4]

Since there is no gravestone to mark his nearly four centuries-old grave, we cannot know for sure who JR102C actually was. Still, archaeological and written facts enable us, as in a modern death investigation, to string together enough circumstantial evidence to suggest at least the identity of the victim, a possible scenario for the shooting, and a weapon.

We can start with the facts, established by JR's remains, that in or around James Fort a young gentleman in his late teens to age twenty or so died of a gunshot wound to the right side of his right leg, the injury occurring possibly during the first years of settlement.[5] We have seen that George Percy, in what is believed to be accurate eyewitness reporting, named some of the colonists who died during the summer months of 1607. According to Percy, twenty-four men, mostly gentlemen, died by September 1607, after which he himself apparently became too sick or starved to keep up with the death record. The healthier John Smith reported that a total of sixty-six out of the original 104 settlers that Christopher Newport brought to Virginia died by the fall of 1607. One Percy entry listed Jerome Alicock, an "ancient" (meaning ensign, junior officer), as dying from a "wound" on August 14, 1607.[6] Of course, "wound" could mean any number of injuries, including one caused by an arrow. But it may be significant that on August 10, only four days before Alicock's death, William Bruster (or Brewster) is listed as dying from a wound "given by the savages." This phrase seems to be saying that an arrow killed Brewster. Judging from the entry about Brewster, it seems likely that Percy would also have named the cause of Alicock's wound if it had been inflicted by the Indians. So why would Percy use the unqualified word "wound"?

Perhaps Percy knew that the wound was a gunshot wound but hesitated to admit that colonists were in danger not only from the Indians but from each other, as a result of either malicious intent or friendly fire. There is no doubt that August 1607 was a time of great stress among the settlers, with heat, disease, and starvation aggravating their plight. In fact, after September 5, Percy may have felt that he had covered all the previous unattributed deaths in stating that "they were destroyed with cruel diseases as swellings, fluxes, burning fevers, and by wars, and some departed suddenly but for the most part they died of mere famine."[7] Under the extreme conditions Percy describes, it stands to reason that civil unrest might easily have broken out among the struggling colonists, perhaps resulting in the shooting of one of their own, either accidentally or on purpose. In any case, death caused in this way would hardly be good news to send home to England, where the Virginia Company was primarily concerned with promoting their venture and urging other Englishmen to emigrate.

Among those whose causes of death Percy did not specify are a number of other candidates for the identity of JR, by reason of their status as gentlemen, their ages at death, and perhaps their political leanings.[8] They are: John Martin Jr., gentleman, died August 18, 1607, approx. age nineteen; Richard Simmons, gentleman, died September 18, 1607, age seventeen; Robert Pennington, gentleman, died August 18, 1607, age twenty; Stephen Calthrope, gentleman, died August 15 1607, age twenty-two. John Martin Jr. and his father, Captain John Martin Sr., were one of two father-and-son teams who came to Virginia on the first voyage (the other was Anthony Gosnold and his son Anthony). John Martin Jr. seems to have had a well-traveled past even before he took his last and fatal trip to Jamestown. His father, Captain Martin, a mariner and a gold refiner, may have apprenticed John Jr. to his grandfather's ironworks on the Welsh border. Since the Martin family was connected in Italy, John Martin Jr. may have spent time at the university in Padua, a fashionable place for young English gentlemen to study at the time. John Jr.'s death as early as 1607 and his possible early years in or near Wales and Italy seem to make him a strong candidate for JR. He could have acquired the isotopic signature found in JR's tooth during early years at the ironworks, and the corn signature may indeed be a result of eating millet (another $C_4$-isotope-producing plant) in Italy.

There is some evidence that Richard Simmons, too, was from Wales, presenting the possibility that he would have had the stable isotopic signature found in JR's tooth. Besides his death date at Jamestown, nothing more is known of Robert Pennington except that he grew up in Lancashire, England, which would not have given him the same isotopic reading as JR's. Nor would the isotopic test on Stephen Calthrope match JR's, because

Calthrope was from Norwich, England. Also, Calthrope was twenty-two years old when he died, a few years older than JR's estimated age at death. More is known about young Calthrope than about the others, however, and there is some reason to believe that he could have been a target during a time of civil unrest at Jamestown.

Percy wrote that Calthrope (or Galthrop) died the day after Alicock (August 15); no cause of death is specified. Percy might not have known what killed Calthrope, or he might have ceased specifying causes of death by this time. Another alternative, however, is that Percy wanted to hide the details. Calthrope's age at death—twenty-two—is established by church records, which show that a Stephen Calthrope, a resident of Norwich, Norfolk, was christened in the church of St. Peter Mancroft in 1585 in England. As third-born in his family—with two older brothers—Calthrope would have been left out of any chance of inheriting family property in England. So he would have had the typical young gentleman's incentive to risk the Virginia adventure.[9]

Perhaps more significant to our search for JR's identity is the evidence of some sort of alliance between Calthrope and Captain John Smith. Smith, Calthrope, and one other man named Robinson led or conspired to lead a "mutinie" against Captain Christopher Newport and his friends, probably in the Canary Islands, where the original ships stopped to resupply.[10] The unsuccessful mutiny could have served to spawn or intensify the distrust that Newport and his friends—including Edward Maria Wingfield, a relative of Calthrope's and soon to be the first elected president of the Virginia colony—had for the commoner and soldier of fortune, John Smith. Calthrope's class status and his relationship to Wingfield may have gotten him off scot-free. Wingfield could have spoken on Calthrope's behalf to Wingfield's friend, Captain Newport, and perhaps also to the English settler with the highest social rank aboard, George Percy. Historical accounts indicate that Captain Newport took out his wrath only on John Smith, who for the rest of the voyage to Jamestown was placed "in restraint."

While this aborted mutiny led first to Smith's near execution and later to his exclusion for the first two months from the Virginia governing council, nothing seems to have been done to punish Calthrope. Nevertheless, young Calthrope's part (perhaps even a leading one) in the mutiny attempt against Newport must have fostered permanent distrust in Newport, Wingfield, and the rest of the governing council. Living conditions in the colony may have further magnified personal distrust and political differences. Men were dropping like flies that first August in Jamestown, as disease, bad water, native arrows, and lack of food took their toll. Percy's report sums up the situation clearly: "There was never Englishmen left in a foreign country in such misery as we were in this newly discovered Virginia."[11] Power struggles, for those strong enough to stand, may have become inevitable.

Stephen Calthrope and his friends could have become marked men, perhaps suspected of plotting against the governing council. Either a preventative shot or a return shot from a military round fired in Calthrope's direction might have been an inevitable result of struggle and suspicion in the early years at Jamestown. Although there is no written record of such shooting, news of political infighting and the death of Alicock or Calthrope as a result would hardly be a topic to report back to England, especially if Percy himself was in the middle of it. It would be little wonder if Percy underreported such a cause for Calthrope's death.

If JR really was the victim of political intrigue, however, why was no one brought to justice when his ally, Captain John Smith, came to power in 1608–9? There is no record of a trial or an execution for such a crime. One execution on record is that of Captain George Kendall, who was tried and eventually shot as an alleged spy. This trial and execution took place after John Ratcliffe, John Smith, and John Martin, led by Gabriel Archer, deposed Wingfield from the presidency, Ratcliffe taking his place.[12] Although the allegation against Kendall is not clearly explained, there is no evidence to suggest that he had put himself in harm's way by supporting any Jamestown faction; it is more likely that he had been involved with the Spanish.

Archaeological evidence has been found for what might have been an early Jamestown execution. In 1896, just after grading was done to stabilize the river shoreline two hundred feet west of the church tower, wave action exposed several human skeletons "lying in regular order." At that time the grading engineer, Colonel Samuel Yonge, thought these skeletons had been originally buried in the early churchyard. Yonge went on to report that "one of the skulls had been perforated by a musket ball and several bits of lead shot, which it still held, suggesting a military execution." Was this the skeleton of George Kendall? Or was it the remains of the man who shot JR, finally brought to justice?[13]

Unfortunately for historians, Yonge further states that "soon after being exposed to the air the skeletons crumbled." Without the crucial dating evidence of artifacts from the burial shaft, and without the skeleton itself to test for other revealing forensic evidence, there is no chance of learning any more about the circumstances surrounding this death. Therefore, to suggest that the wounded skull found by Yonge belonged to JR's killer is pure speculation. In fact, it must be pointed out that great numbers of capital offenses were recorded during the period of strict civil and martial law, between the "starving time" and the late teens of the 1600s. During Jamestown's martial law days, even picking flowers from a neighbor's garden carried the death penalty. The law in effect before that may well have been equally unforgiving.[14]

Finally, it may be relevant to consider a record that does exist of death from a gunshot wound in the knee, probably at Jamestown, although long after that first settlement summer. In 1624 Jamestown's first landowner on record and governor's councilor, Richard Stephens, fought a duel with a George Harrison, who later died from complications from a slight wound in the knee.[15] Stephens himself apparently left the dueling field unharmed. Could JR be Harrison? Probably not. Stephens's age at death is unknown, and JR's wound could hardly be considered slight. Also, there was no sign of healing of JR's shattered leg bones, such as would provide evidence of a lingering death. Nonetheless, in dueling, the traditional firing position was sideways, presenting the smallest possible target to one's opponent. Such a position would present the outside of a right knee up front, an open target for a misguided shot.

So who was JR? Was he Alicock, Martin, Pennington, Calthrop, or even Harrison? Of course, we cannot know in any definitive sense. Based on his status, age, and wound, the most logical choice would seem to be Jerome Alicock. But the study is far from over, given the development of scientific forensic techniques. Biogenetics will likely prove as effective for identifying people of the distant past as it has been in freeing long-jailed but innocent people today. There is no reason to doubt that eventually JR will have his proper gravestone.

While we cannot establish precisely who JR is, who shot JR, or why he was shot, it is possible to determine what shot him. During the course of the Jamestown Rediscovery excavations, a number of gun parts were found in deposits that can be dated to the period 1607–10. All belong to weapons capable of shooting the lead ball and shot found in JR102C's leg wound. The .60-caliber ball, middle-sized shot, and scrap lead found in the bone could have come from a range of weapons, anything from a pistol to a full-sized musket.

The firing mechanisms from four types of firearms were found archaeo-

Musketeer test-firing a caliver with load similar to that recovered from JR.

logically. These include military-issue matchlocks of both the standard-trigger and lever-trigger types. Also among the recovered parts were a lever-fired matchlock of a smaller and more ornate "civilian"-style caliver (a small musket), and a Scottish pistol with a snaphaunce (flint-and-steel) firing mechanism. The most common firearm in the collection is the matchlock, a type that required the musketeer to light and continuously burn a fibrous wick in order to ignite the powder pan and discharge the piece. This type of weapon would have obvious drawbacks in combat, the most serious being accidental premature explosions during the loading process and the revealing light given off by the match during night battle. The humid and rainy climate of a typical Virginia summer would hardly be matchlock-friendly either. The muskets may have been loaded from the bandoliers (single-shot powder containers) found with the gun parts and in other deposits dating to the same 1607–10 period. Soldiers carried these leather-covered tin or copper cylinders, in groups of twelve, from belts draped across their chests.

The five-inch spread of the lead in JR102C's leg can be a clue to the distance between him and the gun that shot him. Testing of a caliver and pistol, two of the weapons that could have fired the .60-caliber ball and shot, determined that at point-blank range (three feet from weapon to target) there is essentially no spread of the projectiles in a load similar to that found in JR's wound. This fact tends to eliminate the possibility that JR was the victim of an accidental, self-inflicted wound from a dropped pistol. Someone else fired the weapon that killed JR. A pistol fired eight feet from the target and a caliver at fifteen feet both produced a five-inch spread pattern. These distances and the trajectory of the bullet and shot in JR's leg suggest a number of scenarios to explain JR's death: a case of friendly fire occasioned by mistaken identity; a freak, accidental discharge in camp; a hunting accident, in which the lead hunter (JR) was shot by a stumbling follower; a gunshot wound inflicted in a close-range battle; feuding among the desperate settlers; or an accident in battle ranks.

All of the above scenarios are possible, but other facts suggest that some are more likely than others. If JR was Alicock, killed in August 1607, the Indians are unlikely suspects, since they would probably not have acquired any English guns that soon. If a fellow settler intended murder, a shot to the leg seems poor marksmanship. The military load combining small shot and a lead ball might have been a bit of overkill for hunting. More likely than any of these possibilities is an accident in rank.

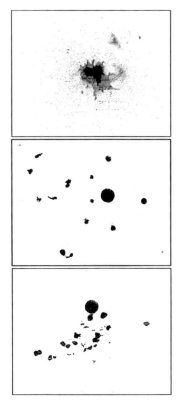

Target shot patterns from modern ballistic test: point-blank from a pistol (*top*), 15 feet from a caliver (*center*), compared with the shot pattern of JR's wound from the x-ray.

In the seventeenth century, military procedure for musketeers was very structured, requiring constant practice. There is clear record of exercise at arms at Jamestown, taking place in the open area known as Smithfield on the western side of the fort.[16] Here the musketeers would form ranks of multiple rows of men with their weapons in various stages of readiness. As soon as each front row fired, the row of men would file to the right, allowing the row behind them to step forward with their fully primed piece to volley, then file right, and so on. In a full rank, there would be enough rows to allow the musketeers an opportunity to advance through the laborious number of steps required to load and prime the weapons. It would not be unusual, in the heat of the action, for someone in the almost-ready row behind to fire accidentally, which could well bring down one of their own in front. A hit to the outside of the right leg of a retiring front-line man could have been common. So friendly fire in the heat of battle, or even during an exercise at arms held in Smithfield, may be the best explanation for JR's demise.

One way to identify a modern crime victim from skeletal remains is to reconstruct the face, hoping to match surviving images or to enable living relatives and friends to identify the victim. Of course, for a four-hundred-year-old skeleton, identification by photographs or the victim's contemporaries is out of the question. Likenesses of any kind have survived for only two of the original settlers: an engraving by Simon de Passe of Captain John Smith, and an anonymous portrait of George Percy. Ironically, these likenesses represent what may have been the two quarreling political factions at James Fort that played a role in JR's death. Nonetheless, by combining science and art to reconstruct the facial features of JR, it is possible at least to know what JR102C looked like.[17]

The first step was to reconstruct the skull by piecing together the 102 fragments left of it, which required days of experienced mending. The skull offered unusual challenges, since it had been seriously damaged in the grave.[18] The pressure of the collapsed coffin and soil resting on it had caused the skull to warp. The grave's position beneath what had become a much-traveled automobile road made matters even worse. In addition, centuries of decay had caused some of the bone either to disappear or to become so brittle that it could not be used in the mending process. Unmendable pieces were reconstructed through computer manipulation, electronically lifted from a photograph of the crushed skull, as it was first found in the grave, and then placed on a digital photograph of the mended skull. Missing parts of the skull were created by copying what did survive on the opposite side, then reversing it, and pasting it into the gaps. Through this mirror imaging, the skull could begin to approach its predeath shape.[19]

No matter how accurate the skull reconstruction, of course it still is not a perfect likeness of the flesh-and-blood face. However, the shape and characteristics of a human skull determine what people look like more than might be expected. Scientific and artistic rebuilding of muscle and tissue thicknesses on a repaired skull can practically bring a face back to life.

Crushed skull
in ground

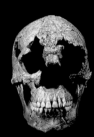
Skull
reconstructed

Reconstruction
completed on a
computer image

Plaster cast
of skull

Connecting tissue
depth markers
with clay

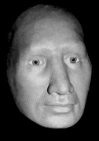
Partially
completed facial
approximation

Completed reconstruction
of Jamestown settler

Steps in the reconstruction of the face of JR.

JR: a composite of a 1606 Dutch engraving, artifacts from James Fort deposits, and facial reconstruction.

Guided by scientifically generated thickness markers on a plaster mold of the skull, an experienced forensic sculptor skillfully applied modeling clay to reconstruct the former appearance of JR's face with an estimated 85 percent accuracy. Eye and hair color, facial hair, and hairstyle were added, based on examination of seventeenth-century portraits and engravings. It is interesting to note that the final rendering of JR could be a distant cousin to George Percy, whose sharply sloping forehead and rather generous nose match the skeletal evidence of JR102C. In fact, Ensign Jerome Alicock might have been a relative of Percy's, as they came from the same town in England.[20]

Archaeology does more than unearth the remnants of dead people and their broken things: as we have seen, it also seeks to picture living people using intact things. The archaeologist's educated speculation about the identity, motive, weapon, and scene of the death of JR is more than an intriguing exercise; it helps bring into clearer focus a number of things about these "able men" in "miserable distress" at early seventeenth-century Jamestown.

JR may represent a typical settler, a young gentleman with some military experience but little hope for bettering his circumstances at home. Such were many of the men who risked life and limb on the Virginia venture. As that first summer at Jamestown ended, Percy poignantly assessed the desperate state of the James Fort outpost these men had come to:

> There were never Englishmen left in a foreign country in such misery as we were in this new discovered Virginia. We watched every three nights, lying on the bare, cold ground . . . which brought our men to be most feeble wretches. Our food was but a small can of barley, sod in water, to five men a day, our drink, cold water taken out of the river, which was at flood very salt at a low tide full of slime and filth. . . . Thus we lived for the space of five months in this miserable distress, not having five able men to man our bulwarks upon any

occasion. If it had not pleased God to have put a terror in the savages' hearts, we had all perished by those wild and cruel pagans, being in that weak estate as we were, our men night and day groaning in every corner of the fort most pitiful to hear.[21]

In these circumstances, it would not have been surprising if civil unrest ran rampant at Jamestown, as there was less and less possibility of getting rich quick, and more and more possibility of dying young. Dreams of what Jamestown would bring to young gentlemen like JR must have died even faster with Smith's institution of military discipline and a "food for work" program.

The dream would take on life again. The Virginia Company started giving land to those who paid their own transport. Eventually Virginia could offer even more: a new commercial crop emerged that could be grown on the rich Virginia land, transforming practically anyone with the slightest ounce of ambition into an instant millionaire. That dream-like transformation would be shadowed by its own tragedy, as native Powhatan and English settlers (some of whom grew tobacco on native land) continued to see each other mostly as "savages."[22] But even these tainted riches were forever out of the reach of the young gentleman JR, who, like the majority of Jamestown's first settlers, never lived to share in this tobacco boom.

## THE FIRST LADY

JR did not lie alone for long in the southeast corner of the Jamestown Fort. Excavations in 1997 uncovered a second burial three feet north of JR's grave, that of a forty- to fifty-five-year-old Caucasian woman (field number: JR156C) who died of unknown causes.[23] The backfilling of the woman's grave contained more European artifacts than had been found in JR's grave. Although the grave, like JR's, was positioned roughly east-west, in the Christian manner, the two graves were slightly out of line with each other. These differences indicated that some period of time had passed between the two interments. Nonetheless, the fragmented pottery in the grave shaft still indicated that the woman's death had occurred probably in the period 1607–10. The woman had been buried in a relatively well-preserved yellow pine coffin. Coffin nails survived, and their positions and a ridge of coffin wood down the center of the burial indicated that the coffin had a gabled lid, a common style for the period. The eggshell thin skull was practically the only recoverable bone, and only five teeth were in place at the time

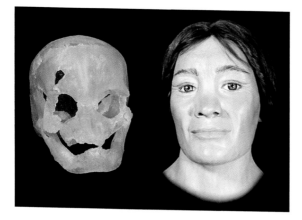

The reconstruction of the face of the female buried near JR required a CT scan-generated stereolithographic reconstruction of the fragile skull before creation of this likeness, perhaps that of one of the first few women living at Jamestown.

of the woman's death. Some of her teeth had been missing so long that the tooth sockets had completely closed. There was evidence that she had spent a lifetime of fairly strenuous physical work.[24]

So who was JR156C? Her identity as an older European woman may narrow the possibilities. Women did not come to Jamestown until the second supply, September 1608, when Mistress Forest and her maid, Anne Burras, arrived. Anne Burras went on to marry John Laydon, a laborer who came to Virginia with the first 107 adventurers in 1607; their first child, named Virginia, became the first Anglo-American born at Jamestown.[25] The Laydons were still alive in 1625, when a census lists John, his wife Anne, then aged thirty, and their four children as living at Elizabeth City (today's city of Hampton, Virginia). Records do not mention Mistress Forest again, which may mean that she did not live long. Since so few women lived in the colony in the first two years, there are good odds that a female buried in a coffin in precious ground inside the fort would be the wife of a gentleman, perhaps Thomas Forest. As the wife of a gentleman with a thirteen- or fourteen-year-old maidservant, Mistress Forest might have been at least in her thirties when she arrived in the colony in 1608. But the wife of a gentleman with a maidservant would hardly develop signs of hard labor. JR156C is more likely one of the females who came from England to Jamestown after the arrival of Mistress Forest. Radiocarbon testing indicates a burial date of circa 1620/40 for JR156C. In the absence of names and dates on a gravestone or further relevant documents, JR156C would be harder to identify positively than JR himself.

Like JR102C, our woman JR156C deserved a facial reconstruction. The delicate skull, too fragile to use for molding, made the effort more challenging. In this case, a computer-generated process known as stereolithography was able to produce the mold even more accurately than plaster, without so much as touching the original fragile skull. The process began with a computed tomography scan (CT) that produced a three-dimensional file. That information was then transferred to a stereolithography apparatus that guided a laser beam to recreate the skull exactly in a light-sensitive epoxy material.[26] At that point, a forensic sculptor produced a face through the same casting and reconstructive processes used to recapture JR's appearance. The physical condition of JR156C at the time of her death did not result in an especially pretty face. The image, however, may be more reflective of the reality of rugged early Jamestown than most want to imagine. Regardless, the 1617 engraving of Pocahontas is now no longer the only existing image of an early Jamestown woman.

## THE CAPTAIN

While the interplay of archaeological/scientific facts and documentary reference surrounding these two burials can offer at best possible identification, the identity of another discovered burial can be established with something approaching probability. Excavations within the Civil War earthwork in search of the western 1607 fort wall not only turned up a well (see chap. 2) but also another unmarked grave.[27] The very siting and soil composition of the burial shaft immediately brought great attention to this grave. The burial was aligned with the predicted (and eventually discovered) west wall of the fort—a compass direction that only made sense in light of the sought-for triangular plan of the original James Fort. In addition, part of the discolored soil outlining the shaft was found to be under a circular, well-like feature jammed with seventeenth-century brickbats. Since the brick deposit had to postdate the burial, this group of circumstances, too, suggested an early seventeenth-century interment.

Removal of the brickbats and about a foot of fill containing domestic trash exposed the bottom, not of a well, but of a shallow pit. The mixed clay in the burial fill was still visible at the bottom of the pit, as was an outline of a posthole, which slightly penetrated the shaft. Artifacts from the pit fill, notably tobacco pipes including a local coarse-ceramic type probably first made at Jamestown after 1630, indicated the date of deposit: these undisturbed strata were at least as old as the 1630s. This inadvertent sealing of the forgotten grave created a time lid on the age of interment—a date, circa 1630, before which the burial must have taken place. This dating, the location adjacent to the fort, and the alignment of the grave with the wall of the

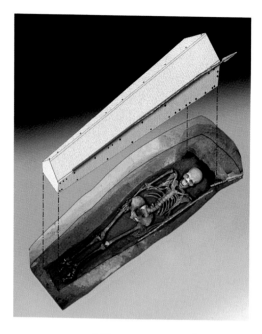

A European man in his mid-
to late thirties buried with
a captain's leading staff, laid
along a gable-lidded coffin.
(Reconstruction based on nail
patterns and wood stains in
the soil.)

original fort pointed to the possible discovery of the most important of lost burials at Jamestown, that of Captain Bartholomew Gosnold.

When a decorative iron captain's leading staff appeared at the excavation level of the coffin lid, finding Gosnold below seemed inevitable. The superbly preserved skeleton lying within the coffin outline offered more reason to hope. The well-preserved pelvis enabled our steadfast forensic anthropologist, Dr. Douglas Owsley, to determine that this five-foot, three-inch European man died in his mid- to late thirties. It is known that Gosnold was thirty-six years of age at his passing on August 22, 1607, the day when George Percy reported that after a three-week illness "there died Captain Bartholomew Gosnold, one of our council; he was honorably buried, having all the ordinance in the fort shot off with many volleys of small shot."[28]

Finding Gosnold was a goal for the Jamestown Rediscovery project from the beginning. Why? His vital importance to both the planning and reality of the Jamestown adventure was unquestionable but not widely known. The discovery of his remains might help inspire a more careful reading of the record of initial English colonization.

We already know that Gosnold's success as a mariner and privateer led him to briefly colonize one of the Elizabeth Isles and explore and name Cape Cod and Martha's Vineyard.[29] This exploration was a prelude to Gosnold's planning, fundraising, and recruiting for the Virginia colony of Jamestown, transporting the settlers, and laying the colony's foundations. Upon Gosnold's passing, even the self-promoting Captain John Smith and his archenemy, Edward Maria Wingfield, the colony's first council president, agreed on Gosnold's value. Smith named Gosnold the "prime mover" of the planting of Jamestown. Wingfield, in an apologia after his removal from office, lamented, "divers of our men fell sick . . . amongst whom was the worthy and religious gentleman, Captain Bartholomew Gosnold, upon whose life stood a great part of the good success and fortune of our government and colony."[30] In the absence of Gosnold's support, Wingfield felt it inevitable that he would be deposed as council president—a strong statement about Gosnold's great value to the colony.

Gosnold's death so early in Jamestown's history robbed him of a chance to produce his own memoirs. The loss of his gravesite further helped relegate him to historical obscurity. But just as the archaeological discovery of James Fort has offered posterity a chance to reassess the Jamestown experience, so the probable discovery of the lost Gosnold grave brings to the forefront the significant accolades of Smith and Wingfield.

The high status accorded to this burial is established by the captain's leading staff or half pike found in the grave. Only the metal parts survived: the decorative point fashioned into a cruciform, and two metal fastening straps (lanquets). However, the decay of the pike's wooden shaft left enough of a dark stain in the ground to reveal its original length, five and one-half feet. During excavation, the corrosion on the metal point disguised its true shape, but laboratory x-rays left no doubt that it was the head of a captain's leading staff. A search in the collections of European military staff weapons and period illustrations produced early seventeenth-century examples of officers' half pikes.[31] A 1626 woodcut shows an identical pike, describing it as a type of captain's half pike intended to be deployed in combat.[32] Examples remain of more decorative ceremonial captains' staffs, but such staffs would have stayed in England, while the more weapon-like half pikes went to the Jamestown frontier.

The presence of the wartime staff at Jamestown might seem to contradict the Virginia Company's instructions to the colonists not to appear menacing to the Virginia Indians. Following these instructions, at first Gosnold and the rest of the council even delayed constructing the fort. It is apparent, however, that Gosnold (or whoever the buried captain may be) had a more realistic understanding than the London-based Virginia Company of the situation they would face at Jamestown. The captain seemed to have known that no matter how peaceful the settlers tried to appear, sooner or later relations with the natives would indeed require the combat version of his leading staff. In fact, combat followed upon first contact at Cape Henry, and as we know, after only a few days of incoming arrows at Jamestown Gosnold and the rest of the council "contrived" and directed construction of James Fort.[33]

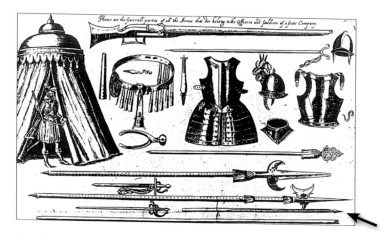

"Drill Postures," a detail from an engraving by T. Cockson (English, 1615–20), showing a leading staff identical to the Jamestown burial staff. (Copyright The Trustees of the British Museum)

Whether or not this burial is Gosnold might be further determined by comparison of its skeletal DNA with that of a known relative, dead or alive. The challenge would be to find the right relative, which means only a maternal descendant. Why? Cells contain two kinds of DNA: nuclear and mitochondrial. Mitochondrial DNA—that contained in the mitochondria of the cell—preserves well in bones, is relatively stable, and can be compared across several generations.[34] Mitochondrial DNA is only passed along the maternal family line, so in order to compare a sample from the bones of a deceased individual, a sample from the mother, or from any of the female siblings who share the same sequence of mitochondrial DNA as the mother of the deceased, would have to be found.

To find a living relative, documentation of about sixteen generations of maiden names going back to Gosnold's mother, aunts, or sisters needed to be researched. Such research has proven that no living maternal line relative can be found. The other option is to find the burial of a female relative of Gosnold and sample it for comparison.

This option appeared to be possible through genealogical research.[35] In fact, with skillful deduction from evidence found in various wills and church records, two possibilities were located in England: Elizabeth (Gosnold) Tilney, Bartholomew's sister, buried in All Saints Church, Shelley, near Ipswich, and Katherine (Bowtell) Blackerby, Bartholomew's niece, buried in St. Peters and St. Marys Church, Stowmarket. Elizabeth, the sister of Bartholomew Gosnold, married Thomas Tilney Esq. of Shelley Hall around 1598.[36] Her husband died circa 1618 (will dated 1618, proved 1620). Their son, Philip Tilney, sold Shelley Hall circa 1627. Elizabeth lived on at Higham St. Mary, and in 1646 she made her will. In that document, she commended her "body to the earth to be buried in decent maner in Shelly chauncell by Thomas Tylney Esquier my late husband." There are no Shelley parish registers for burials for this period, but luckily the Higham St. Mary register records that on April 10, 1646, Elizabeth, widow of Thomas Tylney Esq., died "and was buried in Shelley chauncell the day followinge."[37]

There is more to suggest Elizabeth's burial place. In the later seventeenth century, Shelley church was visited by William Blois (or Bloys; 1600–1673), an antiquarian from Grundisburgh in Suffolk. He saw and recorded:

> An Isle in the church built by the Tilnys. Their coat in stone. And stools.
> 1) A monument for a Tilny
> 2) Another for Dame Margaret wife to Philip Tilney Esq., whose son Freder. Tilny Esq. by Anne, da. of Francis Framlingham of Debenham, had issue Charls [sic] that dyed without issue Anno 1595.
> 3) A stone. Hic iacet Wm. King fil. Joh. King, Do'o huius ville circiter 1500. His coat (not there) a lion ramp &c.[38]

Then in 1825 Shelley church was visited by another Suffolk antiquarian, David Elisha Davy (1769–1851), who recorded the following information:[39]

> The church . . . consists of a Chancel, Nave and Isle on the S[outh] side.
> The chancel is 19ft 10ins long, & 18ft 3ins wide, covered with tiles, and ceiled. The Communion Table is not raised, but railed around. . . . On the north side was a large opening into what was probably a chapel or burial place for the family residing at the Hall [originally the Tilney family], but now used as a vestry, the entrance to which is through a narrow modern door.
> The whole floor of the church is paved with white brick, and the church is kept in very neat and clean order.
> Monuments, inscriptions etc.
> In the chancel
> In the floor below the rails, on a small slab of Purbeck stone, were brasses
> On another small one [stone], near the Vestry door, was a brass of this shape [Davy sketches a simple narrow rectangle]
> In the Vestry
> Against the north wall is fixed a square frame of stone, in the centre of which is the following shield of arms:

Tilney quartering Thorpe. Over it: crest: from a ducal coronet, a double plume of 5 and 4 feathers, and arising thence a griffon's head.
Supporters: two griffons, but broken.

From the descriptions given by Blois and Davy, it was possible to identify and locate some of the graves in the chancel. Through the process of elimination, a possible occupant of the grave marked by the slab with the rectangular brass (now missing) can be identified. Members of the Tilney family unaccounted for by Blois and Davy include Philip Tilney (who died in 1602)[40] and his wife, Anne Framlingham. There are no burial records at Shelley or wills to identify where they were living when they died. Another unaccounted-for Tilney is Emery (brother and heir of Philip; died 1606) and his wife Winifred Davis. Again, there are no burial records at Shelley or wills to identify where they were living when they died. Emery had lived in London and also had a house at Syleham in north Suffolk, so his burial at Shelley is unlikely. So the best candidates are Thomas Tilney (son of Emery) and Elizabeth Gosnold, his wife, as both are known to have been buried in Shelley church.

In 1882–83 Shelley church was "thoroughly restored," having been "very much in need of repair."[41] The restoration included the removal of the old pews and their replacement with solid oak benches. The restoration also involved the tiling of the chancel, during which, documentary research suggested, the stone with the missing brass, likely marking the Thomas and Elizabeth Tilney burials and lying directly in front of the Tilney Chapel, was paved over.

Katherine Blackerby's genealogy also created a likely trail to her grave, although a bit of a leap of faith is required along the way. In a *Heralds' Visitation of Suffolk* in 1665, Thomas Blackerby named her as his wife and stated that she was the "daughter of Francis Bowtell of Parham Hall."[42] In his will, dated 1687, Thomas's marriage to a Bowtell is also established, as he mentions his deceased "brother" (in-law) Bowtell and his children.[43] The children's names match with those of Barnaby Bowtell Esq. (1609–84) of Parham Hall, confirming that he was Katherine's brother. Barnaby himself was baptized in 1609 at St. Matthew's, Ipswich, the "sonne of Francis Bowtell and Marie his wife." A record of his marriage to "Marie" has not been found; however, there is good reason to believe that she was Mary Gosnold, Bartholomew's sister. But this is where the leap of faith comes into the

All Saints Church, Shelley, Suffolk, England, where Bartholomew Gosnold's sister, Elizabeth, was buried in the chancel in 1646. This is the site of the 2005 excavation to obtain bone samples and thus DNA from the remains, hoping to further link the captain to the remains of Jamestown leader Bartholomew Gosnold.

St. Peters and St. Marys Church, Stowmarket, Suffolk, England, the burial place of Captain Bartholomew Gosnold's niece Katherine Blackerby. This was another predicted site to obtain bone samples with DNA to identify the Jamestown captain's remains.

Choir pews in All Saints Church, Shelley, are located upon the likely burial site of Elizabeth Gosnold Tilney.

picture. Davy, the Suffolk antiquarian, recorded this about Bartholomew's family in his manuscript *East Anglian pedigrees:*[44]

> Gosnold of Otley:
> Anthony Gosnold of Grundisburgh and Clopton married Dorothy, dau. of [blank] Bacon of Hessett.
> Issue: [all given without first names]
> [blank] Gosnold, married Thomas Tilney of Shelley, living 1606; [blank] Gosnold married Edmund Goldsmith; [blank] Gosnold married [blank] Bowtell of Ipswich; [blank] Gosnold married Zachary Norman of Dunwich; Capt.[blank] . . . Gosnold; Ursula Gosnold, buried at Grundisburgh 10 July 1688 [*sic*]; Bartholemew Gosnold, son and heir, of Virginia . . . Captain of a vessel, died in Virginia 1607.

Combining Davy's list with information gleaned from family wills and other sources, the following list of Gosnold daughters can be drawn up: Elizabeth (married Thomas Tilney), Margaret (married Zachary Norman), Dorothie (married Edmund Goldsmith), Anne, Mary, and Ursula. From this list it can be deduced that the daughter who married a Bowtell was named either Anne or Mary—but which? Probably Mary, because the name Bowtell is uncommon in Suffolk, and the only gentry family of the name is the one descended from Francis and Mary of Ipswich. The dates match well for Francis to have married Mary Gosnold. Unfortunately, there is no known will for Francis or Mary, his wife. Here is where the slight leap of faith is required to draw the conclusion that Katherine Bowtell Blackerby's mother was, in fact, Mary Gosnold.

In any event, Katherine's husband, Thomas Blackerby (ca. 1612–88), was a wealthy and influential man. Although a native of Suffolk, he had spent much of his life as a merchant in London, rising to be an alderman in 1667 and Master of the Skinners' Company in 1668. In Suffolk he served as sheriff in 1668–69. He also purchased the lordship of Stowmarket. Katherine is named as his "deare and loveing wife" in his will, dated 1687.[45] Combining these specific connections with one assumption, it can be concluded that Katherine Bowtell Blackerby at Stowmarket is very likely to have been the niece of Bartholomew Gosnold, being the daughter of his sister Mary. While all these fairly complicated relationships do not seem to get us to her exact burial place, they did make a ledgerstone in the floor in a Stowmarket church, St. Peters and St. Marys, a possible key to locating Katherine's grave.

The Stowmarket church parish registers record the burial of Katherine's husband on November 4, 1688, and her own burial on December 22, 1693. In 1811 the antiquarian Davy visited Stowmarket church, where he recorded the monuments, including, "In the chancel within the communion rails, on the south side, Memorial to Thomas Blackerby, died 2 November 1688, aged 76." The Rev. A. G. H. Hollingsworth (vicar of Stowmarket, 1837–59) in his *The History of Stowmarket,* states that Thomas Blackerby was buried "under the altar steps—the most distinguished place in the church, and chosen expressly to mark the high estimation in which his character and person were held by the townsmen."[46] Stowmarket church was re-pewed and beautified in 1840.[47] A further restoration was carried out in the 1860s under the direction of architect R. M. Phipson. Despite the reno-vations, a black floor slab commemorating Thomas Blackerby lies in the center of the chancel. The extreme eastern end of the slab appears to go under the Victorian altar step. The slab carries a long inscription in praise of Thomas:

> Esq. who was elected ALDERMAN of the City
> of LONDON in the year of our Lord 1666
> fined for the same and for Sheriffe
> of the said City. He was HIGH SHERIFFE
> of this County in the year of our Lord 1669
>
> He was a man of very great TEMPERANCE
> of exemplary CHARITY of profound
> HUMILITY and strict PIETY very ZEALOUS
> in the discharge of his duty both as a
> MAGISTRATE and as a private person
> He did much good both in this Town
> and other places whilst he lived
> and is gone to receive his Reward
> He dyed 2 Nov^r 1688 Ætat Suæ 76

There is no mention of Katherine. However, it seems very unlikely that Katherine would have been buried separately from her husband. Her ab-sence from the inscription could be due to a lack of space on the stone or could indicate that, as a childless widow, at her death she left no relatives behind to see to it that the stone was properly inscribed. So there was a chance that Katherine could lie with Thomas under his ledgerstone. True, the central position of the stone today does not agree with Davy's description of the grave slab as being on the "south side" of the chancel. It is possible, however, that the stone was relocated during one of the Victorian restorations. At any rate, in light of the wealth and prominence of Thomas Blackerby, together with the date of the burial, he and his wife would likely be laid to rest in either a brick-lined shaft or an actual vault beneath the stone or nearby. That type of interment for people of prominence was common in the late seventeenth century.

Having exhausted the possibility of a living relative and theoretically located the place of burial of Bartholomew's sister, Elizabeth Tilney, at Shelley and his niece, Katherine Blackerby, at Stowmarket, the next steps were to uncover the remains, identify them more precisely, then obtain bone samples for DNA profiles. This was not to be as simple as it sounded.

First of all, official permission had to be in hand before there was any hope of excavation. These Gosnold relatives are buried in consecrated ground, both inside churches, and therefore under the legal and spiritual care of the Anglican Church of England.[48] The churches are also protected from any damage to structure by the Council for the Care of Churches. This protection is all the more strict because of the dangers posed elsewhere to the evidence of England's past: because England is such a tightly packed treasure chest of archaeological sites stretching over many millennia, and land development is always putting this valuable legacy at risk, the country's archaeologists must concentrate their efforts on rescuing sites in harm's way. Research archaeology, especially any studies of burials in an otherwise "safe" environment—that is, inside churches—has to be of paramount significance and well planned in order to obtain permission, in this case permission from the Church of England, to proceed. It was also vital that the parishioners in both churches be convinced that the work would proceed with a minimum of disruption to church fabric and worship services and would be done with the utmost respect for the deceased. In the end, all of these conditions were met, the authorities convinced, and for the first time in the history of the Church of England, permission was granted. Why? The international significance of Gosnold won the day. This was not to be just a case of some individual trying to prove relationship to someone famous by violating a church grave for DNA. Identifying Gosnold was part of a project with great educational potential.

In 2007 America would commemorate its four-hundred-year-old English heritage, with Jamestown as the focus. The Association for the Preservation of Virginia Antiquities (APVA) and the National Park Service would contribute to the memorial event by completing a $45-million interpretive plan that includes expansion of a state-of-the-art archaeological collection facility meeting the highest museum standards for the preservation and protection of 700,000 Jamestown artifacts and the creation of two educational museum facilities for the anticipated 1 million visitors. One facility, the Archaearium, would exhibit many of the artifacts from the James Fort excavation and would include a section dedicated to explaining to the public the scientific value of the study of early English Jamestown burials. With respect and taste the Archaearium would display two burials symbolizing the struggle to establish the colony: a young soldier and the captain, who was likely Gosnold. That exhibit would teach visitors about the forensic analysis of the remains of these two men while also addressing medical practices and colonial diet. In addition, the Archaearium would have an atrium in public view where most of the Jamestown burials would be reinterred and properly commemorated, with particular emphasis on names and individuals. A positive identification of Bartholomew Gosnold among those interred, or even an explanation of the efforts to identify him through the proposed DNA study, would add tremendously to the educational impact of this monument.

More precisely identifying Gosnold also held the potential to illuminate the experience of the British in the New World in a special way. This burial outside the fort—and therefore in plain view of Indian adversaries—flew in the face of Virginia Company instructions not to show any signs of illness or death to the native population. If the DNA comparison proved positively that the buried captain was Gosnold, however—a man particularly respected by the other leaders as the moving force behind the success of the American colony—the motives for breaking that rule would become clearer, shedding light on the human side of the Virginia story: such a burial with full honors would be a prime example of how, in a difficult situation, the leaders of the colony did their best to maintain British religious and social order even as they adapted to their circumstances in Virginia.

In addition to a clear statement of the purpose the project would serve, the church authorities needed to know how the project would be executed. Indiscriminate digging through the church floors, disrupting grave after grave in the hope of finding a likely candidate for Gosnold DNA, could never be allowed. To assure that such destruction would not occur, the process had to include fail-safe controls along the way. The digging would

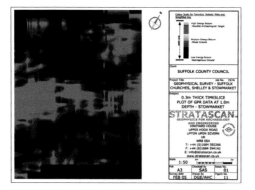

Diagram of the ground-penetrating radar test at Stowmarket showing the existence of burial vaults (*in yellow*). The largest signal was from the area beneath and beside the ledgerstone marking the burial of Thomas Blackerby.

be done in phases, with repeated reassessment of the chances of finding the right grave without irreversible damage to the churches. That analysis would be performed by a committee of individuals representing the church, the church archaeologists from the Suffolk County archaeological unit, and the two sponsoring institutions, the APVA and the National Geographic Society.

Digging would be preceded by ground-penetrating radar (GPR) reading of the chancels, which would have virtually no physical effect on the churches. That testing could proceed even without a full sanction by the church. An electronic device was rolled across the chancel floors, emitting electrical pulses and recording the echoes they produced as they encountered different densities of material beneath, such as masonry walls and voids in burial vaults. Two strong signals were found at each church. The two at Shelley were not in the most likely burial place for Elizabeth Tilney. At Stowmarket, however, an obvious sign of a vault lay under and to the right of the Blackerby ledgerstone. But despite the apparent mixed success of the GPR testing, the decision was made by the churches at both the parish and diocese levels to grant permission, known as a faculty, to begin the phased operation.

At Shelley, the pews and a wooden floor had to be removed to conduct the ground radar test. This revealed part of the ledgerstone with the now-missing nameplate seen by Davy. So far so good. The committee agreed to remove the stone, along with a surrounding unmortared eighteenth-century brick floor, both of which lay in a few inches of bedding sand. Delicate dusting of the soil beneath the sand revealed discrete patches of soil discolorations, signs of filled-in burial shafts. There were indications of at least three grave shafts, one clearly cutting through all the rest—proving it to be the most recent interment. This finding was encouraging, since Elizabeth Tilney's grave would likely intrude upon the space in which her husband, Thomas, had been buried twenty-eight years before her. So to move on, only one grave would be disturbed.

Digging began, and five feet below the ground surface signs of a decomposed coffin holding the skeletal remains of what appeared to be a woman were discovered. If Elizabeth's nameplate were found on the coffin, or if the remains were those of a woman who died in her seventies, Elizabeth's estimated age at death, we would have the needed assurance that the right grave had been located and would proceed to the bone-sampling. But the complete clearance of the remains had to be left for the next day.

Meanwhile, work continued back at Stowmarket. At St. Peters and St. Marys Church, workmen had removed two floor stones next to the Blackerby ledgerstone, which revealed the domed roof of a brick vault lying beneath loose rubble used to raise the chancel floor in the Victorian-era renovations. This was a good candidate for a Blackerby vault, likely containing both Thomas and his wife, Katherine. But the bricks and mortar appeared to date to the Victorian time, well over a century later than the burials of Thomas and Katherine in the late seventeenth century. Nonetheless, the decision was made to drill a small hole in the roof of the vault and insert a fiber-optic viewer to look for

Careful brushing of the dust found beneath an unmarked ledgerstone at Shelley exposed the outline of a burial shaft with no apparent postburial disturbance of the ground.

two coffins. The fiber-optic viewer, a five-foot-long cane-like device with a tiny swivel video camera on the end, sent images of the vault interior to a viewing monitor. The monitor image clearly showed that the vault was completely intact and contained what appeared to be a stone shelf, possibly an inner tomb. This was encouraging enough to justify the enlargement of the excavation, which revealed the walled-up vault entrance. The subsequent removal of a few bricks opened a hole large enough to permit flash photographs to be taken of the vault interior.

At that point the committee halted the work to assess the photographs and to reconsider how much excavation would be required to gain access to the room. If there was any reason to believe that there might be two burials in the vault and that the vault itself had been rebuilt during the Victorian renovations, then there would still be a good chance that the Blackerbys lay inside, and we would push on. The photos did in fact show that there was a stone tomb inside, exactly wide enough to hold two side-by-side coffins. Some of the bricks in the wall farthest from the camera appeared to be the color of seventeenth-century bricks, a possible sign of a rebuild.

Masons proceeded to open the vault entrance just enough to provide access to the vault. They then lifted one of the stones that sealed what appeared to be one part of a double stone tomb. This revealed a collapsed wooden coffin originally covered with black cloth fastened with decorative rows of large brass tacks. Resting on the wood in a chest-high position was an elaborate but very rusted sheet-metal plate known as a "depositum plate." The plate was in the form of a tracery crown below angels and at the center was a mostly illegible epitaph. Only the scrolled handpainted letters "—ed" and the partially legible number "74" could be read. This appeared to be the last line in the epitaph, which traditionally records the person's age at death: "aged —." This man had died "aged 74." According to his ledgerstone, Blackerby died at seventy-six. So this was not our man. Also, the depositum plate was of a style much more recent than the 1688 date of Thomas Blackerby's burial.

There still remained the possibility that an earlier burial, possibly of a woman, lay next to him in the unopened side of the inner vault. The masons returned and removed another stone, opening enough of the remaining tomb to reveal its contents. There lay another collapsed but smaller wooden coffin with a depositum plate, but this time made of lead. The lead was cause for one last flicker of hope, until a closer look at the plate revealed eighteenth- to nineteenth-century-style angles with no epitaph. Indeed, both plates could be no older than circa 1770.[49] But it turned out the burials were not even that old. The final evidence came from high up on the south chancel wall. There a ledgerstone clearly stated, "Near this place are deposited the remains of John Boby, Gen: (late of Stowupland) who died 7 April, 1817 aged 74 years Also Ann, relict of John Boby, Gen: who died 25th of January 8, 1834, aged 84 years." So there was no need to expose any of the bones beneath the wooden coffin lids. Instead, we made a hasty retreat from the vault, leaving the Bobys once again to rest in peace.

Another avenue remained to be pursued. When the archaeologists had cleared space at the Boby vault entrance, a dome-covered vault with brick and mortar of a much older appearance was found. Unfortunately, a fiber-optic peek into that vault dashed hope once again. The monitor clearly

A photo taken through a test hole in the Stowmarket vault showed an inner stone tomb that was wide enough for two individuals as well as brickwork that could be as old as the Blackerbys' interment, 1688, and revealed a decaying wooden brick mason's mallet left by mistake or perhaps by design before the vault was sealed.

Fiber-optic inspection of the inside of the possible Blackerby sealed burial vault distinctly showed an intact room and an inner tomb.

Smithsonian forensic anthropologist Dr. Douglas Owsley and Suffolk archaeologist and historian Edward Martin inspect the wooden coffin and plate found in the Stowmarket inner tomb. The style of the plate and the age of death, seventy-four, still legible on the plate established this to be the tomb of John Boby, who died in 1817 at the age of seventy-four, and next to him, his wife, Ann, who died in 1834.

showed what had to be scattered broken coffins, probably disarticulated bone among them, and brick rubble spilling down the entrance. It was wisely decided that even if this was the Blackerby vault, chances of coming up with a reliable sample were not worth the expense and damage that entry would cause. At that point it was extremely comforting to know that the possible remains of Elizabeth had already been found at Shelley. The Stowmarket venture had ended.

Back at Shelley All Saints, the Suffolk archaeologist, donning his sanitized suit, gloves, and mask to prevent his own DNA from contaminating the woman's remains, proceeded to uncover as much of the skeleton and trace of the coffin as the deep, narrow shaft would allow. At that point, Dr. Owsley arrived to assess more precisely signs of sex and age. After an agonizing hour, there were great sighs of relief when he concluded that this was indeed a woman of advanced age. But the fact that she had almost all of her teeth and that they were not overly worn cast some doubt in Owsley's mind that this was a woman old enough at her time of death to be Elizabeth.

Again, Elizabeth's birth date is unrecorded, but her age at time of death can be estimated by reviewing other documented family history. Her first child was born in 1600 and the last in 1612. Therefore, one can assume that she married Thomas Tilney in the late sixteenth century, perhaps at age twenty to twenty-six, the latter being the average age that women married at that time. Therefore, she would probably have been between sixty-eight and seventy-four when she died in 1646. Owsley could not determine in the field whether the Shelley woman was as old as her late sixties to early seventies, so he took additional bone samples for future laboratory age testing. The grave was left otherwise undisturbed. Following this sampling procedure, the All Saints vicar offered a eulogy and prayer, and the burial shaft was refilled.[50]

DNA does not always survive in buried remains, and because more than three and a half centuries had passed since Elizabeth Gosnold Tilney died, there existed the possibility that no DNA would be found in the Shelley samples. Fortunately, that was not the case; scientists were able to extract a DNA sequence. And although the sequence was considered "minimal and degraded," there was enough of a DNA signature to compare with the sequence from the Jamestown captain. So far so good.

The results of the comparative test proved as surprising as they were disappointing. The disappointment came in that the comparison soundly "excluded" the possibility that the Jamestown captain and the Shelley woman were maternal relatives.[51] That would seem to rule out Bartholomew Gosnold as the Jamestown captain. But at the same time, that could only be true if the Shelley woman was in fact Elizabeth Gosnold Tilney. Failure to find a coffin plate positively identifying the Shelley woman as Elizabeth and the less-than-certain determination made at the church that the Shelley woman could be as old as sixty-eight to seventy-four left the DNA mismatch inconclusive.

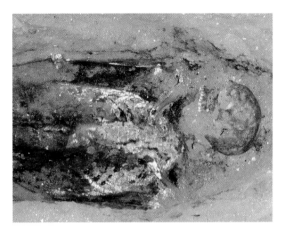

The Shelley woman, Elizabeth Gosnold Tilney (?), in the remnants of her hexagonal wooden coffin. The remains were only partially uncovered, minimally disturbed, and respectfully and quickly reburied.

Further testing of the samples to more precisely determine age provided the surprise. Scientists analyzing the Shelley burial samples for calcium and their closer inspection of her teeth together convinced the specialists that the Shelley woman was thirty-eight to forty-six when she died.[52] She was far too young to be Elizabeth Gosnold Tilney. Consequently, it appeared that after all the months of historical research and negotiations with the church officials, the Shelley burial might be of no help at all in identifying the Jamestown captain.

But there is more evidence to consider. Just as in the JR analysis, the case for proving that the Shelley burial is not Elizabeth Gosnold Tilney may not be as ironclad as it appears. Some of the tests that determined that the Shelley woman was too young to be Bartholomew's sister were called into question by the Advisory Panel for the Archaeology of Christian Burials in England (APACBE).[53] That organization is made up of a group of archaeologists and scientists who work regularly on burial issues in England. They concluded that the possibility that the Shelley burial was Elizabeth Gosnold Tilney cannot be ruled out, basing their decision on what British archaeologists had learned by aging burials removed by archaeologists in 1984 to 1986 from tombs at Christ Church in East London.[54] There were records of the age at death of many of these burials. The Christ Church archaeologists submitted selected skeletons to anthropologists to determine each burial's age based on standard macroscopic and microscopic methods. But the archaeologists also made sure the tests were not influenced by prior knowledge of the recorded ages of the deceased. As a rule, the scientists aged the older burials as much as fifteen years younger then their historically recorded age. Based on the results of the Christ Church study, the Advisory Panel concluded that the Shelley burial determined by testing in the United States plus the likely fifteen-year error factor brought her close to the known age of Elizabeth, sixty-eight to seventy-four years. If this were true, of course, the failure of the DNA from the Shelley woman and the Jamestown captain to match would indeed rule out Bartholomew Gosnold as the Jamestown burial.

But the American and British scientists did then agree that other tests besides determining age at death could add to the evidence chain. They agreed that a reading of the Shelley burial's stable isotopes, the same test conducted on the remains of JR, should give similar dietary statistics to those of the Jamestown captain, that is, if he was in fact raised in the wheat-rich county of Suffolk, England. Also, a C14 reading of the Shelley sample could pin down the date of the burial, which would give additional evidence to determine if the Shelley woman is Ann Framlingham (who preceded Elizabeth Gosnold Tilney as lady of Shelley Manor) or Elizabeth, who had died more than fifty years later. The isotope test showed similar $C_4$ readings for the Shelley woman and the Jamestown man, suggesting at least that the Jamestown man like the Shelley woman could have been raised in Suffolk. This can be considered one more shred of evidence that the Jamestown burial is Bartholomew. The C14 reading of the Shelley samples turned out to be the year 1690, plus or minus fifty years, which tends to rule out Ann, who died in 1590, but offers the possibility that the Shelley burial is Elizabeth, who died in 1646.[55]

So is the Jamestown captain Bartholomew Gosnold or not? Obviously, a final, unequivocal conclusion is not possible to attain without a perfect DNA match. There was no such match. There are certainly good reasons to doubt that the Shelley woman is not Elizabeth Gosnold. If she is not Elizabeth Gosnold, of course, the mismatch identifies no one. Nevertheless, one can still review the other evidence to determine the most likely identity of the Jamestown man. The captain's staff, the well-constructed coffin, the age at death, the orientation of the burial, the record of Gosnold's ceremonial August 1607 interment, his English and possible Suffolk diet, signs of a healthy gentlemanly lifestyle, the TPQ of artifacts covering his grave, and of course, the DNA comparison with a nonrelative has to be a mismatch if the Jamestown captain is Bartholomew Gosnold.

Remember that the Jamestown burial's location, outside the fort, could be testimony against this captain's being Gosnold. Discovery of the twenty-one 1607 burials inside the west wall of the fort seems to establish that the colonists did strictly follow the Company's directive to hide any sickness and death from the Indians. Why then would the settlers break the rules and advertise the death of anyone, especially a leader like Gosnold, by burying him in plain sight outside the fort wall? One possible explanation is that the burial ceremony, with all its pomp and gunfire, could have been intended as a sign of strength rather than of weakness; that is to say, a feigned show of force outside made to disguise the rash of deaths within could still point to Gosnold.

Looking from another perspective, if this burial is not Gosnold, then who could it be? If this man expired after 1607, the year Gosnold died, then he did so at a time when it is likely the Indians knew full well the Englishmen were mortal. In that case the unknown captain might be none other than the chronicler of 1607, Gabriel Archer, who died during the 1609–10 "starving time." But given the tremendous numbers dying that winter and Strachey's grim description of the condition of the few fort survivors in May 1610, one would hardly think that Archer would get a ceremonious burial in a well-built coffin either inside or outside the fort.[56]

Another prominent settler died at Jamestown in 1610, Sir Ferdinando Wenman, appointed Master of the Ordinance by Lord De La Warre. But it is unlikely Wenman, a knight, would be buried with a captain's leading staff. Rather, he would probably be interred with a sword. If that tradition survived at Jamestown, then Wenman's grave may have been found in the late nineteenth century by the Jamestown property owner's son, J. P. Barney. He claimed river shoreline erosion exposed the grove near the church tower of a man buried with a claymore (sword) and breastplate.[57]

And the presence of the captain's leading staff rules out any possibility that the Jamestown burial is that of the most prominent of all the settlers, the Lord De La Warre, who died en route to Jamestown in 1618 and whose body was brought to Virginia (undoubtedly Jamestown) for burial. The royally appointed Governor De La Warre, a lord, would certainly have been buried in Argall's new church, even if the church was not completely finished by the time his body arrived in 1618.[58]

But back to our earlier question, is the Shelley woman Elizabeth Gosnold Tilney? On the one hand, she is identified by the same type of circumstantial evidence identifying Bartholomew Gosnold: documents (ancestry, burial place, and "older" age at death), archaeology (grave stone, undisturbed condition), and forensic anthropology (sex and field assessment of age). On the other hand, the combination of the anthropological tests (teeth and calcium minus the possible fifteen-year error factor, stable isotopes, carbon 14) tends to establish that she is not Bartholomew's sister. As it stands, then, while the results are not incontrovertible, the evidence leans strongly toward the conclusion that the Jamestown burial is that of Captain Bartholomew Gosnold.

Regardless of any definitive conclusion, the Shelley-Jamestown DNA research process itself is a significant achievement in historical archaeology and anthropological science. The fact that DNA could survive in burials over three centuries old and survive to the degree that it was even possible to compare samples from two graves separated by an ocean is a milestone. Perhaps of more significance yet, the exercise in DNA detective work managed to rescue from historical obscurity Captain Bartholomew Gosnold, the overlooked principal figure in the planting of the Virginia colony.

## DEPARTED GENTLEMEN, 1607

Near the captain, removal of plowzone that lay over the longest fort rowhouse revealed more signs of burials. Seventeen soil stains the size of single graves and two apparent double burial shafts were found aligned parallel or perpendicular to the fort wall. The position of one of the apparently double-sized shafts suggested that it might possibly be a backfilled cellar in front of the building hearth instead of a burial site. The other apparent double shaft seemed to have been disturbed at one corner by the construction of a chimney in the long rowhouse. Since there was every reason to believe the rowhouse was built in 1611 or earlier, this construction above them would indicate that these were very early graves. Datable objects in the shafts might also help date the burials and provide the TPQ for the building of the rowhouse.

In order to establish the nature of the ambiguous shaft and the date of the possible double graves, both features were excavated. Digging proved that the shafts were in fact double burials holding the skeletal remains of four European men. The two men who lay partially beneath the chimney

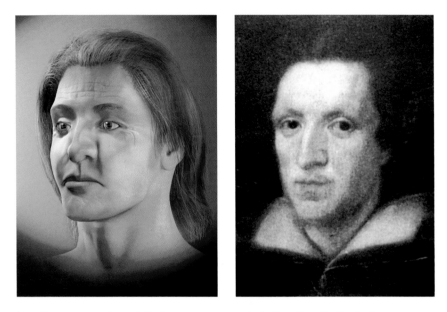

Facial reconstruction of the Jamestown captain believed to be Bartholomew Gosnold and portrait of Robert Gosnold V (1611), Bartholomew Gosnold's second cousin. (Reconstruction by Keith Kaznot; portrait courtesy of Nicholas Hagger)

died in their late teens or early twenties. One of the two men in the other grave died in his mid-twenties, the other in his mid-forties. No artifacts were recovered from the burials or the graveshaft fill except for a few fragments of Virginia Indian pottery and flakes of rock from Indian manufacture of stone tools or weapons. Again, the absence of European artifacts in colonial deposits like this graveshaft suggests that the men died very early in the James Fort period. Again it might be asked, as it was of JR and the first lady, why early burials were allowed to take up useful space within the fort—unless the dwellers were hiding death from their Virginia Indian adversaries. If this was the explanation for the location of the graves, it could be likely that these burials were the final resting places for the twenty-five gentlemen, a surgeon, and two "others" George Percy listed as dying between August 6 and September 19, 1607.[59] In that case, the ages at death could be clues to their identities, especially those of the two men with the great difference in age. On August 24, 1607, Percy recorded that Edward Harrington and George Walker died and were buried on the same day. English church records of christenings established that an Edward

Harrington would be twenty-five and a George Walker would be forty-five in the year 1607. If these are our men, and as they have such common English names there can be some doubt, then it is likely that the other double grave and the single graves about them are the resting places of those unfortunate colonists of that late 1607 summer.

One of the first to fall in the fateful 1607 summer was the boy who was killed during the assault on the colonists by the Virginia Indians on May 25. Excavation of a single burial of a male in his mid-teens, oriented and adjacent to the fort's west wall, may well be the remains of that boy. Just like JR there could be little doubt what killed him, a wound to the leg. But this burial was different; the wound was caused by an arrow tipped with a stone point that was found next to his leg. Preliminary analysis also suggests that he had injuries to his shoulders.[60] Four boys were among the first settlers: Samuell Collier, Nathaniel Pecock, James Brumfield, and Richard Mutton.[61] There is some evidence to suggest that Collier and Pecock

Excavation of two double burials, likely to date to the summer of 1607, beneath the foundations of the James Fort rowhouse and surrounded by seventeen other single burials.

were alive in the 1610s, but there is no record that Brumfield or Mutton lived that long. Either Brumfield or Mutton could well have been this arrow victim.[62]

## BURIALS OUT OF TOWN

In his 1623 will, John Atkins, resident of Jamestown, asked to be buried "at the usual place out of town."[63] It is likely that that burial ground was inadvertently discovered in the mid-1950s during the National Park Service excavations of the foundations of the 1665–98 Jamestown Statehouse, on a ridge of higher ground 700 feet west of the James Fort site. The excavations were prompted by the impending three hundred and fiftieth anniversary of the Jamestown settlement. That burial ground became the focus of the Jamestown Rediscovery excavations as well. Before the recent study could begin, however, it was important to restudy the details of the earlier Park Service digging.

In 1955 clearing of topsoil around the Statehouse foundations uncovered the soil stains of approximately seventy grave-shafts. The NPS archaeologists found skeletons in ten of the seventy graves and were able to recover bones from six. The extremely fragmentary remains then became part of the collections at the Colonial National Historical Park, Jamestown. Recent analysis by forensic scientists indicates that among the six skeletons that could be reliably studied were three males and three females, the women ranging in age from fifteen to thirty-four years old, and the men from fifteen to twenty-nine years old.[64]

While too little of these skeletal re-

Skeletal remains of a boy in his mid-teens found buried just inside and along the fort's west wall show how he met a violent death: an arrow wound in his left leg and apparent injuries to his shoulders.

mains survived to permit any hope for establishing cause of death, their vast numbers (archaeologists at the time estimated that there might be as many as 300) and their haphazard alignment strongly suggested that this was most likely the final resting place of the estimated 155 of the 215 settlers who died during the "starving time" winter of 1609–10.[65] The reasoning was that the few left alive during that winter might not have been strong and healthy enough to bury the bodies properly.[66]

Such considerations among others prompted the Jamestown Rediscovery team to study further the apparently early, unmarked burial ground lying below the foundations of the Statehouse complex. Even if this graveyard was not the final resting place of the victims of the "starving time," the burial ground's location beneath the 1660s Statehouse suggested a date in the early years of Jamestown settlement. Systematic recovery and preservation of at least fifty burials would make it possible to reconstruct a profile, otherwise largely lacking, of the population of early Jamestown.[67] This profile could include details on the ratio of females to males, ancestry, social and economic status, life expectancy, foreign-to-native birth ratios, general health, disease, causes of death, burial customs, and possibly dates of death. That data could be compared to other broader studies of seventeenth-century burials in the Chesapeake region, in order to measure physiological and cultural change across the region and over time from the earliest evidence of the Anglo-American population.

Over an eighteen-month period, excavation of sixty-three graves resulted in the recovery of the skeletal remains of seventy-two individuals.[68] While many deep graves contained carefully positioned individuals, a number of graves were rather shallow and haphazardly aligned. Some individuals appeared to have been placed in the shaft in a careless manner, and there were a number of cases of multiple burials in the same shaft: ten graves held two burials, and one shaft held three. The multiple graves may have resulted from an effort to minimize contact with the bodies of the deceased by throwing them into hastily dug graves.

In-situ buttons, pins, and other artifacts were found with the remains of three skeletons—two men and one woman—indicating that they were buried wearing clothing. Clothed burial was an extremely unusual custom for the time, as clothing was in extremely short supply and considered part of a person's estate.[69] It is likely that these individuals were buried in their clothes because the survivors knew the deceased had died from a contagious disease that could infect the survivors. One clothed man had gone to his grave with a tobacco pipe and spoon in his pocket or purse. The style of this pipe dates to circa 1610–30, suggesting the years when the burial ground was active (see p. 89).[70] A number of graveshafts appear to have been purposefully reused for second burials, and several burials actually cut through earlier burials, suggesting a significant time difference between the early and later burials and/or that no grave markers were used to identify individual graves.

The clothing, multiple burials, misalignment, careless disposal, shallowness of some graves, and the possible 1610 beginning date for the cemetery suggest that some burials indeed could date as early as the "starving time" winter of 1609–10. According to Smith, only sixty of 215 settlers survived that tumultuous winter. But disease was not the sole sign of trauma among the burials. Lead pistol balls were found in the skeletal levels of three graves, although none of the bullets was embedded in surviving bone in such a way

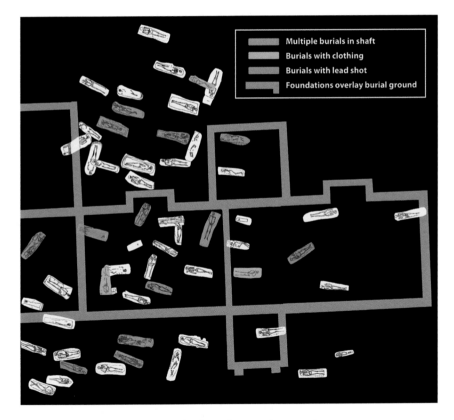

Record of the Statehouse Complex burial ground excavation, 2001.

as to prove death by gunshot. There is an outside chance that gravediggers dropped the bullets accidentally while filling the shafts. If that was the case, however, one would expect to find dropped lead balls at different levels in the fill as well. None was found. Most likely, then, these three people were indeed shot, their resulting injuries probably leading to their deaths.

Analysis of fifty of these graves gives more insight into the harsh James-town experience. While the age of death ranged from infancy to late for-ties, almost half of the population died in their twenties, men twenty-one to twenty-five, women twenty-six to thirty. Fourteen percent died before age two.[71] Most are adult males, but the sample also includes adolescents, young adults, and middle-aged adults. There is some evidence for child-hood malnutrition and disease. The development of muscle attachment sites on many of the skeletons indicates that when alive they had regularly engaged in strenuous physical activity. Initial impressions, therefore, sug-gest a mostly male, not so healthy, working-class population.

This was likely no potter's field. Seven people were buried in coffins, which were expensive to acquire and typically purchased only by wealthy families. Among the coffin forms used, two were trapezoidal (tapered), two were rectangular, and one was hexagonal. One of the seven coffins may not point to high status. A woman wearing copper hair styling, or cap wires, was found wedged in a narrow, reused wooden shipping crate. The rest of the people were unceremoniously wrapped only in shrouds or were completely uncovered. Initial analysis of the burials beneath the Statehouse Complex confirms that this burial ground held a true cross-section of the Jamestown population. Buried there until about 1630 were people from all walks of life. Some likely died during the winter of the "starving time," oth-ers during times of rampant disease, while still others died during times of conflict. Before these skeletal remains are reburied at Jamestown, ever-improving (if slow and expensive) forensic scientific analysis, including chemical and DNA testing, promises to establish more precisely the time of burial, the ages, the causes of death, other trauma that may have been suffered, the ratio of male to female and of immigrants to native-born, and perhaps even family relationships, among the signs of life still held in the graves at Jamestown.

Signs of life and death in bone at Jamestown have not all come from burials. Fill in the west bulwark trench, almost certainly thrown there after 1611 and maybe as late as Argall's rehabilitation of the town, contained not only the rich evidence of Anglo-Indian presence in the fort but also, and surprisingly, a third of a human skull. Enough of the complete skull was there to determine that it came from a middle-aged man who, before apparently dying as a result of a violent blow to the back of the head from a stone implement (like a stone axe), had undergone attempted surgery.[72] Two circular cuts into the skull before death indicate that the "chirurgeons" at Jamestown attempted to cut a nickel-sized hole in the victim's head, a process known as trepanning, apparently in order to relieve the pressure of a swelling brain. The drill never made it through the skull in either attempt; in fact, two cuts were made at one location, perhaps indicating that the patient could not be restrained enough to finish the job. The patient may have died in surgery, since there are signs that the surgeons decided to perform an autopsy, presumably to inspect and learn from the injured

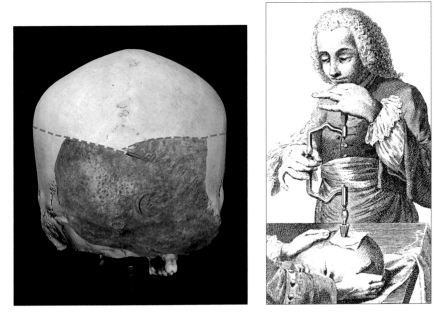

*Left:* Fill in the west bulwark trench yielded this rear section of a human skull amid discarded garbage and trash of ca. 1610. Forensic analysis determined this to be from a mature European man who may have died during a surgical procedure known as trepanning—an attempt to cure his broken skull by drilling a hole in it. Saw marks indicate the procedure was unsuccessful and that an autopsy was performed. *Right:* Eighteenth-century drawing illustrating the trepanning procedure initiated on at least one Jamestown colonist. (Science and Society Picture Library, London)

brain. The upper edge of the fragment had been sawn, the marks indicating the complete removal of the top of the man's skull. Forensic analysis was able to determine that the man was a European. The bone fabric was full of lead absorbed unknowingly through life by someone probably eating from lead-laden pewter or lead-glazed plates with pewter spoons and drinking from pewter or lead-glazed cups. A person carrying so much residual lead in his bones, and dying during the first years of the colony, would have to be an immigrant and certainly not a Virginia Indian.

Excavation of the rest of the ditch failed to reveal any more parts of a skeleton, so the single skull fragment must represent the medical waste of one of the surgeons. The rest of the body may well lie among the seventeen burials found beneath the nearby governor's house. This partial skull underscores again the great risk of living at Jamestown. It shows, too, that the chirurgeons were hard at work not only in trying to save the injured, but also in trying to improve their own skills.

The clear archaeological indications of death throughout the site of early Jamestown underscore the enormous courage it took to come to Jamestown from England during those first few years. There was danger from every quarter: salt in drinking water from the river, well water fouled from unsanitary use, disease from insects, empty food stores, accidents, warfare with the Virginia Indians, and, of course, jealousy and political battles within ranks. After the first few months of settlement, it is unlikely that the great risk for an "adventuring person" who wanted to join the Virginia colony was totally unknown back in England. One can only conclude that even the slim chance for a better life in Virginia outweighed the prospects of death amid the foul marshes at Jamestown or simply staying at home.

# FOUR

# REANIMATING JAMESTOWN

By studying the documentary records left behind by the Jamestown settlers, the four-hundred-year-old footprints of the fort the settlers built, and
the remains of the settlers themselves as well as the artifacts they created or
brought with them, we have been able to generate images of the built landscape of Jamestown and of those who dwelled in it. These varied remnants
have also deepened our understanding of many episodes in Jamestown's
history. These artifacts—especially the over 700,000 individual objects so
far discovered at Jamestown—can also shed light on the states of mind of
those who came to Jamestown. The things the settlers brought with them
and the things they created while at Jamestown are the most literal as well
as symbolic embodiments of what the adventurers thought they would
find in Virginia and how they adapted to what they did find. Perhaps even
more than the documentary, architectural, and skeletal evidence the colonists left behind, these artifacts enable us to trace a process that began the
transformation of Englishmen into Americans. All of these remnants of
Jamestown life yield the most meaning when juxtaposed to a document
that states explicitly the intentions and preconceptions of the Jamestown
colonists—the Virginia Company shareholders' instructions to the settlers.
This juxtaposition can help us take a fresh perspective on the colonists'
anticipations as well as their accomplishments, leading to a more complex
story than the simpler tale of poor preparation and incompetence.

It is undeniable that the Virginia Company officials and the adventurers
made some big mistakes. Wearing body armor in the blistering Virginia
summer certainly could take a far greater toll on the population than the

The Jamestown Rediscovery collection includes more than 700,000 artifacts, at least one-third found in undisturbed deposits dating to the early James Fort period (1607–10).

best Powhatan archer. Whatever food made it to the colonies must have quickly spoiled in the heat and humidity. And the crew that had to deal with these inappropriate supplies was described by John Smith as "poor gentlemen, tradesmen, serving men, libertines . . . ten times more fit to spoil a commonwealth than either to begin one or to help to maintain one."[1]

But we have already seen that poor preparation and incompetent management are hardly the whole story of what went on at Jamestown; they do not even suffice as explanation for the hardships the settlers suffered. We know, too, that Jamestown was not wholly a failure—that a permanent English presence in America did, in fact, take hold. Careful study in particular of artifacts great and small testifies to the level of skill and knowledge of both the Virginia Company leadership and its Jamestown adventurers, offering a new and potentially more objective way to learn what the colonists did, driven by the Virginia Company plan, for the well-being of themselves and their sponsors.

The Virginia Company crafted the instructions for settlement with which the colonists arrived on the Virginia shore before the would-be colonists even left England. This survival manual speaks most directly to the preparation the colonists received. Richard Hakluyt (1552–1616), a geographer, clergyman, translator, collector and editor of adventure narratives, and advocate for the westward expansion of English power, was most likely the author. He edited, translated, and inspired many volumes of first-hand narratives of adventure and discovery, the most notable of which are his *Divers Voyages* (1582), *Principal Navigations, Voiages, and Discoueries of the English Nation* (1589), and its second edition, much enlarged, *The Principal Navigations, Voiages, Traffiques and Discoueries of the English Nation* (three volumes, 1598, 1599, 1600). Thanks to Hakluyt, although the English at Jamestown were late in New World colonization, they would not face Virginia without benefit of the experience of those who went before them. In 1606 Hakluyt was likely one of the chief promoters of the petition to the king for a patent to colonize Virginia. When the ships, supplies, and men set sail from Blackwall for the voyage to Virginia, Hakluyt and the Company made sure they carried the "instructions to the colonists from the Virginia Company shareholders 1606" with them. These directives laid down precise rules for locating, defending, feeding, supporting, and ruling the Virginia colony. The list was well drawn, and, as it turned out, much of it was crucial advice.[2]

In the following summary, the Virginia Company's instructions can be organized by category:

*Location*

The strongest, most wholesome and fertile place is to be chosen, on a river that has a safe entrance harbor and is navigable farthest inland—

For defense, a town site is to be chosen 100 miles from the sea, if possible, or, if nearer, on an island; at a point on the river narrow enough to protect the settlement from ships by musket fire from both banks; and with no natives living between the site and the sea coast.

For trade, the town site should be near the river channel, providing easy access between ships and the shore.

For cultivation, the site should already be cleared of trees and undergrowth.

*Defense*

Scouts should be stationed at the river mouth.

Twenty men should be assigned to fortify the settlement.

Above all else, any death or sickness should be hidden, lest the Indians discover the settlers are mortal men.

Indians should never be allowed to carry the guns.

## Cultivation

Twenty men should be assigned to clear, cultivate, and plant.

Planting should not be done in low or marshy ground.

The Indians should not be offended, but traded with for corn, in order to conceal the colonists' own planting until it can be determined if the English corn will grow in Virginia.

## Economy

Forty men under Newport and Gosnold should be assigned to seek precious metals inland.

The high value of trade goods should be protected by prohibiting the wage-earning sailors or any other unauthorized persons from trading with the Indians.

## Governance

Sails and anchors should be taken off the ship to stop anyone from escaping the colony.

Official reports of the colony's progress should be sent to the Company.

No unauthorized person should be allowed to return to England.

All letters should be censured, deleting any discouraging words.

God should be served and feared or the colony will fail.[3]

Did the colonists follow these orders? And were the orders wise? As to the first question, the buried record of Jamestown makes a strong case that the settlers most often did obey the instructions. When they did not, it can often be established that they had good reason for diverging from the rules; in such cases, we can see these early English settlers beginning to transform themselves into Americans. On some occasions failure to honor the Company rules—whether by negligence or simply the inescapable facts the settlers confronted—attested to the wisdom of those rules by leading to regrettable consequences.

The exact location of the fort itself, as determined by archaeological excavation, indicates that the directives for choosing a settlement site were taken seriously. The James Fort site was, in fact, the strongest location for the settlement: an island defensible by its natural water hazard. The site also followed instructions in being located on a Virginia river that had a safe entrance harbor, reached the farthest inland, and had a deep-water channel close to shore. And the settlement was built on an abandoned, open Indian field.[4] But Jamestown was not one hundred miles from the sea, was not built at a narrow point in the river, and was certainly not lacking in native neighbors. How to account for these features of the island that should have disqualified it by Company standards?

The answer is simple. Rather than ignoring those qualities, the leaders, faced with the actual Virginia geography that confronted them, threw out the unrealistic terms of the shareholders. There simply is no Virginia river with a deep channel between banks that are musket-range apart (200 yards), one hundred miles from the sea. Nor was there any site up any river with no Indians living between it and the sea.

Unfortunately, meeting the first Company priority directive—a secure location—did lead the colonists to compromise on the second Company priority directive: a "wholesome" location. Swampy James Island is definitely not wholesome. The threat of attack from the Spanish and the reality of the initial Virginia Indian assaults appeared a greater threat to survival than any difficulty getting fresh water and fresh air. Still, the concern for a wholesome location was not jettisoned entirely. The Jamestown marshes were interspersed with enough rich and elevated ground to build a fortified town and to plant crops. The fort was built, as archaeology has discovered, on the island's highest ground. In addition, the river must have appeared fresh enough during that May landing time to make the lack of a freshwater spring on the island seem a minor drawback. So in choosing the location for their settlement, the colonists did follow some of the Company's wise advice while reasonably adapting the rest of it to the realities of the Virginia geography.

As to the Company's other instructions for achieving security, the signs in the ground make clear the men's attempt to follow the Company directive to "fortify." A bulwark made of tree branches went up at once. Virginia reality struck quickly, however. The Indian assault of May 25 made it quite clear that a brush fort would not do. There followed a frantic construction program that archaeology shows was nothing short of Herculean. Consider the following: If the council followed the Company directive to assign just twenty of the men to build the fort, then in just under three weeks' time, according to archaeological evidence, these few men, some likely even gentlemen, cut, hauled, divided, and sometimes split at least

Even relatively minor experimental attempts at cutting, hauling, and seating palisade posts have given Jamestown Rediscovery archaeologists insight into the Herculean efforts the original colonists undertook to build James Fort in only nineteen days.

*The New World* movie set, based on some of the Jamestown Rediscovery architectural evidence, accurately depicts James Fort of 1607 and its early shelters. (*The New World*, copyright MMVI, New Line Productions, Inc. All rights reserved. Photo courtesy of New Line Productions, Inc.)

610 four- to eight-hundred-pound trees, then dug a trench at least 1,030 feet long and two and a half feet deep to seat them in. That meant each of the twenty men had to fell, haul, dig, and plant one or two trees a day, and so a total of twenty to forty, for nineteen days straight (May 28–June 15, 1607) in what would likely have been a hot, humid Virginia early summer.[5] For comparison purposes, it might be noted that the contractors who built the Jamestown set for the New Line Cinema film *The New World* in 2004 also constructed a triangular palisaded fort, slightly smaller than the original, with trees of the same size, in about three weeks—using power equipment. And at the same time, the settlers split trees for enough clapboards (rough planks) to load the three ships returning to England. Little

An iron scupper found in the east bulwark, a special seventeenth-century tool for digging the narrow, deep trenches required to seat palisades.

wonder that by August Percy listed exertion from carrying palisades as one of the causes of the rash of deaths afflicting the new outpost. Although at a great cost, the men were successful at least in this: they had fortified themselves against Indian attack. Arrows do not seem to account for many of the losses.

Archaeological investigation has also made it clear that whoever did perish very early on was buried inside the fort. The settlers' losses would be out of sight, just as the Company directed. There was one exception, however: the burial of Gosnold, the captain. His grave, outside the fort walls, looks like a big mistake, a refusal to follow the Company's overarching rule never to let the enemy see death and sickness. Advertising weakness, especially the death of a leader ceremoniously buried, could indeed convince the Indians that the English were not immortal—that they were, in fact, in dire straits behind the walls. There is a plausible explanation for Captain Gosnold's very visible funeral, however. Perhaps the funeral with all its pomp and gunfire was meant to be not only a proper farewell to the Jamestown prime mover but also a feinting show of force to the enemy. In any case, someone as revered as Gosnold had to get the full traditional twenty-one-gun salute and the traditional space of honor outside the fort/town walls in Smithfield, the military parade ground. Still, even if the honor shown Gosnold was strategically unwise in the New World context, all of the other twenty-one burials located so far that can be dated to the very earliest fort occupation are located within the fort walls. As the Company had advised, deaths were hidden from the enemy—or at least, they were for a while. Discovery of the circa 1610–30 mass burial ground on the high ground far west of the fort shows that the Indians soon enough would have learned not to buy the immortality charade.

Of course, the best way for the Company to hide from the Indians any physical problems was to make sure there were none. In preparation for fighting health hazards, the Company sent medicines, physicians, pharmacists, and surgeons. These professions combined to make up the healing arts of the time: the surgeons cut, the physicians collected and philosophized, and the apothecaries drugged.[6] There are archaeological signs of the presence and the practice of these healers at Jamestown. Drug jars (alberellos) are the most numerous of pottery vessels in the artifact collection, and they are commonly found among the oldest deposits. Used by apothecaries—two of whom were named among the first supply—these vessels were designed as containers for medicines and salves. It is likely that the settlers had access to whatever medicines were considered helpful against the known diseases of the times. The Company also sent a leading university-trained physician, a plant and herb specialist named John Fleischer. He likely searched the alien Virginia wilderness for new miracle cures, but there is no record that he succeeded before dying himself in 1608. Still, it is logical to assume that some of these alberellos were intended to double as containers for the export of any new medical discoveries. As it turned out, however, great quantities of sassafras, thought to be a cure for syphilis, are the only documented Virginia medicine sent back to England.

Medical instruments and what can be considered medical waste from an operation testify to the presence of surgeons and their practice. The spatula mundani, an iron tool used to cure constipation, and part of a boring instrument used to extract bullets were found, both surgeon's instruments that could have come from a surgeon's tool chest sent to the colony in 1609. The most graphic archaeological sign of surgery, however, was the human skull fragment found in the fill of the west bulwark ditch, circa 1609–12 (see chap. 3). The three circular marks on the bone are clear signs that someone, likely one of the surgeons, attempted to heal the man by performing trepanation (drilling a hole in the skull to relieve pressure and remove bone

Delft drug jars, made to hold medicines and salves, are the most common European pottery form recovered from James Fort–period deposits.

splinters) before he finally died. Death did not stop the surgeons, the saw marks on the upper edge of the skull fragment indicating an attempt to study the effects of the injury by an autopsy. The surgeons were actively pursuing their practice even in the harsh conditions under which they had to operate.

Did the settlers follow the Company regulations by keeping guns out of the hands of Indians? There is no archaeological evidence to speak to that question. We cannot know, for example, if Indians or colonists pulled the trigger to kill JR102C or the three others lying in the unmarked burial ground west of the fort. From hints in the documents as well as from the discovery of great numbers of contact-period Indian artifacts (like pottery) and signs of the Indian manufacture of stone tools, weapons, and shell beads, we do know that some Indians were inside the palisade walls. Weapons were surely within their reach at any time. John Smith complained about the Dutch glassmakers instructing the Indians in the use of firearms. Smith wrote as well of Indian brothers stealing pistols and of an Indian who accidentally turned into a suicide bomber when he tried to dry out powder on a breastplate over an open fire. So the arms restriction, an obviously key Company directive, seems to have been ignored in the long run by the colonials, if not at first, then eventually. That was a tragic mistake. In the 1622 Indian revolt, some of the Indians living in close contact with

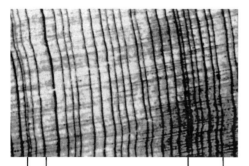

| Lost Colony | Jamestown |
| Drought: | Drought: |
| 1587–1589 | 1606–1612 |

Bald cypress growth-ring stress indicates two droughts, each during the very difficult years of English attempts at Virginia settlement. (The University of Arkansas Tree-Ring Laboratory)

English settlements in the Virginia hinterlands actually used the colonists' own weapons and iron-cutting tools against them.[7] On the other hand, the Jamestown home base was spared by an Indian forewarning. In the end, despite the neglect of this particular rule, James Fort itself never fell to an enemy during its lifetime.

As for the colonists' attention to Company rules relating to cultivation, archaeology gives some clues. The discovery of palisade lines branching out from the triangular footprint of the fort suggests the existence of protected spaces outside the fort, likely locations for gardens. The flag-shaped enclosure on the Zúñiga map is probably one such garden, located on easily secured high ground near the fort. The choice of such a location indicates an effort by the twenty assigned farmers to avoid clearing and planting in low marshy ground, just as the Company advised. The garden depicted on the Zúñiga map also seems to include carefully divided rectangular planting beds. This evidence lends credibility to Percy's report that the colonists had planted two mountains (ridges) that by mid-July produced corn that "sprang a man's height" despite the late planting in the middle of May.[8] Crop failure must have followed, however. Famine is the primary culprit Percy cited in his listing of the deaths of twenty-five gentlemen in August and September. The 1606–13 drought, recently discovered by archaeologists, must have gone against any chance of success for the late planting.[9]

Artifacts discovered in the fort attest to the colonists' effort to obey another of the Company's rules regarding cultivation, that early gardening attempts be hidden until the viability of the English seeds in Virginia soil had been determined. These artifacts—European beads of glass and copper, jettons, and squares of sheet copper, all undoubtedly traded to the more accommodating Indians in exchange for corn—show the colonists' effort to conceal their own efforts at self-sufficiency. Indian-made bowls found among the colonists' rubbish and trash possibly were the means of getting the corn into the fort.

Samples of the collection of copper found in ca.-1607–10 fort deposits. Captain John Smith reported of the great value of copper and glass beads in the earliest trade for food between colonists and Powhatan's Tsenacomacans.

A variety of trade beads.

As this late sixteenth-century painting depicts, copper pendants were worn by the coastal Virginia Indians. There is evidence that the colonists at Jamestown brought great quantities of copper with them to Virginia to trade for food. (From *The American Drawings of John White*, vol. 2; copyright The Trustees of the British Museum)

Among the artifacts that tell the most about the colonists' efforts to fulfill the charge of the shareholders are the many signs of manufacture for profit.[10] After all, Jamestown came into being for one overarching reason: to make money for the Virginia Company investors. Fortification and self-sufficiency were to be achieved primarily so that the settlers could turn their attention to generating whatever Virginia had to offer for export. The artifacts unearthed at Jamestown give plentiful proof of the colonists' focus on this mission.

Again the first ships home carried the most readily available commodity for export, split planks. Well-used iron axes and wedges found in the early deposits are evidence for the production of these rough boards. Excavations also uncovered signs of early pit sawing. Just short of the point where the west fort palisade line met the now eroded shoreline, digging revealed a rectangular pit containing what appeared to be decayed sawdust at the bottom. This regularly shaped and backfilled hole lay beneath a ditch parallel to the fort—the latter apparently the beginning of a bulwark ditch, since its shape mirrors that of its sister defensive outwork at the south corner of the triangle (see p. 60). The fact that the sawdust-filled, squared pit lay beneath the bulwark ditch shows that the saw pit was set up very early in the fort's life. Pit sawing was a simple way to produce wainscot (fairly dressed planks), another timber product to send home. These pits were operated by two men, one at the upper and one at the lower end of the saw, who alternately pulled down and pushed on the saw handles to carve boards from logs laid between their stations. Toiling with timber for export was certainly in keeping with Company policy.

The fort was also meant to serve as the base from which forty men under the command of Christopher Newport and Bartholomew Gosnold could probe inland for precious metals—especially for gold. The president and council did indeed send men upriver, probably to conduct the Company-directed "mineral search." Voyages to the hinterlands of the Chesapeake and its rivers followed. No gold turned up, although "gold refiners" and mineral men came to Jamestown in 1608–10, probably bringing with them the metallurgical equipment found during the excavations of the earliest deposits.[11] These included the lower ceramic boiler (cucurbit) and the upper glass-collecting cover (the alembic) from a still (possibly intended to create the nitric acid required for separating gold from silver), distilling dishes, dippers, and melting crucibles. Whether this equipment was ever used or was just broken and tossed away as the dreams of gold proved unfounded cannot be known. Still, the colonists arrived equipped for prospecting, however unrealistic their hopes.

Another of the Company's hopes for getting rich quick lay in the discovery and export of precious stones. While diamonds and rubies were not to be found, among the artifacts datable to James Fort's first three years are a number of colorful semiprecious stones such as amethysts, garnets, and quartz crystals. These were possibly appraised—undoubtedly to great disappointment—by the jewelers the Company sent to Jamestown in 1608.

Site of a saw pit at the west bulwark.

Another scheme for exploiting minerals was the making of brass, which required copper and zinc. Certain Company shareholders were connected with the English copper industry, and over 8,000 strips and shavings of English copper were found on site, most in 1607–10 contexts.[12] There is no doubt that some of the copper was there to trade with the Indians for corn, venison, fish, and fowl, a plan that quickly fell apart when the sailors flooded the market with copper, leading to its devaluation. The Company's explicit warning against such an eventuality apparently either went unheeded or was out of the colonists' control, but the wisdom of that warning was demonstrated by the event. The devaluation of copper seriously added to the food shortage. However, much of this hoard of copper scraps was likely sent to Jamestown to be processed with Virginia zinc into brass for export. Crucibles with copper residue and a plug of copper from a crucible show that these scraps were used in experiments in the colony. Was brass produced? There is no processed brass in the archaeological collection, implying that this hope, too, proved false. A report by Don Pedro de Zúñiga as early as August 22, 1607, confirms that the colonists hoped to find the material to make the copper alloy "bronce" (brass).[13] In any case, archaeological evidence demonstrates that the colonists made a concerted effort to live up to the Company's industrial expectations.

Documents and artifacts also give hard evidence of the Company's hope for profit from another industry: glassmaking. In 1608 "eight Dutchmen" and a "Pole"—probably meaning Germans—arrived at Jamestown at Com-

An alchemist surrounded by his metallurgy equipment; similar pieces have been found at Jamestown. (*The Alchemist,* Cornelis Pietersz Bega, Haarlem 1631–1664, Eddlemann Collection, 00.03.01, Chemical Heritage Foundation Collections, Philadelphia; photo by Will Brown)

Evidence of copper smelting, which may have been used in attempts to produce brass.

*Below:* Ceramics made for metallurgy found at Jamestown, including a distilling dish (*left front*), earthenware dipper (*center*), and German crucibles.

pany expense, sent there to make "trials" of glass as well as pitch, tar, and soap ash. Evidence of glassmaking at the fort site abounds. Among the collections are heat-resistant clay crucibles and melting pots containing melted sand and glass residue, glassmaking slag (froth), and over 7,000 pieces of European window-glass "cullet" (broken fragments typically used during glass manufacture)—all clear signs that the Germans practiced their craft. In two short months, enough had been produced for a "trial of glass," probably ingots, to be sent back to England. It does appear, however, that the industry was short-lived: the "Dutchmen" eventually threw their lot in with the Indians and smuggled weapons. This life of espionage ended with the death of the imported glassmakers at the hands of the natives by late 1609. Apparently no other attempt at glass production was made until the Company sent Italian glassmakers to Virginia in 1620. A site of glass furnaces made of cobble was found on the mainland next to the Jamestown Island isthmus by National Park Service archaeologists in the 1940s.[14] They concluded that this effort was also short-lived; no evidence was found that this operation produced anything more than glass ingots.

The recovery of a multitude of locally made clay tobacco pipes and pieces of a broken ceramic vessel (a sagger) used in pottery firing indicate more efforts to live up to the Company business plan. Pipemaker Robert Cotton was sent to Virginia with the second supply in 1608. There is every reason to believe that the distinctive pipe type found everywhere in deposits dating to the early fort period—made of local clay and impressed with a multiple fleur-de-lis diamond-shaped mark—was molded by Cotton and fired in his small saggers. These pipes, along with bricks found in the same early deposits and in fort building hearths, must represent the first successfully mass-produced, finished commodity of Anglo-America. The pipes were also apparently exported, for an identical example was found in the English city of Plymouth.[15]

Virginia-grown tobacco, of course, eventually came along to fill the colonial pipes and to give the Company and individual settlers a return on time and money.[16] But it was years before a tobacco strain was discovered that would produce sufficient bulk for export. That might be why hoes are conspicuously absent in deposits dating before 1610, although the circa-1620s well held three, all of them narrow grubbing hoes suited for tending tobacco fields.

The colony's economic viability required a number of support industries, and the Company accordingly sent out a number of skilled men—carpen-

Evidence of glassmaking at James Fort includes crucibles with melted sand and glass in them and broken fragments of English window-glass waste (cullet), brought over to aid in the glassmaking trials at Jamestown.

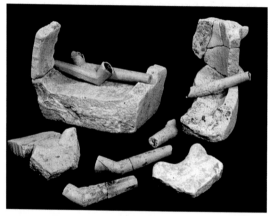

These distinctive tobacco pipes and fragments of a pottery-making device known as a sagger suggest that the 1608 colonist Robert Cotton, "tobacco-pipe-maker," made these, one of the first commercial Jamestown products.

Two hoes, perhaps for tobacco cultivation, from the Smithfield well, which was filled during the beginning of the Virginia tobacco boom.

ters, blacksmiths, brickmakers, bricklayers and masons, coopers, tailors, hunters and fishermen—many of whom left their mark on the archaeological record.[17] Felling axes, hatchets, and gouges, all tools of carpentry primarily for the gathering, dressing, and joining of timbers and boards, were found. Blacksmithing left its traces in slag, waste iron, and some finished products. The "clinker" that appeared in practically every 1607–24 deposit is another sign of working iron. The smiths also adapted standard body armor, such as breastplates, to the Indian guerrilla warfare they faced. The plates were cut up to make more flexible arrow-proof jackets, and gun support tabs riveted to breastplates made them more fit for the musketeers. Smiths hammered one breastplate into a bucket or kettle, and the recovery of a horseshoe from one of the earliest contexts on the site, the store cellar, indicates that one blacksmith typically doubled as a farrier. Waste nail rod suggests that the local smiths produced some of the over 70,000 nails recovered during the excavations as well.

Fragments of brick in every early site, including at least five hearths in the earliest buildings, suggest the two bricklayers listed among the original settlers also made bricks. While no evidence of brick firing was uncovered, these bricks were likely to have been made in Virginia. Space in the ships' holds was far too valuable to waste on inexpensive bricks. Virginia clay is ideal for brick manufacture as well.[18] On the other hand, the mason who arrived with the original settlers must have been frustrated by the lack of natural stone in the immediate environs. He and his successors did find enough by 1610–11 to build the cobble-footed rowhouses dating to that time found along the fort's western wall—probably the governor's residence. The presence of a probable medieval building block in that footing does, however, show that ballast from England could wind up as building materials at Jamestown.[19]

Excavations also recovered evidence of barrelmaking—likely for domestic as well as export use—and tailoring. One cooper left in the ground his "croze iron," a special type of plane that carves out the locking-groove for barrelheads, and the handle of a "bung hole" drill. Other wood-shaping devices such as a broad axe and an adze could be signs of the cooper's craft. Tailors left their mark on the site by losing over nine hundred straight pins, fifty-five sewing needles, fourteen brass thimbles, and two hundred buttons made of brass, iron, and glass. One cluster of eight buttons attached to a thimble was once apparently part of a tailor's kit. Although these particular copper buttons must have dropped from the tailor's own supply,

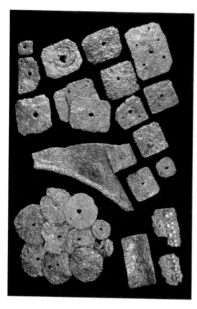

Blacksmiths were busy at Jamestown making body armor known as jacks of plate out of the more rigid and less maneuverable breastplates (*center*).

A breastplate recycled into a basin.

another elaborate button of blown glass must have come from the attire of a very high-status person, perhaps from a councilor's doublet (vest). More than seventy-six lead "bale" seals are further evidence of tailoring. These seals were clinched to rolls or bales of cloth for a variety of reasons, such as to identify place of manufacture or of dyeing, tax status, or length of the roll.

There were no Company directives concerning hunting or fishing. That obvious survival strategy needed no urging since instruction in sport hunting and fishing was standard for gentlemen in England.[20] Artifacts from the excavation include not only the gear required for hunting and fishing but also butchered bones of native Virginia animals and marine life. Although the guns colonists brought were primarily heavy weapons, intended for defense, they undoubtedly were used to acquire some of the fourteen species of wild birds and eight species of wild mammals whose butchered bones were identified in the earliest archaeological deposits.[21] Marine bones and shells abound as well in the garbage deposits of early Jamestown, including twenty-five species of fish and reptiles. While there is much complaint in documentary sources about the lack of fishing skill and equipment, the variety of fish hooks, net weights, and line sinkers in the Rediscovery collections is evidence that the Company did at least supply the colonists with the means to exploit the marine resources for survival. In fact, to judge by representation in one circa-1610 deposit, wild sources made up over half the meat diet. These signs of a wildlife menu seem to contradict Smith's complaint that "[t]hough there be fish in the sea, fouls in the air, and beasts in the woods their bounds are so large, they so wild and we so weak and ignorant we cannot much trouble them."[22] Or was all of this food from the wild acquired by trade with the Indians?

As the Company directed, Newport was in charge until the settlers touched land, at which time a sealed box was opened to identify six governing councilors. These six plus the ex-officio Newport elected a president for a one-year term: Edward Maria Wingfield. The real power, however, lay in the council in England, and the all-powerful final vote belonged to James I. This reality left the resident leader, Wingfield, with unclear authority, subject to removal at the whim of the council. Wingfield was indeed removed, on the charge of hoarding food, after the disastrous summer of 1607 when about half the original settlers died. Archaeology has opened a window on that chaos, revealing the gravesites and burials of the gentlemen who perished by that first September.

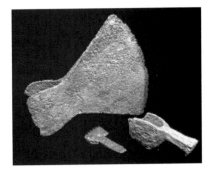

Tools for barrel making including a croze iron used to make barrelhead fastening grooves.

The Company's decision to transfer the seat of power from far-off England directly to Jamestown—another accommodation to New World realities—also left its signs in the ground. Transfer of power came to the fort in the form of the first substantially constructed timber-framed cobble-based rowhouses, one likely fit for a true resident governor. Such a building undoubtedly was intended to command more respect from the men and the Virginia Indians alike.

Construction of the substantial church described in 1608 also showed that the settlers took their charge to colonize "in the name of God" seriously. This early church has yet to be found in the unexcavated area of the fort site. It is curious, however, that almost all the religious artifacts in the Rediscovery collections are Catholic. The sole exception is the hardware from a very thick book, likely a Bible in Robert Hunt's library, burned in the fire of 1608.

Documentary sources prove that the colonists, as required by the Company, sent home periodic official reports. Archaeological discoveries from the

Collection of carpenters' tools recovered at James Fort, including dividers, a felling axe, a hatchet, a socket chisel, and two files.

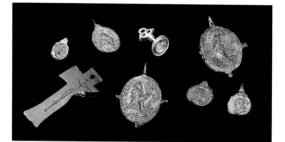

A number of religious objects found at the fort site in a variety of time contexts, including a jet (hard coal) cross depicting a curious stick-figure crucifixion, rosary medallions, and a silver seal with the scallop sign of St. James.

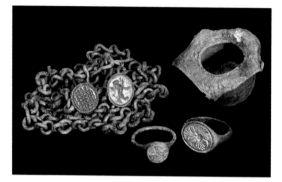

Signs of literacy at Jamestown include (*from left*) two wax seals—a "portcullis" (castle gate) and a standing lion—and a seal chain; two rings—a merchants' sign and a "displayed eagle" signet; and a lead inkwell. The eagle ring may well have belonged to William Strachey, secretary of the colony in 1610–11 and probable friend of William Shakespeare.

A collection of objects used by tailors, including (*from left to right and top to bottom*) an iron, thimbles, decorative copper aglets for laces, straight pins, scissors and sheers, lead cloth seals, and glass and copper buttons.

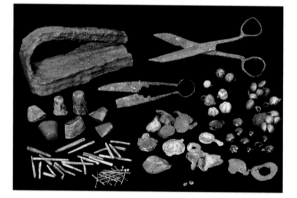

Hunting and fishing tools were plentiful at Jamestown despite Smith's claim that many gentlemen were not skilled with them.

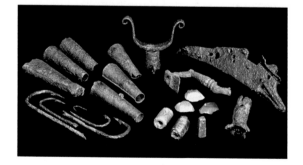

early years of Jamestown include the means for writing such reports: an ink well, pencils, seals, and signet rings. A ring with a crossed eagle, possibly the family crest of William Strachey, is the most dramatic of all of the signet rings for stamping wax seals. Whether discouraging words were censored is harder to establish from documents alone. Certainly, some of Strachey's prose as well as Percy's gruesome reports suggest that the Company directives to paint Jamestown in the best possible light were ignored at times—probably to the detriment of the colony. Still, the negative reports never seemed to stop immigration. All the archaeological signs show the growth and expansion of Jamestown throughout the Company's existence and beyond, until the end of the century.

Documents, architectural remains, and especially artifacts recently recovered at the site of early Jamestown reflect a very busy place, as the settlers, following the instructions they were sent with, sought to make the Virginia Company a profitable enterprise—primarily by establishing a secure colony from which to export whatever Virginia had to offer that would turn a profit. That security almost immediately required the construction of an armed camp. From this fortified town, supported by domestic industry and trade, materials for export were manufactured or searched out by explorers. Security, exploration, and trade required soldiers, manufacturers, merchants, and craftsmen, all of whom were numbered among the settlers. This military and industrial trading center was above all else supposed to become an English colony, literally and figuratively a "New England." Little wonder then that the artifact collection found among the ruins of earliest Jamestown is rich in evidence of a robust, multifaceted community.

Eyewitness descriptions of life at early Jamestown detail other activities that kept the colonists busy. For instance, the men collected sassafras roots and "gilded" soil (soil they thought contained gold) to stock the homeward bound ships. Settlers also built two blockhouses near the fort.[23] The church and the store seemed to be continually repaired or rebuilt. On special days the colonists attended church or court or entertained a visiting emissary from the Powhatan chiefdom. When a supply ship was in port, colonists bargained with seamen for food and whatever luxuries they could get their hands on. The English drilled with their arms, took target practice, stood watch, and mounted ordnance.

All this activity attests to the careful preparation and the hard work of the Jamestown settlers. If that preparation and that work did not always suffice to meet the original objectives of the Virginia Company, the cause for such failures was sometimes negligence, but perhaps most often facts of the New World the settlers found—facts of climate, geography, geology—were to blame. In observing the adaptations made both by the settlers and by the Company in the effort to accommodate these facts, we are witnessing the birth of the first Anglo-Americans.

It is also true, however, that some of the failures can be laid at the feet of the settlers themselves. Not all of Jamestown's gentlemen acted for the greater good: some spent their time black-marketeering and living high on the hog. These were "the saint-seeming worthies of Virginia."[24] But research has demonstrated the undeniable presence of devoted and diligent men, dedicated to the purposes of the colony. These were the truly saintly worthies of Virginia. As a result of their efforts, Jamestown would live on to become the first permanent English settlement in the New World.

# FIVE

# ROYAL JAMESTOWN

In 1624/25 a census showed a total of 1,232 colonists living in Virginia (at least 120 families) in twenty-nine settlements scattered along the James River from Hampton Roads to the Falls.[1] Of these, a total of 121 men, women, and children lived at Jamestown. Most of these 1,232 were the lucky survivors of a massive surprise attack by the Tsenacomacans that had killed 347 colonists two years earlier. Jamestown itself had been spared by an early warning, but the massacre was the final death blow to the Virginia Company: the company was dissolved, and the colony was taken over directly by the Crown.

Although it cannot be disputed that the Virginia Company failed in Virginia, politically as well as financially, the 1,232 colonists of 1624 did not call it quits. They did not go home, nor were they "lost" like their English predecessors of the ill-fated Fort Raleigh colony. For these survivors, Virginia lived on. Strangely, in defeat the Company had succeeded. Jamestown endured.

The fort became a port and Jamestown the capital of the Royal Colony of Virginia, 1624–98. Clearly, there have to be buried signs of life on Jamestown Island after the disappearance of the 1607–24 James Fort. People at Jamestown continued to build houses, go about their daily lives, and add layers to the archaeological soil of the town. And surprisingly, so did Jamestown's politicians. This chapter focuses on what those layers can tell us about Jamestown's and Virginia's government.

Just as Jamestown claims its place among America's premier historic sites as the first enduring English settlement in North America, it also rates national prominence for being the place where the first elected representative government met in English America. The first phase of the story of American democracy begins with the meeting of the first General Assembly in 1619 at the Jamestown church and ends in 1698, with the burning of the Jamestown Statehouse Complex and the move of the state capital to Williamsburg.[2] The nature of the Jamestown meeting places reflects that democracy's evolutionary growth, starting in borrowed space in a building designed for worship and ending in a building complex designed specifically for self-government—with its attached and largely publicly owned living spaces, arguably the largest colonial public building (23,000 square feet) ever built in what would become the United States of America.

Virginia's first governmental assemblies, from 1619 to 1643, comprised a unicameral body consisting of the governor appointed by the Crown, the twelve-member council appointed by the governor, and the burgesses elected from the various plantations and Jamestown. These earliest assemblies, modeled not on the English Parliament but on the Virginia Company's governing body, had quite limited authority. Only after the London-based Virginia Company went bankrupt in 1624 did the General Assembly of the Virginia colony gradually take on the characteristics of a representative legislature.

In 1643 Governor Berkeley encouraged the burgesses to sit apart from the Council of State. Thus was born the House of Burgesses. This decision, of course, made necessary a separate space for each body to meet, and possibly separate buildings. Once split into the two bodies, the governance model in the colony became

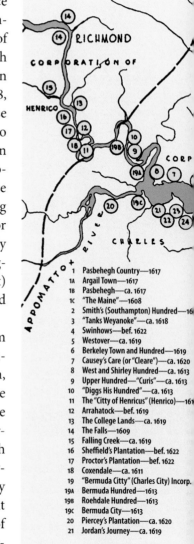

1  Pasbehegh Country—1617
1A  Argail Town—1617
1B  Pasbehegh—ca. 1617
1C  "The Maine"—1608
2  Smith's (Southampton) Hundred—161
3  "Tanks Weyanoke"—ca. 1618
4  Swinhows—bef. 1622
5  Westover—ca. 1619
6  Berkeley Town and Hundred—1619
7  Causey's Care (or "Cleare")—ca. 1620
8  West and Shirley Hundred—ca. 1613
9  Upper Hundred—"Curis"—ca. 1613
10  "Diggs His Hundred"—ca. 1613
11  The "Citty of Henricus" (Henrico)—161
12  Arrahatock—bef. 1619
13  The College Lands—ca. 1619
14  The Falls—1609
15  Falling Creek—ca. 1619
16  Sheffield's Plantation—bef. 1622
17  Proctor's Plantation—bef. 1622
18  Coxendale—ca. 1611
19  "Bermuda Citty" (Charles City) Incorp.
19A  Bermuda Hundred—1613
19B  Roehdale Hundred—1613
19C  Bermuda City—1613
20  Piercey's Plantation—ca. 1620
21  Jordan's Journey—ca. 1619

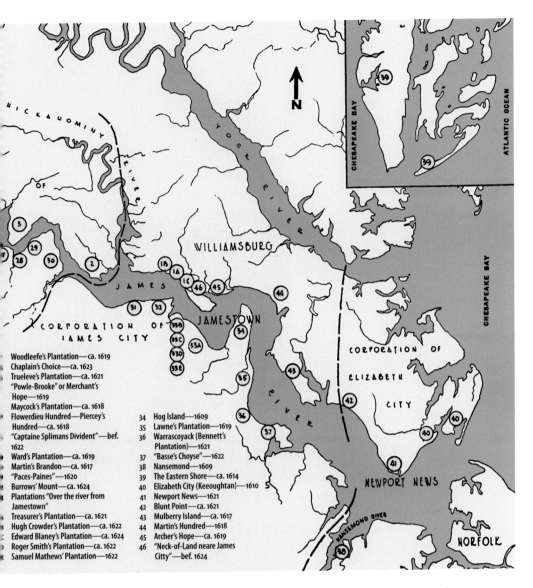

N

HICKAHOMINY

YORK RIVER

CHESAPEAKE BAY

ATLANTIC OCEAN

CHESAPEAKE BAY

OF

3
29
28 30 2

WILLIAMSBURG

1B
1A
1C 46 45

JAMES

44

39

39

31 32

CORPORATION OF
JAMES CITY

JAMESTOWN

33A

34

CORPORATION OF
ELIZABETH CITY

33B

33C 33A

33D

43

42 40

40

33E

35

RIVER

Woodleefe's Plantation—ca. 1619
Chaplain's Choice—ca. 1623
Trueleve's Plantation—ca. 1621
"Powle-Brooke" or Merchant's
Hope—1619
Maycock's Plantation—ca. 1618
Flowerdieu Hundred—Piercey's
Hundred—ca. 1618
"Captaine Splimans Divident"—bef.
1622
Ward's Plantation—ca. 1619
Martin's Brandon—ca. 1617
"Paces-Paines"—1620
Burrows' Mount—ca. 1624
Plantations "Over the river from
Jamestown"
Treasurer's Plantation—ca. 1621
Hugh Crowder's Plantation—ca. 1622
Edward Blaney's Plantation—ca. 1624
Roger Smith's Plantation—ca. 1622
Samuel Mathews' Plantation—1622

34   Hog Island—1609
35   Lawne's Plantation—1619
36   Warrascoyack (Bennett's
       Plantation)—1621
37   "Basse's Choyse"—1622
38   Nansemond—1609
39   The Eastern Shore—ca. 1614
40   Elizabeth City (Keeoughtan)—1610
41   Newport News—1621
42   Blunt Point—ca. 1621
43   Mulberry Island—ca. 1617
44   Martin's Hundred—1618
45   Archer's Hope—ca. 1619
46   "Neck-of-Land neare James
       Citty"—bef. 1624

36

37

41

NEWPORT NEWS

NANSEMOND RIVER

38

NORFOLK

Virginia settlement locations, 1607–20s. (Colored and adapted from the National Park Service book *The First Seventeen Years: Virginia, 1607–1624* by Charles E. Hatch Jr., 1957)

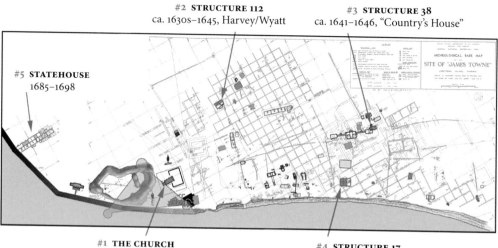

**#2 STRUCTURE 112**
ca. 1630s–1645, Harvey/Wyatt

**#3 STRUCTURE 38**
ca. 1641–1646, "Country's House"

**#5 STATEHOUSE**
1685–1698

**#1 THE CHURCH**
1619–1630s

**#4 STRUCTURE 17**
ca. 1646–1665, Berkeley Row "late/Old State Houses"

Sites where the government met at seventeenth-century Jamestown. (National Park Service, Colonial National Historical Park)

more like the English Parliament, though there were still profound differences between the General Assembly in Jamestown and the Westminster legislature in London. The General Assembly in far-off Virginia grew largely independent of direction from London and reached its zenith of power in the 1660s and 1670s. The 1676 uprising against Virginia's governor, Sir William Berkeley, and the subsequent burning of Jamestown during Bacon's Rebellion, caused the Crown to interfere in the Assembly's business thereafter, with the result that the Assembly lost much of its independence. The principal occupation of the General Assembly became the enactment of statutes that governed the colony's business. Through the process of legislating, however, the colonials acquired the skills to govern themselves.[3]

The first elected burgesses at Jamestown met July 30–August 4, 1619, in the only building large enough at the time to accommodate a sizable group meeting: the Jamestown church, where "the most convenient place we could finde to sit in was the Quire of the churche."[4] Tradition places that first Statehouse/church immediately adjacent to and east of the seventeenth-century brick church tower, still standing. The church in 1619 was not built of brick, nor is the existing tower an original part of that early church. The first reference to the construction of a brick church appears in 1639. The building seems to have been under construction until as late as 1646.

The original church was a mere sailcloth awning, which evolved into a more permanent timber structure in 1608, which appears to have seen a number of years of neglect, until it was rebuilt in 1617.[5] This rebuilt 1617 church was the site of the first Assembly two years later.

Jamestown Church excavation, 1901.

Archaeological evidence that the church of 1617 was technically the first "Statehouse" may have been found during excavations adjacent to the tower, led by Mary Jeffery Galt from 1893 to 1903.[6] Galt wrote that "with her own hands" she had uncovered two brick foundations next to the standing tower: a brick-on-cobblestone footing and a later, shorter, and slightly less wide foundation. Since the dimensions of the brick/cobble foundation seemed to match those specified for the church built by Christopher Newport's sailors in 1608, this footing may have once supported that church.[7] This, Galt concluded, was not the place where the General Assembly first met, as a smaller church replaced it in 1617. It was in that church, presumably on this same site, where the Assembly continued to gather in the choir loft until it outgrew the space.[8]

Mary Jeffery Galt, APVA founder and Jamestown's first archaeologist.

If we believe the later Virginia governor, Sir John Harvey, by 1629 some or all governmental meetings wound up taking place in his house. He complained in 1632 that "his" house had served as the colony's statehouse at his expense for three years running. Harvey might have meant that he held the quarterly council meetings there while the full Assembly met annually in the church (until construction of the new brick church commenced in 1639). Despite Harvey's objections, there is good reason to suppose that Harvey's house continued serving the

Artist's reconstruction of Governor Harvey's house. (National Park Service, Colonial National Historical Park)

government as "State house" (his words) throughout his tenure at Jamestown and even after he left office and Virginia. In 1641 the Virginia government bought Harvey's home lot, which included a "tenement now used as a courthouse and one piece or plot of ground lying and being on the west side of the said capital."[9] Recent land plat research suggests that the Harvey house/Statehouse was located where a substantial house foundation appeared during NPS excavations in 1954–56.[10] This foundation, labeled Structure 112, had supported a sizable building for Jamestown at the time. The digging revealed a construction date in Harvey's governorship, during the second quarter of the seventeenth century. The conclusion that this building was Harvey's house/Statehouse is also strengthened by the archaeological recovery of a plaster leopard's head; that symbol was part of Harvey's family coat-of-arms.[11]

In 1639 King Charles I of England instructed Sir Francis Wyatt, Harvey's successor, to build "a convenient house for the meeting of the council and dispatch of public charge."[12] Until 1643 the burgesses and the council had met together, so this building was apparently intended as the sole meeting place for the Virginia governmental body. There is no direct evidence that Wyatt carried out this mandate. In fact, as late as 1644, a land patent was granted to merchant/burgess John White for half an acre of land relatively close to Structure 112 and bordering on land "appertaining to the state-house" on the east. This description suggests that the former Harvey house and lot, located northeast of and apparently contiguous to the White property, still functioned as the Statehouse.[13] Alternatively, the Harvey house could have been put back in government service in 1643 after the governor, Sir William Berkeley, had the burgesses agree to meet separately from the council.[14]

After 1643 the separated House of Burgesses' need for its own meeting space could have necessitated a totally separate building. It is possible that a building referred to as the "country's house" (i.e., a building belonging to the "country of Virginia") may have served the council and court, while Harvey's old house (Structure 112), now publicly owned, likely would have been used by the new House of Burgesses.

In any event, land records and archaeological excavations in 1934–41 appear to locate the "country's house" some 350 feet from the river toward the western end of New Town.[15] The 53' × 20' foundation of a brick house found there (labeled Structure 38 by NPS archaeologists) could well be the remains of this "country's house," which served as a meeting place for the Virginia colony's council and court until 1652, when a directive was issued calling for it to be repaired "and the cellars [let] for the public benefit."[16]

The relatively scant remains of Structure 38 are difficult to interpret because they were disturbed by the construction of another, slightly smaller, later seventeenth-century building (Structure 31).[17] What does remain, however, suggests that Structure 38, like Structure 112, was a sizable and permanent brick building. So the "country's house" and Harvey's house may have served as the major governmental meeting places while the next governor, Sir William Berkeley, established himself at Jamestown and began directing Virginia's affairs.

Governor Berkeley came to Jamestown carrying yet another charge, to build "at ye public charge of ye country a convenient house to be built where you and the council may meet and sitt for dispatching of public affairs and hearing causes."[18] By February 1645 Governor Berkeley's "house" in town was well underway. Even though it was not built "at ye public charge" (with public funds), this house appears to have been Berkeley's version of a "convenient house where you and the council may meet and sitt." The cellar units of the governor's new house had been completed before the builder ran into a shortage of brick. In a letter to Governor Berkeley, Secretary Richard Kemp wrote that "at Towne for want of materials [your building] is yet not higher than ye first storye above ye cellar."[19] Later descriptions reveal that, once completed (1646), the building was a three-part brick rowhouse. Certain units of the governor's new house at Jamestown hosted the General Assembly and served as Berkeley's town residence.

Berkeley left the governorship in 1652 when he surrendered to the Commonwealth troops at Jamestown's door. He then retired to his country home, Green Spring, five miles from Jamestown. Thereafter he sought to get rid of his three-unit Jamestown building, hereafter referred to as Berkeley Row. Documents relating to these real-estate transactions consistently refer to Berkeley Row as the "State house."[20] On March 24, 1655, a land patent refers to "the middle brick house in James Citty bought of . . . Sr. Willm Berkeley" as "the late State house." Then, on March 30, 1655, it is recorded that, for 27,000 pounds of tobacco, William Berkeley sold to "Richard Bennett, Esq., Governour of Virginia . . . my house in James Cittie, lately in the tenure of William Whittby being the westernmost of the three brickhouses which I there built."[21]

These documents establish that during the last few months of his governorship, Governor Richard Bennett bought the westernmost unit of the "late State house." Berkeley Row may have been so designated because it was the former governor's house, it was likely the meeting place of the council, and it was possibly the meeting place of the burgesses. It is tempting to assign the governor's residence, the council chamber, and the burgess assembly room to each of the three units. In particular, the middle unit, or possibly the middle and easternmost units together, seems to have been called the "late State house" and therefore must have once been known as, or functioned as, the Statehouse.

It is equally tempting to conclude that the westernmost unit of the row became Governor Bennett's house because it had already served as Governor Berkeley's house, and so was conveniently designed for a governor's residence and possibly somewhat furnished as such. As a tavernkeeper, Thomas Woodhouse, who was given the "late State house" by the March 30, 1655, Berkeley grant, might well have been interested in the units formerly used for the Statehouse: a building large enough for gatherings of some size would be easily adaptable for use as the public rooms of a tavern.

Why didn't the Jamestown colony itself buy "the late State house" building from Berkeley? The explanation may have been an ailing public treasury. At General Assembly time, the colony's government occasionally opted to rent the space, a fact lamented by the burgesses in 1656 and 1660.[22]

Later real estate transactions involving Berkeley Row offer more clues to its use, plan, and location. It continued to be named as "the State house" or "late State house." After 1665, by which time the final and most substantial Statehouse had been built, Berkeley Row became the "old State house." In 1667 half an acre of land "adjoyneing to the westernmost of those three houses all wch jointly we formerly called by the name of old State house" was granted to Thomas Ludwell, secretary of the colony, and Thomas Stegg, councilor and auditor general of the colony, provided they build another house on the property.[23] Apparently they never occupied the "old

State house" unit, nor did they construct another house on the property. The January 1, 1667, grant describes Berkeley Row as three units running 34 degrees south of east, sixty-seven feet from the James River shore.[24] These details are critical to identifying the building site at Jamestown today.

Sometime between the 1667 Ludwell/ Stegg acquisition and 1670, Berkeley regained all three units of his rowhouse, and the western unit burned. Today we know about the reacquisition and fire because in April 1670, for £25 sterling, Berkeley sold the western unit to Henry Randolph, clerk of the House of Bur-

Structure 17 during National Park Service excavations. (National Park Service, Colonial National Historical Park)

gesses.[25] Since Governor Bennett is named in the 1670 transaction as the last occupant, it may be concluded that Ludwell/Stegg never occupied this unit. Perhaps the burning of the westernmost unit quelled their plans for occupation and additional construction. Presumably as a result of their failure to meet the condition of the grant, the land reverted to the now-reappointed Governor Berkeley.

By 1671 Randolph owned Berkeley Row in its entirety, since records from April 7 show that he sold off all three units, one by one, to council members or former council members.[26] Bennett was still listed as the last occupant of the westernmost unit, suggesting that, like Ludwell and Stegg, Randolph never occupied the property. Since that unit is no longer called a ruin, it may have been repaired by Ludwell or by Randolph. The parcel's jump in price from £25 to £150 by the time Berkeley bought it back by later in 1670 suggests that Ludwell did rebuild it.[27]

So where on the town site did Berkeley Row actually stand?[28] A three-part brick building foundation with the Berkeley Row dimensions and compass alignment is on the riverbank. Known as Structure 17, this building was in all likelihood the Statehouse, circa 1646–52—that is, from the time Berkeley returned to the colony and could oversee the building's completion until his surrender to the English Commonwealth and temporary retirement to Green Spring. The archaeological evidence pertaining to Structure 17 dovetails with the documentary record pertaining to Berkeley

Row. Structure 17 is the only brick building found on the town site that was built as three attached units of equal size. The compass orientation of its walls, 34 degrees south of east, matches perfectly the axis recorded for the "old State house" in 1667. No other building yet found at Jamestown was built in three parts and on the 34–degree axis. Although the town site has not been completely excavated, another fact makes possible a more definite identification of Structure 17. A sales record of 1667 states that the "old State house" was sixty-seven feet from the riverbank—and we can be certain that the various Jamestown excavations, beginning in 1901, have together revealed any sizable brick foundation that has ever been built that close to the shore.[29] This certainty is made possible by the history of the land on which the town stood.

As the town evolved into a plantation and its buildings disappeared in the eighteenth and nineteenth centuries, the land reverted to agriculture. We know that practically all of the seventeenth-century Jamestown site went under the plow. Consequently, except at the Civil War earthworks area, removing the upper foot or so of blended soil was all that was necessary for archaeologists to reveal surviving seventeenth-century foundations. Everything that was left intact from as early as 1607 shows up in excavations at the same relatively shallow depth. In addition, the spaced cross-trenching during the extensive NPS excavations would have exposed any substantial brick construction there was to see in a given area or trench. In particular, the National Park Service's north–south trenches would have intersected every sizable brick foundation built on the odd angle recorded for the Statehouse in the 1667 sale.[30] Finally, the Jamestown Rediscovery excavations have revealed all buildings along the river from its property line east of the church for 460 feet to the northwest. For all these reasons, Structure 17 is indeed the prime candidate for Berkeley Row.

The architectural evidence is similarly conclusive. When NPS excavations led by Dr. John Cotter uncovered the three-part brick Structure 17 foundation,[31] the building consisted of three identical 20' × 40' attached units (inside measurements) with identical central H-shaped chimneys. Each chimney had closets attached between the north and south rooms, and each unit had a curious dead space between the chimney and the east wall. These plans are unusual and, more important, identically so. It is reasonable, then, to suppose they were all designed and constructed by the same builder and therefore probably built close in time to each other. Each room of each unit also had identically placed entrances on the north and south. The building was likely all brick, the outer walls thick enough to support a one-and-one-half-story, triple-gabled building above an English basement half below ground. The fact that the long axis walls are one-half course thicker than the end walls indicates the triple-gable construction; that is to say, the long walls had to support two stories above the basement, while the end walls supported a single story to the roof. All four walls of the westernmost section were built at once and apparently first, but not long before the middle and eastern sections, which were added at one time.

The flimsy original partition wall of the western unit may be additional evidence that this was indeed Berkeley Row, since Kemp reported having trouble getting a unit completed for lack of bricks during Berkeley's absence in 1645.[32] The builders' projected shortfall of bricks may have resulted in less substantial construction. The subsequent halt in construction for want of bricks might explain a puzzling wall joint as well. The flimsy partition wall in the western unit cellar bonded into an outside wall, which ordinarily suggests a two-phase building campaign, quite separate in time. But a single-course thick wall could not ever support the exterior wall of a building of Structure 17's proportions. In other words, builders may well have built what they could with the dwindling brick supply, assuming the supply ship would eventually come in so they could complete the original three-part design.

The building remains may also tell us more than the documents do about the building's history. After the three-part building was completed, someone dug another cellar hole and began laying bricks for the cellar of a fourth unit on the west, of size equal to that of the other three units. This aborted beginning may show one consequence of the Ludwell and Stegg grant of 1667, which required them to build

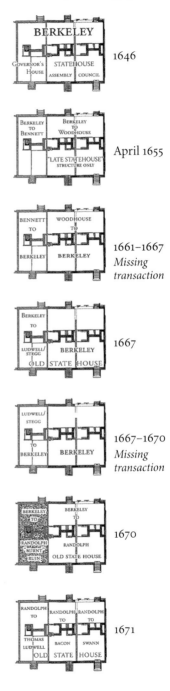

Chain of owners/occupants of Berkeley Row, 1655–71.

1646

April 1655

1661–1667 *Missing transaction*

1667

1667–1670 *Missing transaction*

1670

1671

or forfeit. This physical evidence of intentions unfulfilled may account for how Berkeley came back into ownership by 1670: forfeiture.[33]

Dating Structure 17 is more challenging. Owing to the number of different people digging into the ruins over three decades and the imprecise state of the archaeological art at the time of earlier excavations, little attention was paid to the recovery of artifacts that could have dated the building's construction. The dating evidence from earlier digging amounts to a clay tobacco pipe bowl, some locally made clay pipe stems, and a small fragment of bottle glass, all found sealed beneath the brick floor in the central basement.[34] The most datable piece from this archaeological collection is a molded clay tobacco pipe bowl shaped in a style made circa 1630–40, suggesting a construction date at that time or soon thereafter (see p. 89). This pipe style could have been used into the 1640s, when Berkeley Row was built, making this evidence consistent with other evidence that Berkeley Row, the "old State house" and Structure 17 are one and the same.[35]

The final and most substantial of all the Jamestown statehouses, and the only one built exclusively for the purpose of housing the General Assembly, was first erected in 1663–65. The ruins of this structure form part of what is called the Statehouse Complex, a group of attached and largely publicly owned living spaces located on the extreme western edge of the APVA Jamestown property. The discovery of this group of buildings dates back to the initial construction of the Jamestown concrete seawall by the Army Corps of Engineers in 1901. The engineer in charge of the construction, Samuel Yonge, noticed a brick building foundation falling away from the eroded riverbank along the western side of the APVA's twenty-two-and-a-half-acre portion of the Jamestown site. In his book *The Site of Old James Town*, he describes the ensuing excavation of the foundation.[36]

Yonge traced the entire extent of the brickwork by digging along the walls. He uncovered remains of five connected buildings that had grown from the river side eastward—buildings now labeled 1 through 5. He also discovered the foundations of six chimneys and two building additions to the main block, each with filled-in cellars. Yonge removed the cellar fill and saved what turned out to be the late seventeenth-century artifacts he found in it. He concluded from charred debris that the building had burned. To Yonge, this evidence, together with the plan of the largest foundation on the eastern end of the series, seemed to fit documentary references to the Jamestown Statehouse. The Statehouse had first been built at public expense in 1663–65, burned in 1676, repaired by 1685, burned again and abandoned in 1698.[37] While Yonge's excavation was crude by modern standards, it was valuable nevertheless. His study of erosion rates of the shoreline and land records throughout the town site was remarkably thorough and insightful. He was one of the few who prophetically thought that remains of James Fort still could be found on land in the vicinity of the church tower.[38]

Samuel Yonge's 1901 excavation of the Statehouse Complex.

Yonge's digging at the Statehouse Complex cleared away some of the debris presumably either from the destruction by fire in 1698 and/or from the 1676 Bacon's Rebellion fire. The excavated foundations were eventually capped with concrete and the cellars rebuilt from bricks salvaged from them.

The artifacts Yonge found survive in the APVA archives.[39] One of the cellar floors was littered with military items, including a number of hand grenades, bills, hooks, and cannonballs, evidence consistent perhaps with public use of the building. A number of architectural objects such as iron hinges and a distinctive door-lock plate, identical to a lock found at the 1665 house of William Allen known as Bacon's Castle, located just across the James River from Jamestown, are among the Yonge collection. Yonge also found a distinctive decorative brick known as a mullion brick, typically used in church windows. These all are clues to the design, construction history, and use of the buildings.

In preparation for the three-hundred-and-fiftieth celebration of Jamestown's founding, the APVA and the National Park Service seriously considered reconstruction of the easternmost unit of the Statehouse Complex, identified then as the third and fourth Statehouse. Two major investigations of the eastern end

Some of the artifacts from Yonge's excavation of the Statehouse Complex cellar, including building hinges, a door lock (*left*), and seventeenth-century bill hooks and grenades.

unit were conducted by NPS archaeologists in the hope that archaeology might offer up details for architects to use in recapturing the original design. Louis Caywood led the first excavation of the Statehouse Complex in 1954.[40] He dug along the exposed eastern end of the foundations, opening trenches three feet wide on either side of the brickwork. Caywood found evidence of a partition wall undetected by Yonge, burned floor joists, some roofing tiles, and slate. He also recovered bones from six graves.

Joel Shiner took over the Statehouse dig the following year, chiefly to explore the burial ground.[41] He cleared away all of the topsoil and whatever accumulated building debris Caywood had missed, then dug down to the top of prebuilding subsoil in order to locate and test additional graves. Shiner found seventy grave outlines and uncovered the bones from seven. He also recovered a large number of artifacts within the actual Statehouse footing and tested an area adjacent to the chimney foundation of Building 1. Artifacts from these excavations are mostly building materials. The sparseness of domestic objects may be more evidence of public use. Shiner also recovered lead bearing dates of 1678, 1683, and 1686 from casement-type windows in a disturbed soil area outside Buildings 4 and 5. These windows were likely installed during repairs or a rebuild in the later seventeenth century.[42]

Jamestown Rediscovery excavations of Buildings 2, 3, and part of 4, Statehouse Complex.

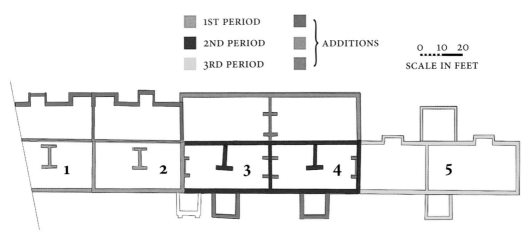

1  2  3  4  5

Plan of Statehouse Complex building phases.

Further excavation of the masonry footings of the Statehouse Complex by the Jamestown Rediscovery team, together with architectural and archaeological studies, has led to more precise conclusions about the date of construction.[43] These excavations confirmed Yonge's conclusion that Buildings 1 and 2, 3, 4, and 5 were built from west to east. The brickwork of each successive foundation abutted rather than bonded onto its predecessor to the west, confirming the west-to-east building campaign. The first of the two double units in line, Buildings 1 and 2, had continuous foundations, indicating they were built at the same time. The mortar in them was identical, further evidence that the units were contemporaneous. Identical mortar in Buildings 3 and 4 indicates that they, too, were built close in time, one onto the other.[44] How much time passed between the construction of the first two buildings and Buildings 3 and 4 cannot be determined.

Buildings 1 and 2 were doubled in size and augmented by cellars, but whether this happened before or after Building 5 existed at the eastern end of the line of buildings is not evident. No artifacts excavated in 1903 can be reliably ascribed to deposition during construction, so a precise time for the expansion remains unknown. Also, the relatively scant fragments of builder's fill that survived the 1950s excavations along the Building 5 foundation produced nothing datable. Nor were datable artifacts found in the original construction scaffold holes recently excavated, with one exception. A probable repair scaffold hole produced a fragment of Virginia-made pottery, Challis type, which dates to circa 1690. This may indicate a repair to Structure 5 after that year. A preponderance of flat clay roofing tiles were found on the site of Buildings 1 and 2, and yet a shift to a preponderance of curved pantiles from the area of the footings of Buildings 3 and 4. The difference of tile types does suggest some separation in time between the construction of Buildings 1 and 2 and Buildings 3 and 4.

Further evidence corroborates that the additions to Buildings 3 and 4 were constructed after the additions to Buildings 1 and 2. The lowest courses of the foundations of the additions of Buildings 3 and 4 were stone, suggesting a later construction than the all-brick addition to Buildings 1 and 2. Also, the addition footing of Buildings 3 and 4 abutted rather than bonded into the Building 2 footing, proof that the additions to Buildings 3 and 4 were built later. Building 5 had two additions to the original main body of the structure, a porch chamber on the south and a massive stair tower on the north. How soon after the original construction these were added could not be determined.

The interior plans of the buildings, including the location of fireplaces and stairs, provide further details of the construction of the complex. It is clear that the main body of Building 5 had an original brick cross-wall dividing the building into two spaces of unequal size. The original H-shaped, back-to-back fireplaces of the other buildings indicate rooms of equal size and lobby entrances south of the chimneys. Tests of the interior fill of Buildings 2, 3, and 4 indicated that they had all burned and that thereafter the H-shaped chimneys in Buildings 3 and 4 were removed and replaced by end chimneys. Scaffold holes apparently from the construction of the replacement chimney at the east end of Building 3 were found inside and cutting through burned levels in Building 2, indicating that Building 2 was in ruins when the alteration took place. The discovery of a reused decorative gauged (rubbed smooth) brick, a type not used in Virginia until the late seventeenth century, suggests that the move from central to end chimneys took place toward the end of the 1600s. The stair towers centered on Buildings 3 and 4 also abutted the main body of the buildings, showing that they were later additions, probably part of the late-seventeenth-century remodeling.[45] Central fireplaces were also added to the partition walls in the additions to Buildings 3 and 4, probably indicating the relocation of cooking hearths for the main body of the buildings to the addition. Partition walls may have divided the main block of Buildings 3 and 4 into two rooms, the hall and parlor. Future excavation of the fire and occupation levels tested so far should provide concrete evidence for this supposition.

Yonge reported finding an additional "porch" foundation, which he proceeded to cap in concrete as he had capped all the other footings. Since its location, straddling the union of Buildings 2 and 3, makes no logical architectural sense, this footing was excavated further in 2002. No brick footing was found under the concrete. The absence of such a footing is puzzling, given Yonge's report and the reliability of his other conclu-

Globe Tavern, London, trade token (1667) from fill inside Yonge's mystery "porch foundation."

sions. Yonge's guess that this odd footing belonged to some earlier structure was also not borne out by the datable artifacts from this so-called footing. These artifacts dated with unusual precision to the last third of the seventeenth century, including window leads of 1671 and 1686, a tradesman's token from the Globe Tavern dated 1667, and Green Spring and Challis pottery, circa 1660–1710. Artifacts from disturbed contexts over Building 2 produced the earliest materials from the site, including types of local tobacco pipes and a sword pommel from the second quarter of the seventeenth century.[46]

An in-depth architectural study produced a conjectural reconstruction of the entire Statehouse Complex.[47] Details of the reconstruction were based on the foundation floor plan, some building remains, parallel contemporary buildings in England, and mortar analysis, the latter determining that the exterior walls were painted solid red (see p. 208).

How the buildings of the Statehouse Complex came to be, what function they served—and, in particular, which of them was the Statehouse itself—can be illuminated by the documentary record. In 1662 King Charles II charged the restored Governor Berkeley with a renewed and more serious effort to develop Jamestown into the prototypical "Cittie" it was supposed to be. Berkeley himself decided the details, which included a number of brick houses of standard size built at a scale that would command respect for the Crown as well as prominence and permanence for the colony.

On December 14, 1662, the burgesses stated the specifications:

Whereas his sacred majestie by his instructions hath enjoyned us to build a town . . . at James Citty as being the most convenient place in James River . . . the towne . . . shall consist of thirty-two houses . . . brick, forty foot long, twenty foot wide, within the walls, to be eighteen foot high above the ground, the walls to be two foot thick to the water table, and a brick and a halfe thick above the water table to the roof, the roof to be fifteen foote pitch and to be covered with slate or tile. . . . That the houses be all regularly placed one by another in a square or such forme as the honorable Sir William Berkeley shall appoint most convenient.[48]

In all likelihood, this legislation resulted in construction of the earliest of the four westernmost units of the Statehouse Complex. These four units were completed in just ten months. The construction of Building 5, which was evidently the massive Statehouse built specifically for the meeting place of the colonial government, followed, being completed by 1665: "[we have] begun a town of brick & have already built enough to accommodate both ye public affairs of ye country."[49] Next, one of the brick houses belonging to the colony—that is, a "Countrie house"—was converted into a prison. It is possible that the first addition to the earliest unit, Building 1, served that purpose.

In 1672 the threat of a Dutch invasion prompted the colony to construct a fort to protect the new Statehouse nearby. The fort was a substantial brick structure, some 250 feet in breadth. However, according to Reverend John Clayton, rector of James City Parish in the 1680s, it was a "silly fort" in that it was built in the "vale," which was at the head of a branch of the pitch-and-tar swamp that once extended out onto long-eroded Church Point.[50] Its position on the southern slope of that valley appeared to render the fort ineffective. Artillerymen would not be able to train their guns on attacking

Artists' reconstruction of the Statehouse Complex superimposed on the modern landscape. (Architect, Earl Mark; Virginia Polytechnic Institute and State University)

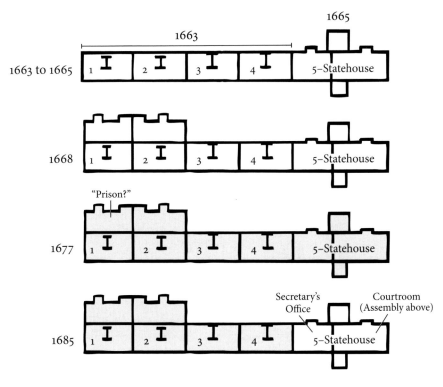

Change through time of the Statehouse Complex.

ships coming up river until the ships cleared the high ground of Church Point, which stood in the line of fire. By that time, the ships would be too close and could fire away point blank at the fort and Statehouse. Apparently this critic did not know that the so-called silly fort had in fact succeeded at least once under fire. In 1673 the fort was effective enough to protect the Statehouse as well as the Virginia tobacco fleet. In that year, Virginia ships escaped the Dutch by retreating up river: by managing to get "above the Fort at James Towne [they] were safe."[51]

By the 1670s the four westernmost houses had been leased primarily to men with political connections, continuing the tradition begun at Berkeley Row. Building 1 was the "country's house" that served as Berkeley's town "apartment," "a coits toss" from the front of the Statehouse.[52]

Next to the "country's house" in Building 2 lived Major Theophilus Hone, burgess for James City County and one of the builders of the brick fort of 1672. After the rebel Nathaniel Bacon destroyed the entire Statehouse Com-

The Ludwell grant of 1694 superimposed on the Statehouse Complex foundations.

plex in 1676, Hone successfully petitioned the Assembly for a fifty-year lease for the ruins of Buildings 3 and 4, described as formerly occupied by Arnold Cassinett and Richard Aubourne, clerk of the council.[53] It is not known whether or not Cassinett played any role in the colonial government, although this seems to be a common trait among most of the other seventeenth-century occupants of Jamestown's public buildings. Aubourne, for his part, was certainly at home among the political leadership of the time as a staunch supporter of Governor Berkeley, especially during Bacon's Rebellion. Aubourne eventually served the colony as a clerk of the House in 1680.[54]

Major Hone's lease would have required him to rebuild Aubourne and Cassinett's house. He evidently never did so, since the ruins next went up for lease to Colonel Nathaniel Bacon (cousin of Nathaniel Bacon Jr., the rebel). Colonel Bacon, a longtime Berkeley councilor, won out over another lease petition by a George Lee. At the same time, Colonel Philip Ludwell petitioned for a lease for Buildings 1 and 2, the jail, and the land belonging to this complex. The identity of these holdings is established by the lease's description of the land on which they stood as a northern boundary of a 1683 grant to Edward Chilton of land we know to have been south of the Statehouse Complex. (Chilton was another politico serving as Assembly clerk and ultimately attorney general.) Chilton's grant also mentions the brick fort as a reference point on the northwest corner of the property. Just as Hone did not rebuild Buildings 1 and 2, however, Ludwell failed to rebuild Buildings 3 and 4, so that they reverted to Nathaniel Bacon. This made Bacon the sole lessee of the entire complex except for Building 5, the Statehouse.[55]

Meanwhile, the Statehouse lay in ruins. A contract was let to Colonel Philip Ludwell in 1685 to rebuild it, the burgesses ordering "that Mr. Auditor Bacon pay to Col. Phillip Ludwell fouer hundred pounds sterl . . . for and in consideration of rebuilding ye state house."[56] Ludwell apparently did not rebuild it: the building was in all likelihood finished by Henry Hartwell by 1685. Records show that the new or rebuilt Statehouse sat on the same site as the 1665 building. There are references as well to the various governmental functions served by different rooms, such as the secretary's office, the courtroom, and the Assembly room.

In 1685, after Ludwell/Hartwell rebuilt the Statehouse, legislation directed the construction of a prison. A prison is also mentioned in records of the fire that ended the life of the Statehouse and Jamestown as capital in 1698. If this is the same prison mentioned in the 1685 legislation, the prison may well have been, like the Statehouse itself, rebuilt from an existing ruin.

Colonel Nathaniel Bacon died in 1692, leaving Buildings 2, 3, and 4 to his niece, Abigail Smith, the wife of Lewis Burwell II. It is likely that Bacon's lease of Building 1, the "country's house," terminated with his death, and that the colony reclaimed ownership. Following the death of Colonel Bacon's niece, also in 1692, ownership of Buildings 2, 3, and 4 passed to her brother-in-law, Philip Ludwell II.

On April 20, 1694, Philip Ludwell II received a grant for an acre of land to adjoin his holdings. The metes and bounds leave no doubt that these holdings are Buildings 2, 3, and 4 of the Statehouse Complex:

> Edward Andros, Governour . . . give and grant unto Phillip Ludwell Esqr. One acre and halfe of Land adjoyning to the ruins of his three Brick houses between the State house and Country house in James City which land is bounded Vizt beginning Near Pitch and Tarr swamp Eight Cheyes [N] of the Eastrmost End of the said houses and running by the said End south two degrees westerly sixteen Cheynes thence North Eighty Eight degrees westerly three and three quarter Cheynes thence North two degrees Easterly sixteen Cheynes by the other End of the said houses and thence south Eighty Eight degrees Easterly three and three quarteres Cheynes to the place it began.

The Jamestown pitch-and-tar swamp, cited as the northern boundary, is also the northern boundary of the Statehouse Complex. The parcel's width—124 feet—is exactly that of the foundations of Buildings 2, 3, and 4, measured east to west. This grant also confirms that Building 1 did revert back to a "country's house" after Nathaniel Bacon died, and that the 1685 Statehouse and Building 5 of the Statehouse Complex are one and the same.[57]

It seems logical that since Ludwell owned Buildings 2, 3, and 4 and the one acre of land adjoining it, Ludwell would have been the person who rebuilt, doubled in size, and modernized the ruins of Buildings 3 and 4. This

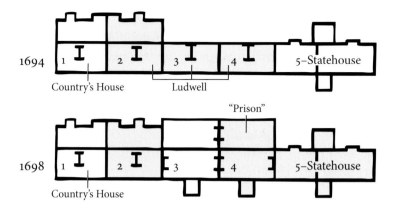

1694
1 — Country's House
2
3 — Ludwell
4
5–Statehouse

"Prison"

1698
1 — Country's House
2
3
4
5–Statehouse

Final phases of the development of the Statehouse Complex.

effort included moving the kitchen to the north addition, replacing the old fashioned central H-shaped fireplaces with end chimneys, and adding porch tower entrances to replace the old-fashioned lobby entrance.

The last event in the chronicle of Jamestown statehouses is the fire of 1698 that sealed Jamestown's fate as the meeting place of Virginia's government, the capital then moving to Williamsburg. The fire began in an adjoining building, in what must have been Building 4 and/or its addition, which seems to have become the prison. According to records, on October 20, 1698, "fire broke out in a house adjoining the State-house, which in a very short time was wholly burnt, and also the prison." It may be that one Arthur Jarvis, sentenced to death for "Burglary & Felony," took revenge on the colony for his sentence by setting fire to the jail. If Jarvis set the fire, however, he did it in such a way that the authorities could not prove it.[58]

The evolution of representative self-government at Jamestown in the seventeenth century, as reflected in the buildings that can be associated with it, is one of the most significant of Jamestown's stories. The 1665–98 Statehouse Complex in its day was the largest secular public building in seventeenth-century America. With its two stories and garrets, additions, porch chambers, cellars, and a stair tower, the complex totaled 23,000 square feet under one roof. No other governmental/public building in colonial America was even close to that scale. And it can be argued that what happened there of significance was equally beyond the scope of the government in the other colonies in the seventeenth century. "It was the place where the habits of self-rule and legislative politics were sorted out."[59]

Within the walls of the Jamestown Statehouse Complex, the legacy of the

1619 first representative assembly in North America evolved into the form of self-government that latter-day native sons, such as Thomas Jefferson and George Washington, would consider a birthright worth dying to preserve. It cannot be denied that Jamestown's legacy of self-government is mixed. In the beginning only a landed few had the right to have their voices heard. Within the walls of the Jamestown capital buildings the enslavement of Africans evolved toward rigid law in the 1660s. But at the same time, the legislative mechanism

A gentlemen's silver "ear picker" made for scraping teeth and cleaning ears, found in the plowed soil of James Fort. They were simultaneously frivolous (a status symbol) and practical (a hygienic necessity).

to enfranchise a diverse and vibrant country of the future—and to outlaw slavery itself—grew from a process born in the statehouses at Jamestown. Such is the precious value of these Jamestown places of America's political beginnings.

So the interplay of history and archaeology rediscovers Jamestown. The lost 1607 James Fort is found. Burials reveal its people. Thousands of objects open windows on daily life. And documents and digging lay bare the places of American democracy.[60]

These discoveries so far have brought the Jamestown experience into greater focus. They reveal some successes. The highest point of land on Jamestown Island, the site of the remains of James Fort, was a strategically secure place to plant the settlement. With the guidance of experienced military leaders, the colonists enclosed a place with three timber walls in less than three weeks. Neither resistant Virginia Indians, the Spanish, nor any other enemy ever breached those barriers by force. Whether the native Tsenacomacans would not or could not exterminate or expel the immigrants is a question open for debate. There is archaeological evidence, however, that the Indians were not all of one mind on the issue.

Still, death threatened the English immigrants from innumerable other causes. Climate, exertion, impure water, disease, starvation, and accidents

An English gentleman, 1610. (From *A Tudor Atlas* by John Speed. By permission of the British Library)

took their toll. Captains, gentlemen, craftsmen, laborers, women, and children alike dropped by the way, often exceeding the ability of the living to bury them properly. Despite these hardships, the survivors went about their mission, primarily to experiment in industry, trade, and agriculture. Eventually that mission included experiments in self-government. At the end of the beginning, a number of original colonists and thousands of immigrants were still standing when the Virginia Company passed the reins of government to the Crown. Jamestown would endure.

So it is that archaeological remains and the sense of reality they convey reflect the buried truth about modern America's birthplace. There is evidence that some of the immigrants worked hard and achieved a better life. Those who first met them at the shore usually did not share this good fortune. Still, a political system was born and migrated across the seventeenth-century Jamestown landscape establishing principles that would some day make possible a more equal access to that better life. The American dream was born on the banks of the James River, at a place first called James Fort, in 1607.

# Notes

## Introduction

1. Edmund S. Morgan, *American Slavery, American Freedom* (New York, 1975), 56.
2. David A. Price, *Love and Hate in Jamestown* (New York, 2003).
3. Alison Wangsness Clement, "Rewriting American History: Does the Grade School American History Curriculum Reflect the Native American Experience?," master's thesis, Georgetown University, 1997, chap. 1.
4. William M. Kelso, Nicholas M. Luccketti, and Beverly A. Straube, "A Re-evaluation of the Archaeological Evidence Produced by Project 100: The Search for James Fort," Colonial National Historical Park ms., 1990, Jamestown Discovery Center, Jamestown, Va.

## 1. Reimagining Jamestown

1. George Percy, *Observations Gathered out of "A Discourse of the Plantation of the Southern Colony in Virginia by the English, 1606" written by the honorable gentleman, Master George Percy,* ed. David B. Quinn (Charlottesville, Va., 1967), 15.
2. Philip L. Barbour, *The Jamestown Voyages Under the First Charter, 1606–1609* (London, 1969), 1:49–54.
3. Ibid., 1:16.
4. Dennis Blanton, personal communication, 1996.
5. John Smith, *The Complete Works of Captain John Smith, 1580–1631,* ed. Philip L. Barbour (London, 1986), 1:29.
6. When Newport returned to England in July 1607, 104 were listed as alive, as three had died between the May landing and that time. I am indebted to Dan Brown for the math on the numbers.
7. Smith, *Complete Works,* 2:38.
8. Percy, *Observations,* 16.
9. Ibid., 17.

10. Ibid., 18–19.

11. Gabriel Archer, "A Relatyon . . . written . . . by a gent. Of ye Colony," in Barbour, *Jamestown Voyages,* 1:95.

12. Ibid.

13. Ibid.

14. Percy, *Observations,* 22.

15. Louis B. Wright, *A Voyage to Virginia in 1609: Two Narratives: Strachey's "True Reportory" and Jourdain's Discovery of the Bermudas* (Charlottesville, Va., 1964), 63–64.

16. Archer, "A Relatyon . . . written . . . by a gent," 96.

17. Smith, *Complete Works,* 2:142–43.

18. Percy, *Observations,* 27.

19. Smith, *Complete Works,* 2:143.

20. Percy, *Observations,* 27; Smith, *Complete Works,* 2:144, 145.

21. Smith, *Complete Works,* 2:153–54, 157.

22. Ibid., 2:169, 180, 325.

23. Ibid., 2:180–81.

24. Ibid., 2:187.

25. Ibid., 2:208, 212.

26. Ibid., 2:213, 223.

27. Ibid., 2:225.

28. Ibid.

29. Fred Fausz, "England's First Indian War, 1609–1614," *Virginia Magazine of History and Biography* 98, no. 1 (Jan. 1990): 3–56.

30. Smith, *Complete Works,* 2:232–33; Nancy Egloff, personal communication, May 1997.

31. Strachey, in Wright, *Voyage to Virginia,* 63–64, 76.

32. "Thomas West to Lord Salisbury, September 1610," in *Jamestown Narratives: Eyewitness Accounts of the Virginia Colony: The First Decade, 1607–1617,* ed. Edward Wright Haile (Champlain, Va., 1998), 465.

33. Strachey, in Wright, *Voyage to Virginia,* 79–81.

34. "Pedro de Zúñiga Map of Virginia," Archivo General de Simancas, M.P.D., IV-66, XIX-163, Valladolid, Spain.

35. Ralph Hamor, "A True Discourse of the Present Estate of Virginia, and the successe of the Affaires there till the 18 of June, 1615" (Richmond, Va., 1957). Compare Smith, *Complete Works,* 2:242.

36. Susan Myra Kingsbury, ed., *The Records of the Virginia Company of London* (Washington, D.C., 1906–35), 3:101–2.

37. Don Diego de Molina to Don Alonso de Velasco, May 28, 1613, in *Jamestown Narratives,* ed. Haile, 749.

38. Smith, *Complete Works,* 2:262.

39. Samuel H. Yonge, *The Site of Old James Towne, 1697–1698* (Richmond, Va., 1903), 65.

40. Gravenhage Colectie Leupe Supplement Algemeenrijksarchief, The Hague, Velh 619.89. Michael Jarvis brought this chart to my attention and Jeroen van Driel gave valuable references.

41. Smith, *Complete Works,* 2:242; Hamor, "A True Discourse of the Present State of Virginia," 40, 45.

42. Smith, *Complete Works,* 2:138, 1:35.

43. Strachey, in Wright, *Voyage to Virginia,* 79–82.

44. Ibid.

45. Smith, *Complete Works,* 2:225, 262, 324; I. Noël Hume, *The Virginia Adventure* (New York, 1994), 274.

46. Kingsbury, ed., *Records of the Virginia Company of London* (1935), 4:259.

47. "A Brief Declaration of the Plantation of Virginia during the first twelve years, when Sir Thomas Smith was governor of the Company, and down to this present time. By the Ancient Planters now remaining in Virginia, 1623," in *Jamestown Narratives,* ed. Haile, 893–901.

48. Smith, *Complete Works,* 2:136.

49. Rosemary Taylor, *Blackwall, the Brunswick and Whitebait Dinners* (Blackwall, England, 1991). I am indebted to Ms. Taylor for providing a copy of this booklet.

50. I am indebted to Daniel Brown for alerting me to the exact numbers.

51. Alexander Brown, *The Genesis of the United States* (Boston, 1890), 2:943–44, 977–78, 904, 1006–10, 1055; Jocelyn R. Wingfield, *Virginia's True Founder: Edward-Maria Wingfield and His Times, 1550–c. 1614* (Athens, Ga., 1993); Samuel Merrifield Bemiss, *Ancient Adventurers, A Collection of Essays* (Richmond, Va., 1964); Warner F. Gookin, "Who Was Bartholomew Gosnold?" *William and Mary Quarterly* 6, no. 3, 3d. ser. (1949): 401.

52. Mary Abbott, *Life Cycles in England, 1560–1720: Cradle to Grave* (London, 1996), 135.

53. Catherine Correll-Walls, Jamestown Biographies database project, Jamestown Rediscovery Center (hereafter JRC), Jamestown, Va., 2004. This is a database of biographical information gathered from traditional sources such as first-hand accounts, scholarly publications, and British and Irish manuscript collections. These age estimates are based on the Correll-Walls database.

54. Ibid.

55. Nell Marion Nugent, *Cavaliers and Pioneers* (Baltimore, 1974), xxi.

56. Correll-Walls, Jamestown Biographies database, passim.

57. That Martin does eventually get by grant ten shares (1,000 acres) of choice land in 1616 and stays in Virginia may mean his English prospects were not major. Brown, *Genesis of the United States,* 2:943.

58. Correll-Walls, Jamestown Biographies database.

59. Gookin, "Who Was Bartholomew Gosnold?," 401.

60. Ibid. The author is indebted to Nicholas Hagger, past owner of Otley Hall, the Gosnold mansion, for suggesting sources for Gosnold's biography.

61. Smith, *Complete Works,* 1:203.

62. Percy, *Observations,* 24.

63. Correll-Walls, Jamestown Biographies database.

64. Smith, *Complete Works,* 2:140–42, 160–63, 190–91.

65. Federal Emergency Management Agency Flood Insurance Study and Flood Rate Map, Jamestown Island, Virginia, 1991.

66. Strachey, in Wright, *Voyage to Virginia,* 37.

67. Edward Arber, ed., *Captain John Smith's Works, 1608–1637* (Westminster, 1895), xcv.

68. Strachey, "The Historie of Travell Into Virginia Britania" (1612), in *Jamestown Narratives,* ed. Haile, 58.

69. Frederic W. Gleach, *Powhatan's World and Colonial Virginia: A Conflict of Cultures* (Lincoln, Neb., 1997), 91.

70. Smith, *Complete Works,* 1:173.

71. Correll-Walls, Jamestown Biographies database.

72. Helen C. Rountree, *The Powhatan Indians of Virginia: Their Traditional Culture* (Norman, Okla., 1989), 184–94.

73. Strachey, "Historie of Travell," 619.

74. Smith, *Complete Works,* 2:258, 260–61.

75. Survey Report no. 01538, PRO, Class SP14/90, State Papers, Domestic, James I, Letters and Papers, 1611–1618, Virginia Colonial Records Project, the Library of Virginia, Richmond, 421–56.

76. Smith, *Complete Works,* 2:262.

77. Strachey, "Historie of Travell," 622; Percy, "A True Relation of the procedings and occurrents of moment which have hap'ned in Virginia from the time Sir Thomas Gates was shipwrack'd upon the Bermudes, anno 1609, until my departure out the country, which was in anno Domini 1612," in *Jamestown Narratives,* ed. Haile, 509.

78. Hamor, "A True Discourse of the Present Estate of Virginia," 40, 45; Smith, *Complete Works,* 1:63, 73.

79. Strachey, "Historie of Travell," 622; General Archives of Simancas, Department of State, Vol. 2589, Folio 61, Copy of deciphered letter of the Marquess of Flores to the King of Spain, August 1, 1612, in Brown, *Genesis of the United States,* 2:572.

80. Strachey, in Wright, *Voyage to Virginia,* 64.

81. Arber, ed., *Captain John Smith's Works,* xcv.

82. Pedro de Zúñiga to Philip III [February 23] March 15, 1609, in Barbour, *Jamestown Voyages,* 2:255.

83. Strachey, in Wright, *Voyage to Virginia,* 63.

84. Virginia M. Meyer and John Frederick Dorman, *Adventures of Purse and Person,* 3d ed. (Richmond, Va., 1987), 71.

85. Brown, *Genesis of the United States,* 2:895.

86. Douglas W. Owsley, Parvene Hamzavi, and Karin L. Bruwelheide, "Analysis of the APVA Skeletal Collection Jamestown, Virginia," mss., JRC, January 1997.

87. "Thomas West to Lord Salisbury, September 1610," 466.

88. Brown, *Genesis of the United States,* 1:116, 393.

89. Ibid., 116, 121–22, 125–27, 141, 143–45.

90. Ibid., 243.

91. Frank Hancock, *Jamestown Revisited: A Medical Proposal with Circumstantial Considerations* (Burlington, N.C., 1998); Percy, *Observations,* 24–27.

92. Smith, *Complete Works,* 2:223–24.

93. Brown, *Genesis of the United States,* 1:311.

## 2. Rediscovering Jamestown

1. Haile, ed., *Jamestown Narratives,* 891–915.

2. Smith, *Complete Works,* 1:234.

3. Richard Randolph, "Island of Jamestown," *Southern Literary Messenger* 3 (1837): 303; John L. Cotter, *Archeological Excavations at Jamestown, Virginia* (Washington, D.C., 1958), 17; Thad Tate, "Early Jamestown History," volunteer training lecture, Yeardley House, Jamestown Island, February 1994.

4. William M. Kelso, Jamestown Rediscovery Archaeological Project: The Search for the Site of James Fort (1607), Master Plan, Association for the Preservation of Virginia Antiquities (APVA), Richmond, 1993.

5. Strachey, in Wright, *Voyage to Virginia,* 63–64.

6. Noël Hume, conversation at Jamestown Island, March 1994.

7. Smith, *Complete Works,* 2:212.

8. Cotter, *Archeological Excavations at Jamestown,* 17l.

9. Ivor Noël Hume, *Here Lies Virginia* (New York, 1963), 46; Ivor Noël Hume, "Thinking the Unthinkable," keynote address delivered at the Society for Historical Archaeology Conference, Williamsburg, Va., 1984; Virginia A. Harrington, "Theories and Evidence for the Location of James Fort," *Virginia Magazine of History and Biography* 93 (January 1985): 36–53.

10. Kelso, Luccketti, and Straube, "Re-Evaluation of the Archaeological Evidence Produced by Project 100," 42.

11. Strachey, in Wright, *Voyage to Virginia,* 63–64.

12. Ivor Noël Hume, Fort Raleigh National Historic Site, 1991 Archaeological Investigation, mss., National Park Service Southeastern Archaeological Center, copy at JRC, 25–26.

13. Smith, *Complete Works,* 2:187.

14. Ransome True, ed., "Seventeenth Century Patents from the State Land Office, Richmond, Virginia," mss. no. 83, JRC.

15. Percy, *Observations,* 22.

16. Strachey, in Wright, *Voyage to Virginia,* 81.

17. Smith, *Complete Works,* 2:157.

18. John L. Cotter, personal communication, 1993.

19. See chap. 1, p. 18.

20. Smith, *Complete Works,* 2:180–81, 324.

21. Strachey, in Wright, *Voyage to Virginia,* 79–81.

22. Hamor, "A True Discourse of the Present Estate of Virginia," 33.

23. Mary Jeffery Galt, "Report to the Jamestown Committee," n.d., in Cotter, *Archeological Excavations at Jamestown,* 222

24. Smith, *Complete Works,* 3:295.

25. I am indebted to the research and master's thesis of Eric Deetz for the "discovery" of the mud-and-stud tradition at early Jamestown and his direction of the fieldwork at Building 165. Eric Deetz, "Architecture of Early Virginia: An Analysis of the Origins of Earthfast

Tradition," M.A. thesis, University of Leicester, England, 2001; see also Rodney Cousins, *Lincolnshire Buildings in the Mud and Stud Tradition* (Heritage: Lincolnshire, 2000).

26. Correll-Walls, Jamestown Biographies database.

27. Smith, *Complete Works*, 1:157.

28. Strachey, in Wright, *Voyage to Virginia*, 79.

29. Jeffery P. Brain, "Fort St. George VI," Peabody Essex Museum, Salem, Mass., 2001, 8; Ivor Noël Hume, *Shipwreck!* (Hamilton, Bermudas, 1995), 16.

30. I am always indebted to the unique and precise expertise of Bly Straube, Jamestown Rediscovery senior curator, for the identification and dating of the artifacts discussed in this book.

31. Joann Bowen, "The Starving Time at Jamestown," mss. report, JRC, 1999.

32. Smith, *Complete Works*, 2:232.

33. Nancy Egloff, "Report on the Starving Time Population Figures," mss., Jamestown Yorktown Foundation, Jamestown, Va., 1990; Correll-Walls, Jamestown Biographies database.

34. Strachey, in Wright, *Voyage to Virginia*, 71.

35. "Thomas West to Lord Salisbury, September 1610," 466.

36. Smith, *Complete Works*, 1:259.

37. Smith's Map of Virginia, 1612, detail in ibid., 2:140–41; Scott Weidensail, "Tracking America's First Dog," *Smithsonian Magazine* (March 1999): 45–57.

38. This is a preliminary identification by veterinarians at Virginia Polytechnical and State University, Blacksburg, Virginia. Thanks especially to Dr. Thomas Chamberlain.

39. Percy, "A True Relation of the Occurrents of Moment which have happened in Virginia," in *Jamestown Narratives*, ed. Haile, 505.

40. Copy of deciphered letter of the Marquess of Flores to the King of Spain, August 1, 1612, Volume 2589, Folio 61, General Archives of Simancas, Department of State, in Brown, *Genesis of the United States*, 2:572.

41. "Brief Declaration of the Plantation of Virginia," 894.

42. Smith, *Complete Works*, 2:317–18.

43. "Lord De La Warre to Virginia Company of London, July 7, 1610," in *Jamestown Narratives*, ed. Haile, 466.

44. Strachey, in Wright, *Voyage to Virginia*, 81.

45. Ibid., 64.

46. Kingsbury, ed., *Records of the Virginia Company of London*, 4:259.

47. Smith, *Complete Works*, passim.

48. Beverly Straube, personal communication, 2003.

49. Timothy Easton, personal communication, 2004.

50. Strachey, in Wright, *Voyage to Virginia*, 56.

51. Barbour, *Jamestown Voyages*, 52.

52. Hamor, "A True Discourse of the Present Estate of Virginia," 45; Kingsbury, ed., *Records of the Virginia Company of London*, 4:101–2.

53. "Brief Declaration of the Plantation of Virginia," 912.

54. Thanks to John Schofield and Chris Elmers of the Museum of London for showing me London parallels.

55. Engraving entitled "Van Dun's Almshouses in Petty France," in John Thomas Smith, *Antiquities of London* (London, 1791).

56. I am indebted to Dennis Blanton, past director of the Center for Archaeological Research, College of William and Mary, for assessing the collection.

57. Archer, "A Relatyon . . . written . . . by a gent," 96.

58. I am grateful for the advice of Jamestown Rediscovery staff archaeologist David Givens regarding projectile point manufacture.

59. Smith, *Complete Works*, 2:175. I am grateful to Jamestown Rediscovery conservator Michael Lavin for an explanation of why copper preserves organic material.

60. Archer, "A Relatyon . . . written . . . by a gent," 96, 98. I am indebted to Dennis Blanton, past director of the Center for Archaeological Research, College of William and Mary, for assessing the collection.

61. See chap. 1.

62. Strachey in Wright, *Voyage to Virginia*, 99.

63. Ivor Noël Hume, *Historical Archaeology* (New York, 1968), 145.

64. John G. Hurst, David S. Neal, and H. J. E. van Beuningen, *Pottery Produced and Traded in North-west Europe, 1350–1650*, Rotterdam Papers 6 (Rotterdam, 1986), 63.

65. William M. Kelso with Beverly Straube, *Jamestown Rediscovery, 1994–2004* (Jamestown, Va., 2004), 133; Strachey, in Wright, *Voyage to Virginia*, 82.

66. Brown, *Genesis of the United States*, 1:492.

67. Smith, *Complete Works*, 3:262.

68. I am indebted to archaeologist Danny Schimdt, who spent six weeks in the well shaft, half-submerged at times, to reveal its secrets and for his summary of the results: D. Schimdt, "Excavations Results and Interpretation STR170 at Jamestown," mss., JRC, 2003. I am also indebted for the arduous months of conservation of the well artifacts by Michael Lavin and Dan Gamble.

69. Kelso with Straube, *Jamestown Rediscovery*, 137, 140.

70. William M. Kelso, *Kingsmill Plantations, 1619–1800* (San Francisco, 1984), 55, 56.

71. I am indebted to David Stahle for his analysis of the well curb growth rings. William Kelso to David Stahle, March 2005.

72. Kelso with Straube, *Jamestown Rediscovery*, 132.

73. Dr. Jack Kane, hydrologist, personal communication, 2002.

74. Strachey, *The Historie of Travell into Virginia Britania* (1612; London, 1953), 4.


## 3. Recovering Jamestownians

1. Douglas W. Owsley, Ashley McKeown, William M. Kelso, Karin S. Bruwelheide, Jamie May, and David Hunt, "Two Early Seventeenth-Century Burials from James Fort, Jamestown Island, Virginia," unpublished report, National Museum of Natural History, Smithsonian Institution, Washington, D.C., APVA JRC, 2003.

2. Smith, *Complete Works*, 1:208, 2:140–42, 160, 162.

3. Owsley et al., "Two Early Seventeenth-Century Burials," 39.

4. Paul Budd and Janet Montgomery, "Combined Pb-, Sr- and O-isotope Analysis of Tooth Enamel from JR102C (a seventeenth-century individual from Jamestown, Virginia,

USA) and Related Samples" (ArchaeoTrace Gibraltar House, Halifax, United Kingdom), unpublished report, JRC.

5. Owsley et al., "Two Early Seventeenth-Century Burials," 35.

6. Percy, *Observations,* 15.

7. Ibid.

8. Catherine Correll-Walls, "Possible Identity of JR102C," unpublished report, JRC, 2003.

9. Correll-Walls, Jamestown Biographies database.

10. Smith, *Complete Works,* 2:139.

11. Percy, *Observations,* 25.

12. Smith, *Complete Works,* 1:20.

13. Yonge, *Site of Old James Towne,* 72.

14. Ibid.

15. "William Strachey, for the Colony in Virginea Britannia. Lawes Divine, Morall and Martiall, etc 1611," in *Tracts and Other Papers, Relating Principally to Origin, Settlement, and Progress of the Colonies in America,* ed. Peter Force (Washington, D.C., 1844), passim.

16. Meyer and Dorman, *Adventures of Purse and Person,* 586.

17. Smith, *Complete Works,* 2:181. Fred Scholpp, musketeer reenactor at the Jamestown Settlement Museum, personal communication, 2003.

18. I am indebted to anthropologist/sculptor Janet Long and National Museum of Natural History anthropologist David Hunt for their talented work in reconstructing the face of JR102C.

19. Physical mending of the skull was also laboriously carried out by David Hunt at the Smithsonian Institution.

20. Lucy Tomlin Smith, *The Itinerary of John Leland, 1535–1543* (Carbondale, Ill., 1964), 47, 49, 59.

21. Percy, *Observations,* 26.

22. See Nancy Oestreich Lurie, "Indian Cultural Adjustment to European Civilization," in *Seventeenth-Century America,* ed. James Morton Smith (Chapel Hill, N.C., 1959), 33–60.

23. Owsley et al., "Two Early Seventeenth-Century Burials."

24. Emily Williams, archaeological conservator, Colonial Williamsburg Foundation, letter to Elliott Jordan, March 15, 1998, JRC.

25. Smith, *Complete Works,* 2:192.

26. I am indebted to Dr. Harry Hager and Bruce Wilson for providing the CT scan at Williamsburg Community Hospital and Marc McAllister of Innova International, Dallas, Texas, for processing the CT data into a stereolithography file, and Accelerated Technologies for building the skull model.

27. Tonia Deetz Rock, "Report on Burial 1046 at Jamestown, Virginia," unpublished report, JRC, 2003.

28. Strachey, in Wright, *Voyage to Virginia,* 76.

29. Warner F. Gookin and Philip L. Barbour, *Bartholomew Gosnold: Discoverer and Planter* (London, 1963), 49–177.

30. Haile, ed., *Jamestown Narrative*, 185.

31. This important artifact was identified by the combined efforts of senior curator Bly Straube, conservator Michael Lavin, Professor James Lavin, and arms expert Claude Blair.

32. *Drill Postures,* an engraving by T. Cockson, 1615–20, The British Museum.

33. Smith, *Complete Works,* 1:206.

34. I am indebted to Dr. Ashley McKeown who, with a generous grant from the crime novelist Patricia Cornwell, and under the direction of Dr. Douglas Owsley, Smithsonian Institution, spent two years in residence at Jamestown during the burial study and taught us all some of the science and art of forensic anthropology and skeletal biology.

35. I am grateful for the skillful research of Edward and Joanna Martin of Hitcham, Suffolk.

36. W. C. Metcalfe, *The Visitations of Suffolk 1561, 1577 and 1612* (Exeter, 1882), 170: Tylney.

37. British Public Record Office: PROB/11/136 and PROB/11/199; Higham St. Mary parish register, Suffolk Record Office (Ipswich, England).

38. GC17:755, vol. III, *f.* 178, Suffolk Record Office (Ipswich, England).

39. The original Davy manuscripts are in the British Library (Add. MS 19105), but there are microfilms in the Suffolk Record Office. The Shelley visit is on *ff.* 96r-99v.

40. Death date given in W. Copinger, *Manors of Suffolk* (1910), 6:81.

41. *Kelly's Directory of Suffolk* (1879, 1883).

42. W. H. Rylands, *Heralds' Visitation of Suffolk 1664–1668* (London, 1910): Blackerby of Shackerland Hall.

43. Public Record Office: PROB/11/396.

44. British Library Add. MS 19,133, *ff.* 9v-12r.

45. Public Record Office PROB/11/396.

46. A. G. H. Hollingsworth (vicar of Stowmarket, 1837–59), *The History of Stowmarket* (Ipswich, 1844), 207

47. *White's Directory of Suffolk* (1855), 418.

48. Julian Litten, *The English Way of Death* (London, 1992), 106. This critical dating evidence was confirmed by Mr. Litten by cell-phone call by the Council for the Care of Churches archaeologist Joe Elders, directly from the Stowmarket vault site.

49. Dr. Terry Melton, memo, to Dr. William M. Kelso, Re: Skeletal Remains JR10456B, Skeletal Remains Shelley Church, Mitotyping Technologies Case no. 2477, Aug. 22, 2005.

50. Edward Martin, "Evidence for the Burial Places of Two Maternal-Line Relatives of Capt. Bartholomew Gosnold of Virginia," Rediscovery Center, Jamestown, 2005, n.p.; Mary Abbott, *Life Cycles in England 1550–1720,* (London and New York, 1996), 96.

51. Dr. Terry Melton, memo to Dr. William M. Kelso, Re: Skeletal Remains JR10456B, Skeletal Remains Shelley Church, Mitotyping Technologies Case no. 2477, August 22, 2005.

52. Douglas Owsley and Karin Bruwelheide, "Mitochondrial DNA Sampling at Shelley Church, Suffolk County, England, October 6, 2005," 6, appendix I, "Report provided by Dr. Sam Stout, Department of Anthropology, The Ohio State University."

53. Advisory Panel on the Archaeology of Christian Burials in England (APACBE), "Comments on the Report Mitochrondrial DNA Sampling at Shelley Church by Douglas Owsley and Karin Bruwelheide" (November 14, 2005), Rediscovery Center, Jamestown.

54. For a summary of these aging tests see Margaret Cox, *Life and Death in Spitalfields* (York, England, 1996), 93.

55. Geochron Laboratories, "Radiocarbon Determination of Age, GX-32317, 10/06/2005, JRC." I am indebted to Catherine Correll-Walls, who found the very generous architectural historian Philip Aiken, who in turn connected me with the owner of Shelley Manor, Andrew Scott, who then led me to Shelley Church.

56. Smith, *Complete Works,* 1: xxix.

57. Percy, "A True Relation . . . ," in *Jamestown Narratives,* ed. Haile, 509; Cotter, *Archeological Excavation at Jamestown,* 16. Edward Barney also claimed to have presented the relics he had found in digging around the church to the Virginia Historical Society, but a collections search there could find no trace of them.

58. Peter Wilson Coldham, ed. "The Voyage of the Neptune to Virginia, 1618–1619, and the Disposition of Its Cargo," *Virginia Magazine of History and Biography* (Virginia Historical Society, 1979) 87:32. I am indebted to Martha McCartney for bringing this reference to my attention.

59. Percy, *Observations,* 24–27.

60. Douglas Owsley, personal communication, October 6, 2005.

61. Correll-Walls, Jamestown Biographies database.

62. Smith, *Complete Works,* 2:142.

63. Lothrop Withington, *Virginia Gleanings in England* (Baltimore, 1980), 35–36.

64. Owsley, Hamzavi, and Bruwelheide, "Analysis of the APVA Skeletal Collection Jamestown, Virginia."

65. Egloff, "Report on the Starving Time Population Figures"; Correll-Walls, Jamestown Biographies database.

66. Joel L. Shiner, "Report on the Excavations in the Area of the Statehouse Group at Jamestown, Research Project N. 105," mss. Colonial National Historical Park, Jamestown, Va., June 16, 1955.

67. Ashley H. McKeown, Douglas W. Owsley, and William M. Kelso, "Jamestown Rediscovery Statehouse Burial Ground Research Design," unpublished report, JRC, 1993; rev. 1996, 2000, 2004.

68. Ibid.

69. Ibid.; Ivor and Audrey Noël Hume, *The Archaeology of Martin's Hundred, Part II* (Philadelphia, 2001), fig. 96, 2.

70. Egloff, "Report on the Starving Time Population Figures."

71. Ashley H. McKeown and Douglas W. Owsley, "Jamestown Statehouse Cemetery Skeletal Analysis Progress Report, July 2005," JRC.

72. I am indebted to Dr. Ashley H. McKeown and Dr. Douglas W. Owsley for this analysis.

## 4. Reanimating Jamestown

1. Smith, *Complete Works*, 2:225.

2. Barbour, *Jamestown Voyages*, 49–54.

3. Edward S. Neill, *History of the Virginia Company of London* (Albany, N.Y., 1869), 8–14.

4. Wherever soil layers survived under the 1607 fort deposits, they contained a type of Virginia Indian pottery known as "Townsend series" made and used by late Woodland period people who cleared and farmed in Virginia into the late sixteenth century.

5. I am indebted to Daniel W. Brown for our discussions about palisade construction and engineering.

6. Unless otherwise noted, the references for the facts about the Jamestown "medical men" and other activities illustrated by the *Rediscovery* finds come the fine research of Beverly Straube, senior curator Jamestown Rediscovery, much of which appears in chap. 4 of *Jamestown Rediscovery, 1994–2004*.

7. Smith, *Complete Works*, 2:294.

8. Percy, *Observations*, 22.

9. Stahle et al., "The Lost Colony and Jamestown Droughts."

10. I am indebted to Beverly Straube for her meticulous research that identified most of the artifacts discussed throughout the remainder of this chapter.

11. Smith, *Complete Works*, 2:138.

12. Carter C. Hudgins, "Articles of Exchange or Ingredients of New World Metallurgy?," *Early American Studies* 3, no. 1 (2005): 32–64.

13. Brown, *Genesis of the United States*, 110.

14. J. C. Harrington, *A Tryal of Glasse* (Richmond, Va., 1980), 10.

15. David Higgins, *Devon Archaeological Society Proceedings, no. 54, 1996* (1998): 245.

16. Warren Billings, *Jamestown and the Founding of the Nation* (Gettysburg, Pa., n.d.), 46.

17. Straube, op cit.

18. Thomas Davidson to Beverly Straube, personal communication.

19. Although this cut stone has yet to be specifically identified, it is likely from the banks of the Thames, still littered with similar ancient stones to this day.

20. Daniel Schmidt, "The Role of Fishing in Sustenance of the Early Jamestown Colony: The First Decade," M.A. thesis, Royal Holloway, University of London, 2004, 7.

21. Joanne Bowen and Susan Trevarthen Andrews, "The Starving Time at Jamestown," report submitted to JRC, December 1999, 2.

22. Smith, *Complete Works*, 2:189.

23. Ibid, 1:219, 2:212.

24. Ibid., 2:187.


## 5. Royal Jamestown

1. Meyer and Dorman, *Adventures of Purse and Person*, 7–71. These figures are a minimum.

2. The term *Statehouse* hereafter refers to the building site on the eastern end of a complex of foundations located on the extreme western edge of the APVA Jamestown property. The entire contiguous series of foundations attached to the Statehouse will hereafter be designated Statehouse Complex, an edifice that existed either intact or in partial or total ruin from 1665–1698. An earlier building located toward the eastern end of Jamestown and used for governmental functions will be termed Berkeley Row, although it was also called at times statehouse during the seventeenth century.

3. Warren Billings, personal communication, June 4, 2003.

4. Billings, *Jamestown and the Founding of the Nation,* 49.

5. For a thorough discussion of the succession of the five Jamestown churches, see Lyman G. Tyler, *Cradle of the Republic* (1906), chap. 7.

6. "M. J. Galt Report," in Cotter, *Archeological Excavations at Jamestown,* 222.

7. Tyler, *Cradle of the Republic,* chap. 7.

8. Billings, *Jamestown and the Founding of the Nation,* 49.

9. Martha W. McCartney, *Biographical Sketches: People Associated with Jamestown Island,* An Archaeological Assessment of Jamestown, Virginia, Technical Report no. 5 (Williamsburg, Va., 2000), 164, 168.

10. Martha W. McCartney, *Documentary History of Jamestown Island,* vol. 2, *Land Ownership* (Williamsburg, Va., 2000), 116, 68.

11. Cotter, *Archeological Excavations at Jamestown,* 112–21; Carl Lounsbury, "The Statehouses of Jamestown," Colonial Williamsburg Foundation: unpublished report, October 22, 1994.

12. Instructions to Francis Wyatt, January 1638–39, CO 5/1354, PRO.

13. "Patents from the State Land Office," APVA mss., no. 83, JRC.

14. Warren M. Billings, *A Little Parliament* (Richmond, Va., 2004), 60.

15. Cotter, *Archeological Excavations at Jamestown,* 77–79.

16. McCartney, *Documentary History of Jamestown Island,* 2:44.

17. Cotter, *Archeological Excavations at Jamestown,* 77–79.

18. Billings, *A Little Parliament,* 144.

19. McCartney, *Documentary History of Jamestown Island,* vol. 1, *An Archaeological Assessment of Jamestown, Virginia* (Williamsburg, Va., 1999), 85.

20. McCartney, *Documentary History of Jamestown Island,* 2:404–24.

21. William M. Kelso to Cary Carson, personal communication, April 29, 2002.

22. H. R. McIlwaine, ed., *Journals of the House of Burgesses of Virginia* (Richmond, Va., 1904), *1619–1660,* 96, 101; *1660–1693,* 27.

23. Land Patents, APVA, number 130: "and bounded as followth Vizd beginning on the South side of the said house close to the wall where the said westernmost house joynes to the middle house, thence running S. wesly 34 degr 67 feet to high water mark, thence N. wesly 56 degr up the river side 120 feet, thence N. Ely 34 degr 181 ffeet & halfe, thence S. Ely 56 deg. 120 feet thence S Wly againe 34 degr through the said old State house and the partition wall dividing the sd westernmost house and middle house 114 feet and halfe to the place where it first began."

24. In his will of March 31, 1670, Stegg leaves to Ludwell his part of a house and furniture that they had bought from Henry Randolph. This should not be confused with the

three-part "old State house complex" (Cary Carson, Willie Graham, Carl Lounsbury, and Martha McCartney, *Description and Analysis of Structure 144, Jamestown, Virginia, A Report to APVA Jamestown Rediscovery* [Williamsburg, Va., August 20, 2002], 3-E, 14).

25. Berkeley to Randolph: "all that the remains, foundation and brick works of a certain house or messuage that was burned of 40 feet long and 20 feet broad being the westernmost pt of the ruined fabrick or buildings adjoining to the old State house which said messuage was formerly in the occupation of Richard Bennett Esqr [the former Governor and last occupant] together with the land whereon the said ruined messuage standeth, situated lying and being upon the river side in James city."

26. "one messuage house or tenement of brick building of 40 feet long and 20 wide being the middle pt of that fabrick of building where was the old State house, together with the lands." There immediately followed the sale by Randolph of the other two Berkeley Row buildings.

April 7, 1671: Henry Randolph sold to Thomas Swann of Surrey "one messuage, house or brick building of 40 feet long and 20 wide being the easternmost end of that pile of building whereof the old state-house was pt and next adjoining thereto, which messuage was formerly in the occupation of Thomas Bayly."

April 7, 1671: Henry Randolph sold to Thomas Ludwell of James City County "one messuage or tenement of brick building of 40 feet long and 20 feet wide being the messuage of pt of that fabrick pile of building which contains three tenements, the middlemost whereof was the old State house which messuage was formerly in the occupation of Richard Bennett Esqr."

27. Carson et al., *Structure 144,* 3-D-3.

28. Cotter, *Archeological Excavations at Jamestown,* 50–51.

29. After various remote sensing tests, test holes excavated in a gridded pattern during the Jamestown Archaeological Assessment revealed a target there. It was concluded that there were no seventeenth-century features in the area. It is the opinion of the author that this testing was not extensive enough to lead to that conclusion.

30. Rieley and Associates, "Assessment of Selected 17th-Century Surveys at Jamestown Island, Virginia," unpublished report, APVA, JRC, 2002.

31. Cotter, *Archeological Excavations at Jamestown,* 45–47.

32. The author feels that this can be the only explanation for such a lightly built partition bonded onto the main foundation with no evidence beneath or along the partition of an earlier dismantled end wall.

33. See Ludwell/Stegg, Randolph sale above, n. 26.

34. Cotter, *Archeological Excavations at Jamestown,* 50.

35. Bly Straube, personal communication; Noël Hume and Noël Hume, *Archaeology of Martin's Hundred,* fig. 105, no. 4.

36. Yonge, *Site of Old James Towne.*

37. McIlwaine, ed., *Journals of the House of Burgesses of Virginia, 1660–1693,* 26.

38. Yonge, *Site of Old James Towne,* 18.

39. The artifacts discussed here are described in greater detail in Beverly Straube, "State House Ridge Artifacts, 1903–2002," mss., APVA, JRC.

40. Louis R. Caywood, "Report on the Excavations at the Site of the Third Ridge and

Fourth State Houses at Jamestown, Virginia, November 1–15, 1954," mss., Colonial National Historic Park, Jamestown, Va.

41. Joel L. Shiner, "Report on the Excavations in the Area of the Statehouse Group at Jamestown," mss., Colonial National Historic Park, Jamestown, Va., 1955.

42. Both Caywood and Shiner concluded that the burial ground beneath the Statehouse ruins predated the building of the Statehouse Complex probably by enough years to have erased all memory of it. Shiner concluded that the sometimes helter-skelter orientation of many of the graves might indicate that they were from the 1609–10 "starving time" winter.

43. Carson et al., *Structure 144,* passim; May, "Report of the Excavations of the Statehouse Ridge Complex," passim.

44. Carson et al., *Structure 144,* 1-4.

45. Ibid., 1-6, 1-8.

46. Straube, passim. This may be evidence of the early structure Yonge felt he found, but no other architectural elements were found during the recent excavations.

47. Carson et al., *Structure 144,* chap. 4.

48. William Waller Hening, *Statutes at Large* (New York, 1823), 172.

49. Warren M. Billings, *Sir William Berkeley and the Forging of Colonial Virginia, A Virginian's Biography* (Baton Rouge, 2004), chap. 11.

50. John Clayton to Robert Boyle, Boyle Papers, 3a, Item 3 160–162, Archives of the Royal Society of London, London, 1688, in McCartney, *Documentary History of Jamestown Island,* 1:112–13.

51. McCartney, *Documentary History of Jamestown Island,* 1:112.

52. T. M. (Thomas Mathews) to Robert Harley, July 13, 1705, in *Tracts and Other Papers,* ed. Force, 16.

53. I am especially indebted for the historical research of Bly Straube for sorting out many of the references to the evolving uses of the Statehouse Complex buildings.

54. McIlwaine, ed., *Journals of the House of Burgesses of Virginia,* 121–22: July 6, 1680 . . . "Whereas there is the ruines of two brick houses burnt in the late Rebellion . . . it's the opinion of his Excellencie & the councell that Coll. Bacon may have one of the houses on the same termes . . . the same which did belong to Mr. Auborne."

55. May 22, 1684 . . . "Resolved in the affirmative The report of ye commt for contracting for the building the state house . . . it is Referred to Mr. Wm Sherwood to draw the articles between his Exlncy . . . And the Honble Collo. Phillip Ludwell for ye Rebuilding the state house."

May 22, 1684 . . . "The petition of Collo. Nathaniell Bacon . . . for a stack of building belonging to the Country, formerly granted to Phillip Ludwell Esqr. for 50. yeares . . . [and] Ludwell . . . declaring that he did voluntarily Relinquish the said lease or grant. Resolved that the said Building or Ruine of two houses be leased to the Honable Nathaniell Bacon Esqr. For fifty yeares . . . under the same conditions as . . . June, 1680 . . . November 1682."

May 23, 1684 . . . "the two houses to be granted to Coll. Bacon, Returned from his Exlncy and Councell with their Assent, that a lease shall be drawn."

56. H. R. McIlwaine, ed., *Legislative Journals of the Council of Virginia,* 2d ed. (Richmond, Va., 1979), 1:93–94.

57. Rieley and Associates, "Assessment of Selected 17th-Century Surveys at Jamestown Island, Virginia," unpublished report, APVA, JRC, 2002.

58. Sainsbury, William Noel et al., Calendar of State Papers Colonial Series, America and the West Indies, 16:513, 516.

59. Billings, personal communication, June 4, 2003.

60. The discovery process at Jamestown is far from over. At this writing, August 3, 2005, approximately one-half of the interior of the fort site remains to be excavated, in-depth analysis of the field data and artifacts has only begun, and the expanded fort area on APVA property has only been tested. Despite almost three decades of excavation, about 80 percent of the forty-acre town site that lies on the National Park Service property west of the fort remains basically unexplored.

# Index

*Page numbers in italics refer to illustrations.*

Adling, Henry, 30
Advisory Panel for the Archaeology of Christian Burials in England (APACBE), 157–58
agricultural cultivation. *See* plowing and archaeological evidence
Alicock, Jerome, *30*, 129, 133, 135, 138
Allen, Capt. William, 62, 203
Amarice, 38
"Ancient Planters of Virginia," 11, 26, 46, 96
APACBE (Advisory Panel for the Archaeology of Christian Burials in England), 157–58
Archaearium, 151
Archer, Gabriel, 10, *30*; governance of settlement and, 132; identity of the "captain" and, 159; on Paspahegh Indians' attack (1607), 16, 93, 112, 114
Archer's Hope, 13
architectural evidence. *See individual structures*
Argall, Samuel, 24, 57, 79–80, 119
Army Corps of Engineers excavations (1901), 64, 132, 202–3
arrow points. *See* projectile points
Arundel, Baron, 41–43

Association for the Preservation of Virginia Antiquities (APVA), 3, 5, 47–48, 54–55, 150–51, 203–4
Atkins, John, 163
Aubourne, Richard, 210

Bacon, Col. Nathaniel, 210–11
Bacon, Nathaniel, Jr. (the rebel), 209
Bacon's Rebellion, 194, 203, 209–10
ballistic tests, 134–35
Barbour, Philip, 46, 47
Barney, Edward E., 159
barracks building, 81, 83–93, 97
barrelmaking, 185, *187*
Bartmanns, *90*, 120
Beheathland, Robert, *30*
Bennett, Richard, 198–99
Berkeley, William, 192, 194, 197–99, 207–8
Berkeley Row, *194*, 197–202, 226n2
Blackerby, Katherine Bowtell, 144, 146–50, 152–56
Blackerby, Thomas, 146, 148–50, 153–55
blacksmithing, 51, 185–86
Blackwall, England, 27–28
"blockhouses," 19, 24, 45, 78, 101–2, 189
Blois, William, 145
bone chemistry analyses, 128–29, 158

Booker, Lancelot, *30*

Botwell, Barnaby, 146

boy (killed 1607), 16, *162–64*

brass-making operations, 181–82

Brewster (Bruster?), William, *30*, 129

brickmakers and bricklayers, 185

Brinto, Edward, *30*

Brookes, Edward, *30*

Browne, Edward, *30*

Brumfield, James, 29, *30*, 162–63

bulwarks, 16, 22, 44, 53; artifacts found with, 64–65, *175*; excavation of, 58–66, 69–72, *74*, 78; powder magazines and, 65–66; saw pit and, 180–*81*

burials: Archaearium museum and display of, 151; of the captain (Gosnold?), 141–*61*, *175–76*; first burial of woman found (JR156C), 139–41; inside or near the church, 132, 159; JR102C (gentleman), 126–39; near south wall of fort, 126, 139; near west wall of fort, 141, 159; under or near the factory, 104, 115; outside of James Fort, 163–68, 176; under the rowhouses, 107, 109, 160–63; from "starving time," 52, 164, 165, 228n42; under Statehouse Complex, 39, 163–68, 204; use of in determining fort site, 52–53

Burras, Ann, 19, 140

Burwell, Abigail Smith, 211

Burwell, Lewis, II, 211

Burwell, Nathaniel, 211

Calthrope, Stephen, 33, 130–32

Capper, John, *30*

carpenters, 183, 185, *187*

Cassen, George, *30*

Cassen, Thomas, *30*

Cassen, William, *30*

Cassinett, Arnold, 210

casting counters (jettons), 57–*58*, 88, 100, 103–4

Catholic Church artifacts, 187–*88*

Cawsey, Thomasine, 39

Caywood, Louis, 204

cellars/pits, 81–*82*, *83*; of barracks, 83, 87–93, 97; of factory, *84*, 96–99; north of the factory, 111–15; of quarter, 94–96, 97; as trash deposits, 100–103

Charles I, King of England, 196

Charles II, King of England, 207

Charles Fort (Virginia), 24, 91

Chilton, Edward, 210

Church of England, 150–52

church structures, *51*, *53*, 79–80; artifacts from, 187–*88*; building methods used for, 83; dismantling of, 48; excavations of, 50–51, 52, 79, 195; rebuilding/reconstruction of, 18, 24, 51, 94, 189, 194–95; relocation of, 51, 77, 79–80; as Statehouse, 192, 194–95

Civil War earthwork: archaeological display at, 3–5; construction of, 48, 62, 68, 70; in determining fort site, 51–53; excavations of, 68, 69–70, *71*, *72–73*; graves under, 141; wells under, 72–73

clay tobacco pipes, 88–*89*, 107, *109*, 119, 183–*84*

Clayton, John, 208

climate, impacts of, 33, 85–86, 122–23, 169–70, 178

Clovill, Eustace, 17, *30*, 114

Collier, Samuell, 162

colonists, 27–34; and intermarriage with Virginia Indians, 38, 95; laziness/incompetence of, 2–3, 20, 170; non-English, 19; origins of, 29–31, 85; women arrivals, 19, 39–40, 140

construction methods: for buildings, 83–*86*, *87*, 99–100, 106–7; for wells, 116–17

Cooke, Roger, *30*

copper, 18, 111, 178–*79*, 181

costrels (handled jugs), 119

Cotter, John, 73, 75, 200

Cotton, Robert, 119, 183

Council for the Care of Churches (England), 150–51

Cowper, Thomas, *30*

cratchets, 83–84
Crofts, Richard, *30*
crucibles, 51–52, 60, 88, 181–82

Dale, Thomas, 22–23, 119
Davy, David Elisha, 145, 148–49, 150
De La Warre, Thomas West, 3rd Lord, *21;*
    arrival of, 21–22, 40, 92; burial of, 159;
    renovations by, 57, 66, 78–79, 101, 103
Delft ware, 100, *112, 177*
dendrochronological dating, 122–24, *178*
distilling operations, 103–5
Dixon, Richard, *30*
DNA testing, 144, 151–52, 156–58, 160
documentary evidence, 1–2; eyewitness
    accounts of James Fort as, 11–27, 46; of-
    ficial reports to Virginia Company as,
    187, 189; on the people of James Fort,
    27–43; writers of, 10–11
Dods, John, *30*
dogs, 92–93
droughts, 122–23, 178
drug jars (alberellos), 100, *176–77*
duels, 133

Emery, Thomas, *30*
excavation and analysis strategies: bone
    chemistry analyses, 128–29, 158; den-
    drochronological dating, 122–24, *178*;
    DNA testing, 144, 151–52, 156–58, 160;
    facial reconstructions, 136–38, *140–41,
    161*; ground penetrating radar, 152;
    "quilting," 50, 56; water-quality testing,
    123–24
executions, 40, 132–33
export products, 2, 19, 180–*84*; barrels,
    185, *187*; brass, 181–82; clay tobacco
    pipes, 183–84; glass, 51–52, 59–60, 89,
    181, 183–*84*; precious metals, 2, 16,
    103–5, 172, 180–81; sassafras, 176, 189;
    timber (split planks, wainscoting), 180;
    tobacco, 2, 24, 139, 183–84

facial reconstructions, 136–38, *140–41, 161*

factory, 81, *84,* 96–106
Fenton, Robert, *30*
firearms. *See* military artifacts
fires: James Fort (1608), 18, 25, 68, 86;
    Statehouse Complex (1698), 212
fishing. *See* hunting and fishing
Fitch, Matthew, *30*
Fleischer, John, 176
Flowerdew, Temperance, 39
food supplies and diet, 19–20, 170, 186;
    artifacts of, 94–95, 100; from Bermuda,
    20–21, 39–40, 89–91; bone chemistry
    analyses and, 128–29, 158; droughts
    and, 122–23, 178; garden plots and, 69,
    172, 178; during "starving time," 92–93;
    Virginia Indians and, 18, 21, 88, 104,
    112, 172, 178–79, 181
Ford, Robert, *30*
Forest, Mistress, 19, 140
Forest, Thomas, 140
fort, brick (1672), 208–9, 210
Fort Algernon (Virginia), 24, 91
Fort Raleigh (North Carolina), 57
Fort Saint George (Maine), 88
Frith, Richard, *30*

Galt, Mary Jeffery, 50–52, 79, 195
garden plots, 22, 69, 172, 178
Garrett, William, *30*
Gates, Elizabeth and Margaret, 39
Gates, Thomas: arrival of, 20–*21*; evacua-
    tion ordered by, 21, 39–40; food supplies
    and, 91; martial law declared by, 119;
    renovations by, 78; residence built by,
    23, 26, 109
gemstones, 181
General Assembly, 192, 194
glassmaking operations, 51–*52*, 59–60, 89,
    181, 183–*84*
gold, search for. *See* precious metals (gold,
    etc.)
Gore, Thomas, *30*
Gosnold, Anthony (brother of B. Gosnold),
    *30*, 31

Gosnold, Anthony (cousin of B. Gosnold), *30*

Gosnold, Bartholomew, *30*; alleged mutiny and, 33; death of, 18, 33, 142–43, 175–76; governance of settlement and, 12, 28–29; interior explorations and, 172, 180; Paspahegh Indians' attack (1607) and, 16; as promoter of Virginia venture, 31–32, 142; on site of settlement, 14; skeletal evidence and, 141–*61*

Gosnold, Elizabeth. *See* Tilney, Elizabeth Gosnold

Gosnold, Margaret, 31, 148

Gosnold, Mary, 146, 148

Gosnold, Robert, V, *161*

Goulding, George, *30*

Governor's Row. *See* rowhouses

Gower, Thomas, *30*

ground-penetrating radar (GPR), 152

guns and ordnance. *See* military artifacts

Hakluyt, Richard, 32, 171

half pikes, 143–*44*

Hamor, Ralph, 11; on construction/design of settlement, 22–23, 46, 77–78, 102, 109–10; on laziness/incompetence of colonists, 3

Harrington, Edward, *30,* 161–62

Harrington, Virginia, 52

Harrison, George, 133

Hartwell, Henry, 210–11

Harvey, Sir John, 195–97

Herd, John, *30*

Hollingsworth, A. G. H., 149

Hone, Theophilus, 209–10

Hopewell, Va., 24

House of Burgesses, 192, 196–97

Hunt, Robert, 18, 187

hunting and fishing, 19–20, 92–93, 186, *188*

isotope testing. *See* bone chemistry analyses

jails. *See* prisons and jails

James Fort: barracks building in, 81, 83–93, 97; buildings within, 18, 24–26, 80–115; cellars in, 81–*84,* 111–15; construction of, 16–18, 25, 66, 143, 173–75; dimensions/design of, 22–23, 26, 44–46, 53–54, 69–70, 75–76; east wall of, 66–69, 77, 79–80, 101–2; evacuation of, 21–22, 39–40, 91–92; eyewitness accounts of, 11–27, 46; factory building in, 81, *84,* 96–106; lean-to structures in, 80–82, 86, 103; north bulwark of, 69–72, 78; quarter building in, 81, 93–97, 99; rebuilding/renovation of, 18–19, 57, 71–72, 79–80, 101; rowhouses in, 81, 103, 106–11, 185, 187; site of, 12–14, 34, 47–55, 75–76, 171, 172–73; south bulwark of, 58–66, 78; south palisade of, 55–58, *60;* storehouse in, 18, 24, 110–11; transition from fort to town of, 26–27, 76–80, 102–3; wells in, 19, 72–73, 115–24; west bulwark of, *74,* 180–*81;* west wall of, 72–76

James I, King of England, 27, 34, 40–*41*

Jamestown: abandonment of, 48; Berkeley Row in, *194,* 197–202, 226n2; brick fort constructed in, 208–9, 210; John White building in, 62–64, 78; population of, 90, 92, 191; representative government and, 1, 187, 192, 194, 212–13; Statehouse Complex in, 163, *165,* 192, *194,* 202–13; Structure 38 ("Country's House"), *194,* 197; Structure 112 (Harvey/Wyatt statehouse), *194,* 195–97; transition from fort of, 26–27, 76–80, 102–3

Jamestown Island, 13–*14, 48*

Jarvis, Arthur, 212

jettons. *See* casting counters

Joones, Elizabeth, 39

Jordan's Point, Va., 121

JR156C (first woman's remains found), 139–41

JR102C (remains of probable gentleman), 126–39; bone chemistry analyses of,

128–29; circumstances of death of, 133–36; facial reconstruction of, 136–38; identity of, 130–31, 133

Kelso, William M., 2–6
Kemp, Richard, 197, 201
Kemps, 19, 38
Kendall, George, *30*; construction/design of settlement and, 15; execution of, 40, 132; governance of settlement and, 12, 28–29; Paspahegh Indians' attack (1607) and, 16
Kinistone (or Kingston), Ellis, *30*

Laxon, William, *30*, 85
Laydon, John and Ann Burras, 19, 140
Laydon, Virginia, 140
leading staffs, 143–*44*
lean-to structures, 80–*82*, 86, 103
Lee, George, 210
literacy artifacts, *188–89*
Love, William, *30*
Luccketti, Nicholas, 5
Ludwell, Philip, 210
Ludwell, Philip, II, 211–12
Ludwell, Thomas, 198–99

Mantiuas, *36–38*
manufacturing artifacts, 51, 180–83
maps: of Blackwall, England, *28*; Vingboons chart, 11, *13*, 24–25, 45–46, 110; of Virginia by Smith, *35*; Zúñiga map (1608), 11, *12*, 22, 44–45, 53, 58, 64–66, 69–71, 178
martial law period, 119, 133
Martin, Edward, *155*
Martin, George, *30*
Martin, John, Jr., *30*, 130
Martin, John, Sr., 12, 16, 28, *30–31*, 130, 132
Martincamp ceramic flasks, 103–4
masons, 185
Matachanna, *36*, 37
medical artifacts, *65*, 167–68, 176–77

metallurgical artifacts, 103–5, 180–82
military artifacts, 51, 133–35; from barracks, 88–89; from bulwarks, *61, 91*; from captain's grave, 143–*44*; from factory, 100; from palisades, 57–58; from quarter, *96*; from Statehouse Complex, 203; from wells, *117*, 120–22
Molina, Don Diego de, 23
Morris, Edward, *30*
Muchamps, 38
"mud and stud" building methods, 84–*87, 94*, 99–100
Mutton, Richard, *30*, 162–64

Nantaquawis, *36–38*
National Park Service (NPS): excavations (1940s), 183; excavations (1950s), 3, 5, 47, 51–53, 72, 163, 196, 200, 203–4; interpretative plan and, 151
Native Americans. *See* Virginia Indians
Newport, Christopher, 29, *30*; as admiral of the fleet, 12, 33, 187; alleged mutiny and, 33, 131; construction of settlement and, 17; interior explorations and, 16, 172, 180; return to England by, 19
*New World, The* (motion picture), *82, 174, 175*
Noël Hume, Ivor, 52, 54
non-English colonists, 19
NPS. *See* National Park Service

Oholasc, *36*, 37
Opechancanough, 37
Otley Hall (Suffolk, Eng.), 31–32
Owsley, Douglas, 142, *155–56*

palisade walls, 16, 18, 22, 23–24, 26, 76–79; artifacts found with, 57–*58*, 68; construction of, 55, 174–75; dismantling of, 79–80, 101–2; excavation of, *6–7*, 55–58, *60*, 66–69, *71–76, 77*
Paspahegh Indians, 15–16, 19, 114
Pecock, Nathaniel, *30*, 162
Pennington, Robert, *30*, 130

Pepasschicher, 38

Percy, George, *10–11, 30;* on construction/
design of settlement, 16, 22, 44, 64; on
cultivation efforts, 178; on deaths
of colonists, 18, 33, 109, 124, 129–30,
132, 161, 175, 178; description of Virginia by, 9; on first days of settlement,
15, 132, 138–39; on Gosnold's burial,
142; governance of settlement and, 20;
as possible relative of JR, 138; on siting
of settlement, 13–14, 34; "starving time"
and, 10–11, 93, 132; on well contamination, 124

pewter ware, 120, *122*

Philip III, King of Spain, 40–43

Pickayes, Drew, *30*

Pierce, Richard and Elizabeth, 120

pipes. *See* clay tobacco pipes

Pising, Edward, *30*

pit sawing, 180–*81*

plowing and archaeological evidence, 48–
49, 61–62, 67

Pocahontas, 18, 37–*38*

pottery artifacts: from barracks, 88–*90;*
from bulwarks, *61;* Delft ware, 100, *112,
177;* from distilling operations, *182;*
from factory, 100, 103–4; from rowhouses, *113;* from wells, 119, 120

powder magazines, 65–66

Powhatan, 34–38

precious metals (gold, etc.), 16, 103–5, 172,
180–81

prisons and jails, 97, 99, 208, 211, 212

Project 100, 51–53. *See also* National Park
Service

projectile points, 111–12, *114*

quarter building, 81, 93–97, 99

Raleigh (Sir Walter) House (Blackwall,
Eng.), 28–*29*

Randolph, Henry, 199, 226n24

Randolph, William, 47

Ratcliffe, John, 12, 16, 28, 132

Read, James, *30*

reed matting, 111–12, *115*

representative government, 1, 187, 192,
194, 212–13

road construction, nineteenth–century, 94

Robinson, John, 33

Rolfe, John, 2, 24, 37, 38

Roods, William, *30*

rowhouses, 81, 103, 106–11, 185, 187

Sands, Thomas, *30*

sassafras root, 176, 189

Scot, Nicholas, *30*

*Sea Venture* (ship), 20, 88

seawall construction. *See* Army Corps of
Engineers excavations (1901)

Shiner, Joel, 204

Simmons, Richard, *30, 130*

Sir Walter Raleigh House (Blackwall, Eng.),
28–*29*

skeletal evidence. *See* burials

Smethes, William, *30*

Smith, Abigail, 211

Smith, John, 10, *30;* alleged mutiny of, 1,
12, 33, 131; building of houses and, 19,
85; on the church, 83; construction/de-
sign of settlement and, 14, 46, 57, 77–78;
on deaths of colonists, 18, 33, 90, 129;
on fire (1608), 86; on first days of settlement, 15, *17;* on food supplies, 19–20,
186; on glassmaking, 51; on Gosnold,
32, 142; governance of settlement and,
12, 18–20, 28–29, 132; interior explorations by, 16, 18, 33; on laziness/incom-
petence of colonists, 20, 170; map of
Virginia by, *35;* on relations with Virginia Indians, 97, 99, 112, 114, *179;* return to England by, 20; on the "starving
time," 90, 165; and tale of the "dungeon,"
97, 99; on wells dug for settlement, 19,
115–16

Smithfield (west of fort), 19, *73,* 116,
135–36

Smythe, Thomas, 11, 31, 32, 109

snaphaunce pistol locks, 57–58
Somerset House Conference (1604), 42
Spain, relations with, 23, 27, 40–43
spatula mundani, 65, *65*, 176
"starving time" (1609–10), 20; deaths and burials from, 52, 90, 164, 165, 228n42; diet during, 92–93; relations with Virginia Indians during, 38–39
Statehouse Complex, 163, *165*, *192*, *194*, 202–13
Steen, Jan, *3*
Stegg, Thomas, 198–99
Stephens, Richard, 133
stereolithography, 140–41
Stevenson, John, *30*
storehouse, 18, 24, 110–11
Strachey, William, 11; buildings described by, 25–26, 81, 85–86, 110; on the church, 50, 79; on De La Warre's renovations, 79, 101–2; on food stores brought from Bermuda, 89; on James Fort, 21–22, 25, 46, 53, 66, 68–70, 72, 75–76, 101; literacy artifacts of, *188*–89; on "starving time," 90, 93; on transition from fort to town, 77–78; on Virginia Indians, 34; on wells dug at James Fort, 115–16, 123–24
Straube, Bly, 5
Structure 17. *See* Berkeley Row
Structure 31, 197
Structure 38 ("Country's House"), *194*, 197
Structure 112 (Harvey/Wyatt statehouse), *194*, 195–97
support industries, 183, 185–86

tailors, 185–86, *188*
Tassore, 19
*terminus post quem* (TPQ dating), 56
Throckmorton, Kenelme, *30*
Tilney, Elizabeth Gosnold, 31, 144–*47*, 150, 152–53, 156–58, 160
Tilney, Emery, 146
Tilney, Philip, 145–46
Tilney, Thomas, 145–46
timber products, 180

tobacco cultivation, 2, 24, 139, 183–84
Todkill, Anas, *30*
Tomocomo, 37
TPQ dating, 56
trade beads, 57–*58*, 95, 178–79
trash deposits, 100–103
trepanning, 167, 176
Tsenacomacah, 34–35. *See also* Virginia Indians
Tyler, John, 79

Unger, William, *30*
Uttamatomakkin, 37

Vingboons, Johannes, 11
Vingboons chart (1617–20), 11, *13*, 24–*25*, 45–46, 110
Virginia: climate of, 33, 85–86, 122–23, 169–70, 178; settlements in, *192–93*
Virginia Company: on concealing deaths from Virginia Indians, 107, 109, 151, 171–72, 175–76; council named by, 12, 28–29; cultivation instructions, 172, 178; dissolution of, 27, 191; goals of, 1–2, 16, 106; governance rules, 12, 23, 172, 187; hunting and fishing instructions, lack of, 186; instructions to colonists of, 12, 14, 16, 143, 170–89; land grants by, 139; on selecting a settlement site, 12, 14, 171, 172–73
Virginia Indians, 27, 34–39; artifacts of, 88, 111–14, 178; attack (1607) by, 16, 93, 112, 162; building methods of, 86; concealing deaths from, 107, 109, 151, 171–72, 175–76; conversion to Christianity of, 2; first contacts with, 15–16, 143; food supplies for settlement and, 18, 21, 88, 104, 112, 172, 178–79, 181; genealogical chart of, *36*; guns, access to, by, 20, 135, 172, 177; intermarriage with, 38, 95; relations with, 14, 24, 101–2, 112, 114, 139, 143, 171–72; revolt (1622) of, 2, 26, 37, 79, 177–78, 191; revolt (1644) of, 37; during "starving time," 38–39

Waine, Amtyte, 39
Walker, George, *30, 161–62*
water-quality testing, 123–24
Webb, Thomas, *30*
wells, 19, *72–73, 115–24*
Wenman, Ferdinando, 159
White, John, 196
White (John) building, 62–64, 78
Whittby, William, 198
Whitt Cottage (Thimbleby, Lincolnshire, Eng.), *87*
Williamsburg, Va., 48, 192, 212
Wingfield, Edward Maria, *30,* 31; alleged mutiny and, 131; on Gosnold, 142–43; governance of settlement and, 12, 28–29, 187; impeachment of, 18, 132, 143;

Paspahegh Indians' attack (1607) and, 16; planning of Virginia venture and, 32–33; Spanish, relations with, and, 40
Woodhouse, Thomas, 198
Wotton, Thomas, 18, *30*
written records. *See* documentary evidence
Wyatt, Sir Francis, 196

Yonge, Samuel, 132, 202–3, 206–7

Zúñiga, Pedro de, 11, 39–41, 181
Zúñiga map (1608), 11, *12;* design of James Fort on, 22, 44–45, 58, 64–66, 69–71; in determining fort site, 45, 53; garden plot on, 22, 69, 178